Pro Continuous Delivery

With Jenkins 2.0

Nikhil Pathania

Apress®

Pro Continuous Delivery

Nikhil Pathania
Bangalore, Karnataka
India

ISBN-13 (pbk): 978-1-4842-2912-5   ISBN-13 (electronic): 978-1-4842-2913-2
DOI 10.1007/978-1-4842-2913-2

Library of Congress Control Number: 2017946339

Managing Director: Welmoed Spahr
Lead Editor: Nikhil Karkal
Technical Reviewer: Sanjay Kurra
Editorial Board: Steve Anglin, Pramila Balan, Laura Berendson, Aaron Black, Louise Corrigan,
    Jonathan Gennick, Robert Hutchinson, Celestin Suresh John, Nikhil Karkal, James Markham,
    Susan McDermott, Matthew Moodie, Natalie Pao, Gwenan Spearing
Coordinating Editor: Prachi Mehta
Copy Editor: Karen Jameson
Compositor: SPi Global
Indexer: SPi Global
Artist: SPi Global
Illustrations: Nikhil Pathania

Distributed to the book trade worldwide by Springer Science+Business Media New York,
233 Spring Street, 6th Floor, New York, NY 10013. Phone 1-800-SPRINGER, fax (201) 348-4505, e-mail orders-ny@springer-sbm.com, or visit www.springeronline.com. Apress Media, LLC is a California LLC and the sole member (owner) is Springer Science + Business Media Finance Inc (SSBM Finance Inc). SSBM Finance Inc is a **Delaware** corporation.

For information on translations, please e-mail rights@apress.com, or visit www.apress.com.

Apress and friends of ED books may be purchased in bulk for academic, corporate, or promotional use. eBook versions and licenses are also available for most titles. For more information, reference our Special Bulk Sales–eBook Licensing web page at www.apress.com/bulk-sales.

Any source code or other supplementary materials referenced by the author in this text are available to readers at www.apress.com. For detailed information about how to locate your book's source code, go to www.apress.com/source-code/978-1-4842-2912-5. Readers can also access source code at SpringerLink in the Supplementary Material section for each chapter.

Printed on acid-free paper

Dedicated to the open source community

Contents at a Glance

Contents

About the Author

Nikhil Pathania is the author of *Learning Continuous Integration with Jenkins*. He is currently practicing DevOps at SIEMENS Gamesa Renewable Energy Brande, Denmark. He started his career in software configuration management as an SCM engineer and later moved on to learn various other tools and technologies in the field of automation and DevOps. During his career, Nikhil has architected and implemented Continuous Integration and Continuous Delivery solutions across diverse IT projects. He enjoys finding new and better ways to automate and improve manual processes. In his spare time, Nikhil likes to read, write, and meditate. He is an avid climber, and now hikes and cycles.

About the Technical Reviewer

Sanjay Kurra is a passionate DevOps Consultant with a specialty in Continuous Delivery and DevOps. His love for automation and operations since 2008 has allowed him to implement and lead teams to achieve zero touch deployment using various DevOps tools in a wide range of assignments in industries such as investment banking and finance, accounting, retail, and healthcare.

Acknowledgments

First and foremost, I would like to thank my beautiful wife Karishma, for encouraging me to write another book on Jenkins. I would also like to thank Nikhil Karkal for bringing me this wonderful opportunity to write a second book on Jenkins. And I give great thanks to Sanjay Kurra, who provided me with valuable feedback throughout the writing process. Most importantly, a special thanks to the following people who worked hard to make this book the best possible experience for the readers: Prachi Mehta and Laura Berendson, and the entire Apress publishing team. And finally, a great thanks to the Jenkins, Docker, Kubernetes, CoreOS, and GitHub communities for creating such wonderful software.

Introduction

As more and more software projects are moving toward continuous integration (CI) and continuous delivery (CD), the amount of overhead present on the CI/CD tool continues to increase proportionately, in a way that there are more pipelines to maintain, more users and permissions to manage, and more projects to configure. There is also a proportionate increase in demand for the number of build and test agents along with their maintenance.

The idea behind this book is to answer the demands discussed above using the new features introduced in Jenkins, as well as utilizing the advantages provided by some of the key container technologies and lightweight OS present in the market.

The current book *Pro Continuous Delivery with Jenkins 2.0*, serves as a step-by-step guide to set up an advanced continuous delivery system using all the new features in Jenkins 2.0 such as pipeline as a code and multibranch pipeline. It also demonstrates how tools such as Docker and Kubernetes can be leveraged to create on-demand build/test machines that are fungible and scalable. The book is 13% theory and 87% practical. The first chapter of the book starts with explaining the elements of continuous delivery. The following chapters, thereafter, demonstrate the implementation of the concepts discussed in the first chapter.

What This Book Covers

Chapter 1, "Elements of Continuous Delivery." A short talk on Continuous Delivery and its elements, which are the following: importance of branching strategy, manageable and reproducible pipelines, scalable build/test infrastructure, fungible build/test environment, and more. All the forthcoming chapters (Chapters 2–8) are the practical implementation of the concepts discussed in this chapter.

Chapter 2, "HA Jenkins Setup Using Pacemaker, Corosync, and DRBD." A step-by-step guide to implement a highly available setup for Jenkins using Pacemaker, Corosync, and DRBD.

Chapter 3, "HA Jenkins Setup Using CoreOS, Docker, and GlusterFS." A step-by-step guide to implement a highly available setup for Jenkins using CoreOS, Docker and GlusterFS.

Chapter 4, "Setting Up Jenkins on Docker and Cloud." A step-by-step guide to install Jenkins on various platforms such as Linux (Fedora, Ubuntu), Docker, and Cloud (AWS).

Chapter 5, "Pipeline As a Code." The chapter is all about the Jenkins pipeline, Jenkins multibranch pipeline, Jenkinsfile, and Jenkins improved integration with GitHub. All this using a practical example that involves creating a CI (build-test) pipeline for a Maven project.

Chapter 6, "Using Containers for Distributed Builds." A step-by-step guide to creating a scalable build farm using Docker alone and using Kubernetes.

Chapter 7, "Pre-Tested Commits Using Jenkins." A short note on Pre-tested commits (Gated Check-in) along with a step-by-step guide to achieve it using the distributed nature of Git and the "Merge before build feature" of Jenkins.

Chapter 8, "Continuous Delivery Using Jenkins Pipeline." A step-by-step guide to creating a continuous delivery pipeline using Jenkins pipeline Job along with the required DevOps tool chain. All this using a practical example that involves creating a CD pipeline for a Maven project.

What You Need for This Book

To follow the examples mentioned in the book, it's recommended that you have the following system specifications and OS.

Operating System:

Windows 7/8/10

Ubuntu 16.XX.X (LTS)

Hardware requirements:

A machine with a minimum 8 GB of Memory and a Multi-Core Processor.

Who This Book Is For

The book is written keeping in mind readers that are already familiar with Jenkins and the concepts of continuous integration and continuous delivery.

You already have experience in implementing continuous integration and continuous delivery using Jenkins freestyle Jobs and now wish to use the new Pipeline as Code feature introduced in Jenkins 2.0.

Your source code is on a Git-like version control system (Git, GitHub, etc.) and you wish to leverage the advantages of a multibranch pipeline in Jenkins.

Your infrastructure is on a Unix-like platform and you wish to create a scalable, distributed build/test farm using Docker or Kubernetes.

You are in need of a highly available system for your Jenkins Server using open source tools and technologies.

What is not covered in the book

The book does not cover Jenkins administrative tasks, such as user management, Jenkins backup, plugin management, views management, and other exotic plugins that make Jenkins better.

There is a vast ocean of tools that work in conjunction with Jenkins to achieve continuous integration and continuous delivery for various types of software projects. Therefore it's impossible to cover every case. Hence, the concepts and examples discussed in the book must be treated as a template and must be modified and twisted to suit your purpose.

CHAPTER 1

■ ■ ■

Elements of Continuous Delivery

What Is Continuous Delivery?

Continuous Delivery (CD) is the practice of delivering quality software more frequently. CD practices can include more or less the following entities:

- A good branching strategy.
- A working Continuous Integration (CI) process.
- Distributed builds.
- Automated testing.
- Distributed or parallel testing.
- Automated and quick environment provisioning.
- Automated code promotion.

Branching Strategy

Using a single master branch for all your development might seem the best option for CI. However, having a multibranch-based workflow is more fruitful than doing everything on a single branch. Following are some of the different ways of using multiple branches.

Using Separate Branch for Every Feature/Bug-Fix

A feature branch enables you to isolate your development as per features, allowing you to play with the source code without the risk of breaking the master branch. Every feature and every bug-fix can have its own branch. Figure 1-1 portrays the usage of feature branches.

© Nikhil Pathania 2017
N. Pathania, *Pro Continuous Delivery*, DOI 10.1007/978-1-4842-2913-2_1

1

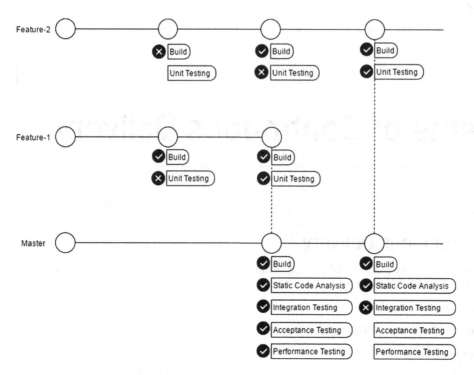

Figure 1-1. *Using feature branches*

In the following workflow, developers work and push their changes to the Feature branches. A CI tool (say, Jenkins), is configured to build and unit test each and every push on the feature branches. Only the changes that pass the build and unit tests are allowed to be merged with the Master branch. In **Chapter 5**, you will see how the Jenkins "Multibranch pipeline" job is used to run continuous integration on every feature branch.

Using the Gitflow Workflow

Gitflow is another way of managing your code using multiple branches. In the following method, the master branch is kept clean and contains only the releasable: ready to ship code. All the development happens on the feature branches with the Develop/Development branch serving as a common place to integrate all the features. Figure 1-2 is a moderate version of the Gitflow.

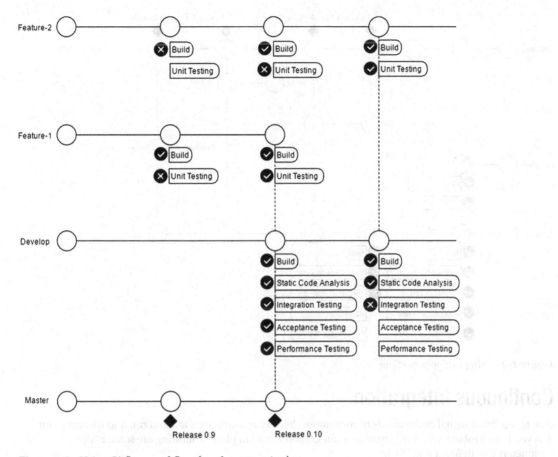

Figure 1-2. *Using Gitflow workflow (moderate version)*

Figure 1-3 illustrates the full version of Gitflow. We have a Master branch that contains only the production-ready code. The Feature branches are where all of the development takes place. The Development/Develop branch (also known as Integration branch) is where the code gets integrated and tested for quality. In addition to that, we have Release branches that are pulled out from the development branch as and when there is a stable release. All bug-fixes related to a release happen on the release branch. There is also a Hotfix branch that is pulled out of the master branch as and when there is a need for a hotfix.

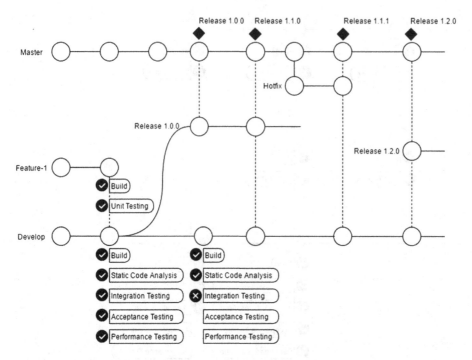

Figure 1-3. *Using Gitflow workflow*

Continuous Integration

One of the fundamental components of continuous delivery is continuous integration. And it's important that you have a robust, working continuous integration model in place. Following are some of the parameters that define a robust CI.

- Codable CI pipelines.

- Reproducible build environments.

- A highly available CI master.

Codable CI Pipeline

A CI pipeline is a set of sequential or parallel jobs (sometimes a combination of both). These jobs are designed to perform a set of tasks and are traditionally configured using a GUI interface. However, as the number of Jobs grows it becomes increasingly difficult for anyone to maintain them. Especially in cases where a Job is a modified copy of another Job, It becomes crucial to maintain consistency.

Nevertheless, tools like Jenkins and Gitlab (to name a few) have come up with the concept of **pipeline as a code**. The idea is to have your CI pipeline written as a code and saved inside a file. The code can be either in the form of Groovy script (Groovy DSL) or as a Declarative Pipeline Syntax. In Jenkins, the file that stores the pipeline script is referred to as **Jenkinsfile**.

A Jenkinsfile or pipeline script gives you the following abilities:

- Jenkinsfile can be a version control along with your source code.

- Jenkinsfile is easily shareable.

- Developers can themselves define what a Jenkinsfile should do.

- You can have different Jenkinsfile for different branches.

Following is an example of a Jenkinsfile:

```
node('master'){
        stage('build'){
                sh 'mvn clean install';
        }
        stage('static code analysis'){
                sh 'mvn verify sonar:sonar';
        }
}
```

How to Use Jenkinsfile?

Figure 1-4 illustrates the Jenkinsfile usage. As you can see from the figure, the Jenkinsfile is stored along with the source code inside a version control system. Whenever there is a code commit on the version control system, the following steps take place:

1. A Source control webhook (commit) is sent to Jenkins.

2. The Jenkins pipeline Job is triggered on receiving the webhook condition.

3. The Jenkins pipeline Job downloads the latest source code as well as the Jenkinsfile from the version control system.

4. Jenkins reads the Jenkinsfile and executes the pipeline steps accordingly.

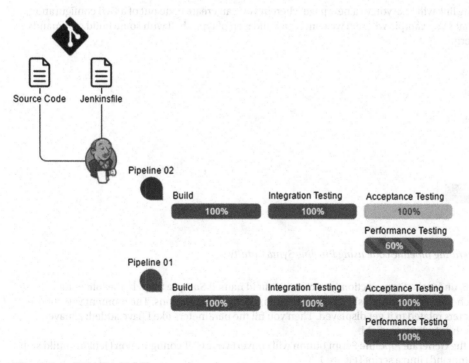

Figure 1-4. Using Jenkinsfile

How to Write Pipeline Steps Inside a Jenkinsfile?

Using the Jenkins Groovy DSL (Domain Specific Language) or using the Jenkins Declarative pipeline Syntax, all of the continuous integration and continuous delivery pipeline steps can be written inside a Jenkinsfile.

To start writing a pipeline, visit the following page *https://jenkins.io/doc/pipeline/steps/*. Here you will find the code for most of the pipeline steps. Nevertheless, you can also make use of the Jenkins *pipeline syntax* utility available right inside Jenkins.

The Pipeline Syntax link is available inside a Jenkins Pipeline Job. Try creating a new Jenkins pipeline and scroll down to the Pipeline section. Under the Pipeline section, you will find a link named Pipeline Syntax, as shown in Figure 1-5.

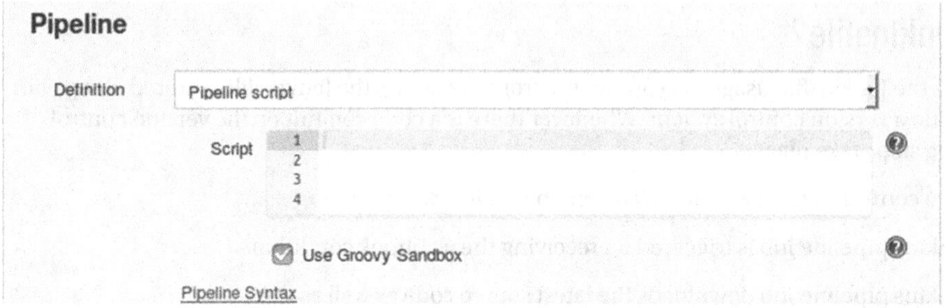

Figure 1-5. *Pipeline Syntax link*

Accessing the link will take you to a new page wherein you can create code out of a GUI configuration. Figure 1-6 illustrates an example wherein we convert a build step of type shell with some build commands, into a pipeline script.

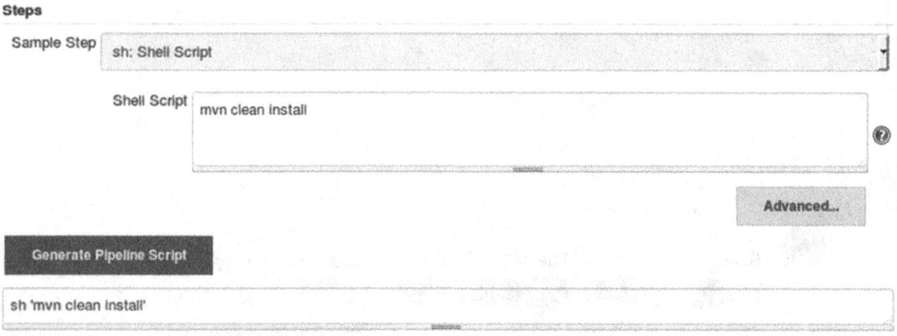

Figure 1-6. *Generating pipeline code using Pipeline Syntax utility*

In Figure 1-6, under the **Steps** section, you can see a field named **Sample Step**. In the following example, I have chosen a step named **sh: Shell Script** from the available options. The moment you choose a step, all parameters related to it get displayed. Then you fill the parameters like I have added: a maven command under the **Shell Script** field.

Clicking on the Generate Pipeline Script button will convert your GUI configuration (Jenkins build step with a maven command) into a script (Figure 1-6).

More about writing a Jenkinsfile for CI/CD is discussed in detail in **Chapter 5** and **Chapter 8**.

Reproducible Build Environments

Traditionally, Jenkins build agents are either individual hardware machines or virtual machines maintained using VMware vsphere or other similar tools. In either case, setting up the build machines requires both time and effort. From the infrastructure perspective, the tasks include procuring hardware, networking, licenses, etc. And from the configuration management perspective, the tasks include installing and configuring the OS and other software.

Nevertheless, most of the tasks pertaining to the infrastructure can be reduced by moving to a cloud-based solution, for example: AWS, DigitalOcean, etc. And, most of the work pertaining to the configuration management can be reduced by using tools such as Chef, Puppet, etc.

However, all these measures do not stop things from going wrong. As the famous Murphy's law states, Anything that can go wrong, will go wrong. Therefore the point is, "what do we do if things go wrong?"

What Do We Do if the Build Agent Fails?

If the build agents are bare metal machines, then it may take a while to figure out what went wrong. Usually, in an organization, hardware machines are maintained by the IT department that has SLAs to provide a resolution. Examples are, Tier1 machines: 3~4 hours; Tier2 machines: 1~2 days, etc.

If the build agents are virtual machines, then it's more or less the same time as discussed above. The only advantage is that there is no need to fetch a new piece of hardware if required. The chances of a machine going down on a cloud are less. Nevertheless, they are still likely to occur. And if they do, the situation becomes the same as it were with the bare metal machines. Even the configuration management tools like Chef and Puppet take some time to configure a new machine.

This is where the container technology comes to the rescue. Tools like Docker enable us to describe a machine as a code that can be saved inside a file (Dockerfile). Dockerfile is a set of instructions that define what a machine should look like, what applications it should have, how they should be configured, etc. Using Dockerfile, we can quickly bring up a lightweight machine with all the necessary software preinstalled.

While Jenkinsfile defines a pipeline as a code, Dockerfile defines infrastructure as a code. And it has the same advantages as that of Jenkinsfile:

- Dockerfile can be a version control along with your source code.

- Dockerfile is easily shareable.

- Developers can themselves define what a Dockerfile should do.

- You can have different Dockerfiles for different types of builds.

How Dockerfile Works?

Following is an example of a Dockerfile:

```
############################################################
# Dockerfile for Maven build container images
# Based on Ubuntu
############################################################

# Set the base image to Ubuntu
FROM ubuntu

# Author / Maintainer
Nikhil Pathania

############################################################
```

```
# Update the repository sources list
RUN apt-get update

# Install Maven
RUN apt-get install maven

# Install Java
RUN apt-get install default-jre
```

To create a Docker image using Dockerfile, we need to build it using the Docker build command:

```
docker build -t <docker image name> <path to your docker file>
```

Example:

```
Docker build -t maven-build-image .

Sending build context to Docker daemon 45.04 kB
...snip...
Removing intermediate container cb53c9d09fff
Successfully built c2c31529076d
```

To check the newly created Docker image, use the following Docker command:

```
docker images
```

The outcome should be something similar to this:

```
REPOSITORY           TAG     IMAGE   ID      CREATED         SIZE
maven-build-image    latest  c2c3152907b5    10 minutes ago  376 MB
hello-world          latest  91c95931e552    5 weeks ago     910 B
```

To run a container using the above Docker image, issue the following command:

```
docker run -it maven-build-image /bin/bash
```

To see all the running containers, open up a new terminal on your Docker host machine and use the following command:

```
docker ps
```

How to Use a Dockerfile with Jenkins?

The idea is to have Dockerfile for each environment. Examples:

- Dockerfile for build & Unit test.
- Dockerfile for build & Integration test.
- Dockerfile for Acceptance testing.
- Dockerfile for Performance testing.
- Dockerfile for end-to-end testing.

All these files can be kept under a version control system along with your source code. Whenever there is a code commit on the version control system. the following steps take place:

1. A Version control webhook (commit) is sent to Jenkins.

2. The Jenkins pipeline Job gets triggered on receiving the webhook.

3. The Jenkins pipeline Job downloads the latest source code as well as the Jenkinsfile and the set of Dockerfiles from the version control system.

4. Jenkins reads the Jenkinsfile and executes the pipeline steps accordingly.

5. The first step inside the Jenkinsfile is to build all the required Docker images using the Dockerfiles.

6. With the required Docker images built, Jenkins can now perform various pipeline steps on the respective Docker containers that are spawned using the Docker images.

Figure 1-7 illustrates how Dockerfile can be used along with Jenkins.

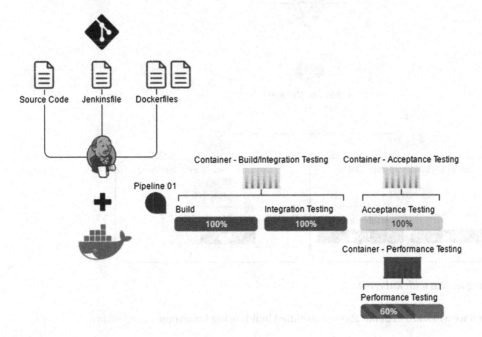

Figure 1-7. *Using Dockerfile with Jenkins*

Kubernetes

In the previous section, we saw how Jenkins along with Docker makes spawning build agents a piece of cake. Surely Jenkins works brilliantly with Docker. However, with Kubernetes it goes even further, that is, by making the build farm (Docker host) scalable. In simple terms, Kubernetes can be thought of as a cluster of Docker hosts that are scalable. It's a tool to manage containers across a cluster of Docker hosts.

How to Use Kubernetes with Jenkins?

Figure 1-8 illustrates how Kubernetes can be used along with Jenkins. The working of it is pretty much the same as discussed in Figure 1-7. The only difference is that we have more than one Docker host. The responsibility of running and maintaining containers across multiple Docker hosts is with the Kubernetes manager. Jenkins is connected with Kubernetes using a plugin.

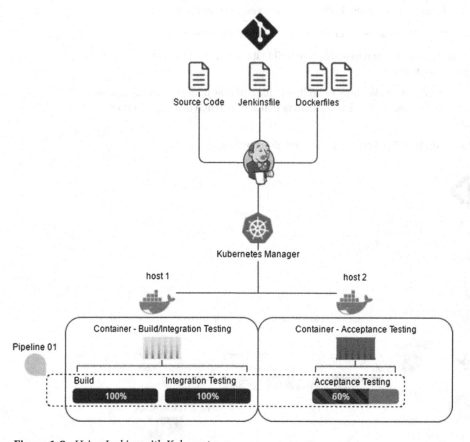

Figure 1-8. *Using Jenkins with Kubernetes*

In **Chapter 6** we will learn in detail about distributed builds using Kubernetes and Jenkins.

A Highly Available CI Master

Tools like Docker help in making the build environment (Jenkins build agents) highly available and fungible. But, what about the CI master? What if the Jenkins Master fails to start? There should be some mechanism to make it available somewhere else with the same address, and without the users noticing anything.

Right now Jenkins does not provide anything for High availability. Nevertheless, using technologies like CoreOS, Pacemaker, and Kubernetes we can make Jenkins Service highly available.

Let's have a look at these technologies.

CoreOS

CoreOS is a Linux-based OS. It is a minimal operating system that supports popular container systems like Docker and Kubernetes. The operating system is designed to work in clusters. Figure 1-9 shows the constituents of CoreOS.

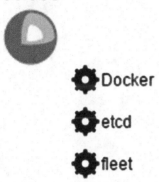

Figure 1-9. *CoreOS constituents*

Docker

Docker is a container platform. Containers contain everything that are required to run an application in an isolated workspace. Unlike VMs, containers do not contain a full operating system; instead, it only has libraries and settings required to make the software work. This makes a container efficient, lightweight, and self-contained.

Etcd

Etcd is a distributed key/value store. In simple terms, etcd is a utility that enables a group of machines that form a cluster to communicate with each other. Etcd serves as a pillar of any distributed system. Kubernetes, CoreOS, and Fleet all rely on etcd (Figure 1-10).

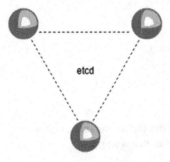

Figure 1-10. *CoreOS cluster using etcd*

Fleet

Fleet is a utility to manage a cluster. It can be considered as an extension of **systemd** that functions at the cluster level. Fleet is used to schedule systemd units across multiple nodes in a cluster.

Figure 1-11 shows an HA Jenkins Master setup using CoreOS cluster. Unit files are used to define services that are to be monitored and made highly available.

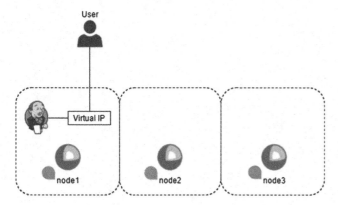

Figure 1-11. *CoreOS cluster for Jenkins HA*

In the case of a failure, the services are moved to the remaining online nodes of the cluster. Figure 1-12 shows a failover scenario.

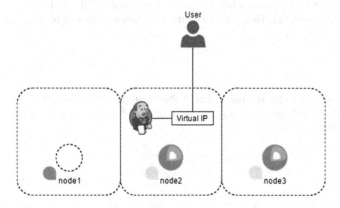

Figure 1-12. *CoreOS cluster for Jenkins HA with a failover scenario*

Unit Files

A unit file defines how and when a service should start, what must be done if the service becomes offline, what should start before the service starts, and what should happen after the service is stopped.

Shown below is a sample unit file to start a Jenkins Master inside a Docker container.

```
[Unit]
Description=Jenkins Master Server

After=docker.service
Requires=docker.service

[Service]
TimeoutStartSec=0
ExecStartPre=-/usr/bin/docker kill jenkins%i
ExecStartPre=-/usr/bin/docker rm jenkins%i

ExecStart=/usr/bin/docker run --privileged --name jenkins%i -p 8080:8080
jenkinsci/jenkins:lts

ExecStop=/usr/bin/docker stop jenkins%i

[X-Fleet]
Conflicts=jenkins@*.service
```

The section **[Unit]** defines the Unit file. The section **[Service]** is where you define **ExecStartPre**, **ExecStart**, and the **ExecPost** steps. The section **[X-Fleet]** defines a few special properties about how a service should run. Using some of the X-Fleet options, you can make instances of the service to run on each CoreOS machine.

The above code can be saved inside a file **jenkins.service,** assuming a CoreOS cluster with three nodes (172.17.8.101, 172.17.8.102, 172.17.8.103). To bring up the service on any one of the nodes give the following fleetctl command:

```
fleetctl start jenkins@1.service
```

You will get an output as shown below:

```
Unit jenkins@1.service inactive
Unit jenkins@1.service launched on b40a8da6.../172.17.8.101
```

To check the status of the units that we just started do,

```
fleetctl list-units
```

And you should see something as shown below:

```
UNIT                MACHINE                     ACTIVE        SUB
jenkins@1.service   b40a8da6.../172.17.8.101    activating    start-pre
```

The status of the units is still **activating**. It will take some time (depending on you network speed) as the fleet is downloading the Jenkins Docker image from the Docker hub.

Run the **fleetctl list-units** command again and now you can see the Jenkins Server is started and active.

```
UNIT                MACHINE                     ACTIVE        SUB
jenkins@1.service   b40a8da6.../172.17.8.101    active        running
```

13

Jenkins service is now running in a highly available mode. Try killing the machines where the Jenkins service is running. CoreOS Cluster will immediately bring up Jenkins on any one of the remaining CoreOS machines.

Highly available Jenkins Master using CoreOS, Docker, and GlusterFS (storage) is the topic of discussion in **Chapter 3**.

Pacemaker

Pacemaker is an open source cluster resource manager. Along with Corosync, it can offer an open source high availability (HA) cluster. Pacemaker can detect system as well as service failures by utilizing the messaging capabilities provided by Corosync. Following are some of the key features provided by Pacemaker.

- Detection and recovering from node and service-level failures.
- Anything that can be scripted can be clustered.
- Uses STONITH for data integrity.
- Can support large and small clusters.
- Can support any variant of redundancy configuration.

Figure 1-13 shows an Active/Passive HA setup for Jenkins. Pacemaker and Corosync run on all nodes of the cluster. Jenkins, Virtual IP, and Storage (DRBD) run as a service on the active node. These services are monitored continuously by Corosync.

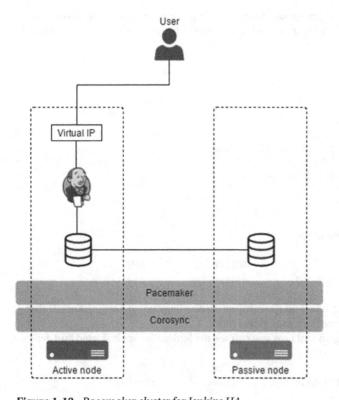

Figure 1-13. Pacemaker cluster for Jenkins HA

In the event of failure, let's say the active node goes offline, all running services on the active node are moved to the passive node. Since the storage is in sync there is hardly anything lost, except the Jenkins Jobs that were running during the failover (Figure 1-14).

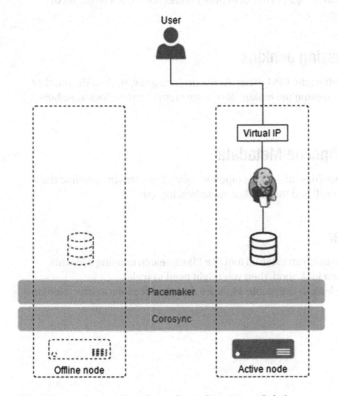

Figure 1-14. Pacemaker cluster for Jenkins HA with failover scenario

Once you bring the offline node back online, the storage syncs again. Highly available Jenkins Master using Pacemaker, Corosync, and DRBD (storage) is the topic of discussion in **Chapter 2**.

Scaling Jenkins Master

Scaling Jenkins involves two different things, scaling Jenkins Master and scaling Jenkins Slaves. We already saw scaling Jenkins Slave in the previous section using Docker and Kubernetes. Let us see the possibilities of scaling the Jenkins Master.

Why Do We Need to Scale the Jenkins Master?

As more and more projects switch to continuous integration and continuous delivery models, the requirements on the Jenkins server increase. And at some point, a single Jenkins Master may not be sufficient to serve a growing number of projects.

The same question can be put another way: "When and how do we know we need to scale Jenkins Master?" Assuming that we perform all builds on the Jenkins Slaves and nothing on the Jenkins Master, we are left with the following things that may eat up hardware resources on the Jenkins server.

Out of Memory Issues While Reading Huge Logs

Some of the pipeline stages in Jenkins could produce a massive amount of logs. Accessing them sometimes might lead to slowness. This slowness can quickly lead to out of memory issues (OOM) if a larger set of people start accessing logs all at the same time.

Growing Number of Users Accessing Jenkins

The number of users accessing Jenkins can affect the CPU usage. As the projects grow, so does the number of users accessing Jenkins. The purpose of accessing the Jenkins server are many: it can be logs, dashboard, pipeline progress, etc.

Growing Number of Logs, and Pipeline Metadata

As the number of projects on Jenkins grow, so does the Jenkins pipeline count. Each Jenkins pipeline has a workspace on the Jenkins Master, where you will find the pipeline metadata, log, etc.

Benchmark Your Jenkins Master

It's possible to monitor Jenkins performance using an external tool like Elasticsearch or using a Jenkins plugin (monitoring) itself. If the reports do not look good, then you might need to scale.

All the above reasons can make scaling Jenkins inevitable. Here are the two directions in which Jenkins can scale.

- Vertical scaling.

- Horizontal scaling.

Vertical Scaling

Vertical scaling is the easiest. It simply requires you to upgrade the hardware. The advantage of using this approach is the following.

A Single Jenkins Master to Maintain

Some of the Jenkins maintenance activities include the following:

- Installing and updating plugins.

- Archiving or deleting old build data.

- Managing users and permissions.

- Upgrading Jenkins.

- Configuring Jenkins.

The list is not comprehensive. However, a single Jenkins master means you need to worry only about a single machine. Adding to that, with careful configuration most of the above tasks can be automated. Nevertheless, following is one disadvantage of having a single Jenkins Master.

Greater Risk

Having a single Jenkins master is pleasant when it comes to maintenance. However, any kind of failure may halt your day-to-day business. Even with proper backup, it would be a difficult task to bring a beefy Jenkins Master up again.

One way to look at this problem is to make Jenkins highly available. However, there is still a problem. A heavy Jenkins master, for obvious reasons, will have a large number of pipelines running at any given point of time. In an event of failure, even with an HA solution in place, all the running Jobs will be lost to the heavens.

To make matters worse, imagine a situation wherein the Jenkins HA itself fails to bring up Jenkins Master on the secondary machine: remember Murphy's law. Therefore, there is a greater risk of having everything inside a single Jenkins master.

Horizontal Scaling

Horizontal scaling requires using multiple Jenkins masters. Each Jenkins master serves a group of projects. Following are some of the advantages of having multiple Jenkins Masters.

Better Management Using Segregation

You can segregate projects based on their requirements and characteristics. Example: all projects that are windows based (say .NET or C++) will have a similar set of plugins, build tool configurations, etc. Hence, keeping all the Microsoft-based projects on a particular Jenkins Master might help in managing the projects better.

Better Reliability

In a multiple Jenkins Master setup, if any one of the Jenkins Master fails, the others still run. And if we make each of the Jenkins Masters highly available, then the probability of a complete business standstill becomes minute since the probability of all the Jenkins Master HA setups failing at once is very minimal.

Maintenance Encumbrance

With multiple Jenkins Master setups, the maintenance tasks also multiply. However, most of the maintenance tasks can be automated to reduce the maintenance encumbrance.

Parallel Testing

The benefits of distributed and scalable Jenkins Slaves are not just limited to software builds, but can also be taken forward to the testing arena. Faster and parallel testing is an integral part of the continuous delivery.

What Is Parallel Testing?

Parallel testing can be defined as the process of running multiple test cases on a distributed testing infrastructure. This distributed testing infrastructure can be a set of virtual machines or Docker containers.

Some of the key advantages of parallel testing are as follows.

Broader Compatibility

Let's say you have a web application that you would like to test on multiple browsers like Firefox, Chrome, Opera, etc. You can do this in parallel in the following way.

In the Jenkinsfile you define parallel stages for each running test case on a particular node (Docker container). In the following pipeline code, you can see three stages ('acceptance test chrome', 'acceptance test opera', and 'acceptance test firefox') defined to run in parallel. Each one of the stages has its own node ('docker-chrome', 'docker-opera', 'docker-firefox').

```
/* CI starts */
node('docker-ci-agent'){

        stage('build'){
        // some build step
        }

        stage('integration testing'){
        // some integration steps
        }

}
/* CI ends */

/* Testing starts */
parallel stage('acceptance test chrome'){

        node('docker-chrome'){
        // steps to perform acceptance test on chrome
        }

},
        stage('acceptance test Opera'){

        node('docker-opera'){
        //steps to perform acceptance test on opera
        }

}

        stage('acceptance test firefox'){

        node('docker-firefox'){
        //steps to perform acceptance test on firefox
        }

}
/* Testing ends */
```

Along with the Jenkinsfile, you also create Dockerfiles for each type of testing. These Dockerfiles are then used by the Jenkins pipeline to create Docker containers (Jenkins nodes) to perform the testing. Figure 1-15 illustrates testing an application in parallel on multiple browsers using Jenkins and Docker.

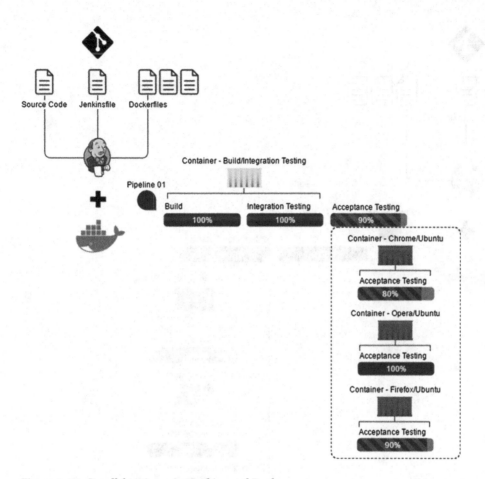

Figure 1-15. *Parallel testing using Jenkins and Docker*

Reduce Testing Time

Using intelligent scripts or plugins, you can divide your test cases into batches and execute them in parallel on a set of testing machines. The testing machines could be just virtual machines or Docker containers. Executing tests in parallel can drastically reduce the testing time.

For example, you are running 1000 concurrent tests on a single testing machine, and it takes you 24 hours. You can divide your test cases into 4 groups of 250 test cases each, and execute each group on an individual testing machine. This will reduce your testing time from 24 hours to 6 hours, theoretically. Figure 1-16 illustrates dividing and running the test cases in parallel across similar testing machines.

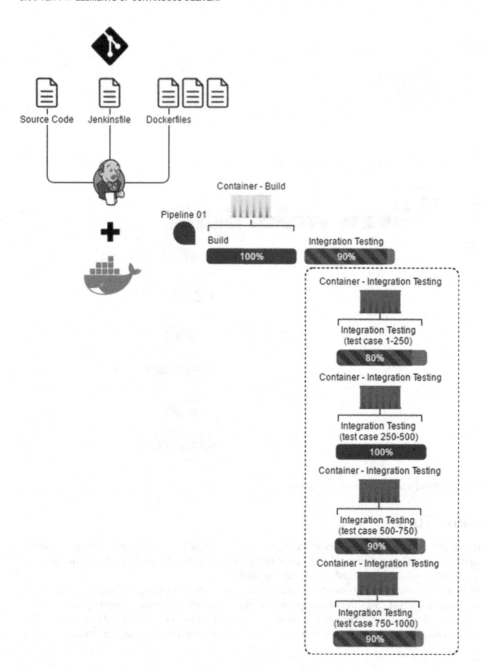

Figure 1-16. *Parallel testing using Jenkins and Docker*

Summary

In the current chapter, we discussed the four key elements that are important to achieve continuous delivery: fungible build/test environment, pipeline as code, scalable build/test environment, and parallel testing. We also learned about the tools involved in achieving it.

Along with this, we discussed the importance of using a branching strategy, the process of making Jenkins highly available, and the importance of scaling Jenkins horizontally. All in all, the current chapter forms a theoretical base for the upcoming chapters.

In the next chapter, we will learn to create a highly available Jenkins Master using Pacemaker, Corosync, and DRBD.

CHAPTER 2

■ ■ ■

HA Jenkins Setup Using Pacemaker, Corosync, and DRBD

In the following chapter, we will build a highly available (HA) Jenkins Server using Pacemaker, Corosync, and DRBD. We will begin the chapter by discussing a HA design along with a failover scenario. Next, we will build and start a HA setup for Jenkins using Pacemaker, Corosync and DRBD. At the end of the chapter, we will test our HA setup by simulating a failover scenario.

Designing a High Availability Setup for Jenkins

Failures could occur at the hardware level (machine shutdown/reboot/freeze), application server level (application server failure), or at the service level (the service fails to start or hangs). High Availability (HA) ensures that a service or a group of services is available continuously without any interruption. Every HA system comes with a **failover** mechanism. This failover mechanism ensures that the controls of the primary system are transferred to a secondary system (replica of the primary system) in case there are any failures observed on the primary system. To detect failures, every HA setup has a feature to check the health of the hardware and the applications that are being served.

Figure 2-1 illustrates a typical HA setup (Active/Passive). This is a two-node HA setup with one of the nodes taking up the primary role and the other acting as a secondary (backup). A user accesses the service through a fixed virtual IP. If the primary node goes down for some reason or the service on the primary node fails, the secondary node is immediately made active (along with the services), and the static virtual IP is shifted to the secondary node.

© Nikhil Pathania 2017
N. Pathania, *Pro Continuous Delivery*, DOI 10.1007/978-1-4842-2913-2_2

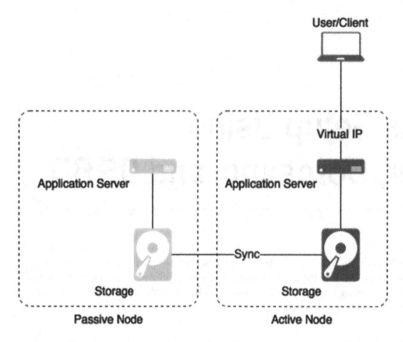

Figure 2-1. *A typical Active/Passive HA setup*

Since the users access the HA services using a static virtual IP, all they notice is a small glitch while the switching takes place.

HA Setup for Jenkins

Figure 2-2 illustrates how our HA setup for Jenkins should look. We have two Ubuntu machines, **node1** and **node2** respectively. Each machine is running Pacemaker, Corosync, and DRBD. Both these nodes are also running Jenkins inside Apache Tomcat Server.

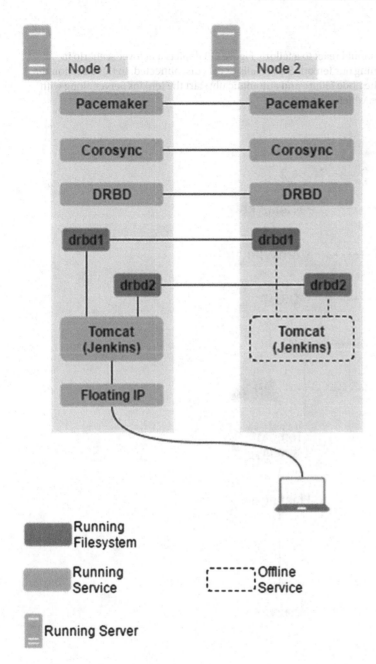

Figure 2-2. Jenkins HA setup

Whether it's a build or a configuration change, everything that happens on the Jenkins Server is stored inside the Jenkins home directory. Thus, making the data inside the Jenkins home directory redundant is of the uttermost importance. We are using DRBD for that purpose, and therefore there is an extra disk (sdb) on each node. These extra disks have two filesystems **drbd1** and **drbd2** running on partitions /**dev/sdb1** and /**dev/sdb2** respectively. These discs are in sync using DRBD.

The Jenkins Server is accessible to the outside world using a Floating IP.

25

Failover Scenario

Let us understand how our HA setup should react to a failure. Figure 2-3 depicts a failover scenario in which the **node1** machine that is running our Jenkins Server fails or gets disconnected. In this situation the Pacemaker/Corosync should detect the node failure and automatically start the Jenkins Server along with the Floating IP on the secondary node, which is **node2**.

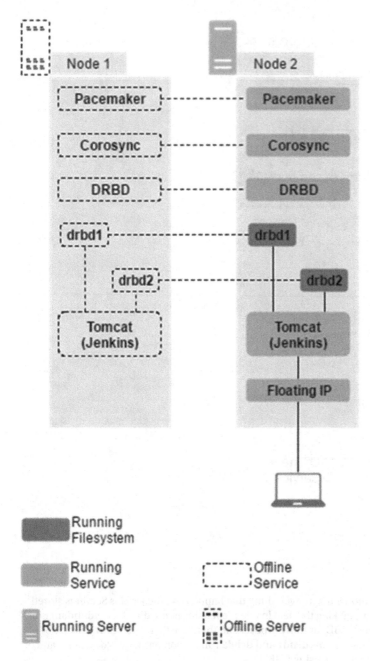

Figure 2-3. *Failover scenario*

Creating a HA Cluster for Jenkins

In the following section we will realize the HA setup design discussed in Figure 2-2. We are going to use **Vagrant** along with **Oracle Virtual-Box** to create the two nodes (Ubuntu 16.04 machines). Once these nodes (node1 and node2) are ready, we will install Apache Tomcat Server and Jenkins on them. After this we will install and configure the cluster software Pacemaker and Corosync.

Once the setup is ready, we will create the cluster resources for Floating IP and Tomcat. To make the Jenkins Server data and the Tomcat Server data persistent, we will install and configure DRBD. Consecutively we will also create cluster resources for the DRBD device and the filesystems.

■ **Note**   While writing this chapter, I have chosen a machine with Ubuntu 16.04 that will host our two nodes HA setup. Nevertheless, you can also choose to use Windows 7/8/10 without any issues.

For simplicity I am using Vagrant along with Oracle VirtualBox to create the two nodes for our HA setup. However, in reality you may choose to create these two nodes on two bare metal machines or on a cloud platform such as AWS.

Installing Vagrant

Make sure you perform the following steps as a root user or with an account having root privileges (sudo access).

1. Open up a terminal and type the following commands to download Vagrant. Or you can also download the latest vagrant package from the vagrant website (Figure 2-4): https://www.vagrantup.com/downloads.html

    ```
    wget https://releases.hashicorp.com/vagrant/1.8.5/vagrant_1.8.5_x86_64.deb
    ```

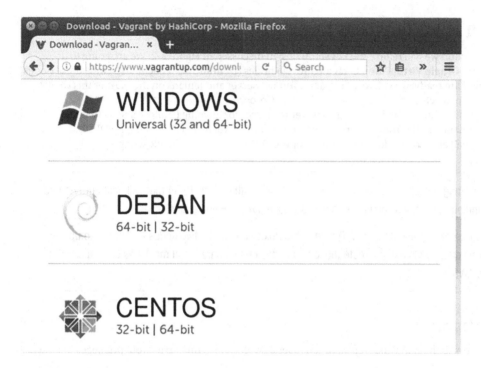

Figure 2-4. *Vagrant download webpage*

■ **Note**   Use the latest version of Vagrant and VirtualBox. Using an older version of Vagrant with a newer version of VirtualBox or vice versa may result in issues while creating the virtual machines (node1 and node2).

---

2. When the download completes, you should see a **.deb** file in the download folder.

3. Change to the location where you have downloaded the Vagrant package and execute the following commands to install Vagrant. You may be prompted to provide a password.

    ```
    sudo dpkg -i vagrant_1.8.5_x86_64.deb

    sudo apt-get install -f
    ```

4. Once the installation is complete, check the installed version of vagrant by executing the following command.

    ```
    vagrant --version
    ```

5. You should see the vagrant version as shown in Figure 2-5.

```
nikhil@dev01:~/Downloads$ vagrant --version
Vagrant 1.8.5
nikhil@dev01:~/Downloads$ ▮
```

Figure 2-5. Check the vagrant version

Installing VirtualBox

Vagrant needs Oracle VirtualBox to create virtual machines. However, it's not limited to just Oracle VirtualBox, you can also use VMware and AWS.

■ **Note** To run Vagrant with either VMware or AWS, visit the following webpage: `https://www.vagrantup.com/docs/getting-started/providers.html`

Follow the below steps to install Oracle VirtualBox on your machine.

1. Add the following line to your **/etc/apt/sources.list** file.

    `deb http://download.virtualbox.org/virtualbox/debian xenial contrib`

■ **Note** According to your Ubuntu distribution, replace 'xenial' by 'vivid', 'utopic', 'trusty', 'raring', 'quantal', 'precise', 'lucid', 'jessie', 'wheezy', or 'squeeze'.

---

2. Download and register the keys by executing the following commands in sequence. The output of these commands is depicted in Figure 2-6.

    ```
    wget -q https://www.virtualbox.org/download/oracle_vbox_2016.asc -O- |
    sudo apt-key add -
    ```

    ```
    wget -q https://www.virtualbox.org/download/oracle_vbox.asc -O- |
    sudo apt-key add -
    ```

```
nikhil@dev01:~$ sudo wget -q https://www.virtualbox.org/download/oracle_vbox_201
6.asc -O- | sudo apt-key add -
OK
nikhil@dev01:~$ sudo wget -q https://www.virtualbox.org/download/oracle_vbox.asc
 -O- | sudo apt-key add -
OK
nikhil@dev01:~$ ▮
```

Figure 2-6. Download and register the VirtualBox keys

3. Update your apt-get package index using the following command.

```
sudo apt-get update
```

4. To install VirtualBox, execute the following commands.

```
sudo apt-get install virtualbox-5.1
```

5. Execute the following command to check the VirtualBox version. The output of the command is depicted in Figure 2-7.

```
VBoxManage --version
```

```
nikhil@dev01:~$ VBoxManage --version
5.1.6r110634
nikhil@dev01:~$
```

Figure 2-7. *Check VirtualBox version*

■ **Note** Ubuntu/Debian users might want to install the dkms package to ensure that the VirtualBox host kernel modules (vboxdrv, vboxnetflt, and vboxnetadp) are properly updated if the Linux kernel version changes during the next apt-get upgrade. For Debian it is available in Lenny backports and in the normal repository for Squeeze and later. The dkms package can be installed through the Synaptic Package manager or through the following command:

```
sudo apt-get install dkms
```

Creating Virtual Machines

Creating the virtual machines using Vagrant is easy. We will use a simple **Vagrantfile** to create two Ubuntu nodes.

1. Create a directory named **vagrant-ubuntu** under your **/home** directory and get inside it.

```
mkdir vagrant-ubuntu
cd vagrant-ubuntu
```

2. Download the official vagrant box image for Ubuntu (ubuntu/trusty64) using the following command. This will take some time to finish.

```
sudo vagrant box add ubuntu/trusty64
```

3. To create a Vagrantfile do.

```
sudo nano Vagrantfile
```

4. Paste the following code inside the Vagrantfile.

```
# -*- mode: ruby -*-
# vi: set ft=ruby :

Vagrant.configure(2) do |config|
  config.vm.box = "ubuntu/trusty64"

  config.vm.define :node1 do |node1_config|
      node1_config.vm.host_name = "node1"
      node1_config.vm.network "private_network", ip:"172.17.8.104"
      node1_config.vm.provider :virtualbox do |vb|
          vb.customize ["modifyvm", :id, "--memory", "1024"]
          vb.customize ["modifyvm", :id, "--cpus", "1"]
      end
  end

  config.vm.define :node2 do |node2_config|
      node2_config.vm.host_name = "node2"
      node2_config.vm.network "private_network", ip:"172.17.8.105"
      node2_config.vm.provider :virtualbox do |vb|
          vb.customize ["modifyvm", :id, "--memory", "1024"]
          vb.customize ["modifyvm", :id, "--cpus", "1"]
      end
  end

end
```

5. I have named the two nodes as **node1** and **node2** with IP address 172.17.8.104 and 172.17.8.105 respectively. However, you are free to choose the IP address. Similarly you are free to choose the node names, number of CPUs, and the memory.

6. Type **Ctrl+x** and then **Y** to save and exit the file.

Starting the Virtual Machines

Starting the virtual machines is simple.

1. Move to the **ubuntu-vagrant** directory and run the vagrant up command to start the virtual machines.

```
cd ubuntu-vagrant

vagrant up
```

2. The vagrant up command should execute without any errors.

3. To check the status of the virtual machines, execute the command vagrant status. The output of this command is shown in Figure 2-8.

```
nikhil@dev01:~/ubuntu-vagrant$ vagrant status
Current machine states:

node1                     running (virtualbox)
node2                     running (virtualbox)

This environment represents multiple VMs. The VMs are all listed
above with their current state. For more information about a specific
VM, run `vagrant status NAME`.
nikhil@dev01:~/ubuntu-vagrant$ █
```

Figure 2-8. *List the running virtual machines*

4. To login to any one of the virtual machines (let say node1) use the vagrant ssh command as shown in Figure 2-9.

    vagrant ssh node1 -- -A

```
nikhil@dev01:~/ubuntu-vagrant$ vagrant ssh node1 -- -A
Welcome to Ubuntu 14.04.5 LTS (GNU/Linux 3.13.0-96-generic x86_64)

 * Documentation:  https://help.ubuntu.com/

  System information as of Mon Oct  3 15:00:36 UTC 2016

  System load:  0.02              Processes:           78
  Usage of /:   3.5% of 39.34GB   Users logged in:     0
  Memory usage: 12%               IP address for eth0: 10.0.2.15
  Swap usage:   0%                IP address for eth1: 172.17.8.104

  Graph this data and manage this system at:
    https://landscape.canonical.com/

  Get cloud support with Ubuntu Advantage Cloud Guest:
    http://www.ubuntu.com/business/services/cloud

0 packages can be updated.
0 updates are security updates.

New release '16.04.1 LTS' available.
Run 'do-release-upgrade' to upgrade to it.


Last login: Mon Oct  3 15:00:36 2016 from 10.0.2.2
vagrant@node1:~$
```

Figure 2-9. *Log in to node1*

5. To know the IP address of **node1**, execute the ip route command. Notice the highlighted IP address in Figure 2-10 that's the IP of our **node1** machine.

```
vagrant@node1:~$ ip route
default via 10.0.2.2 dev eth0
10.0.2.0/24 dev eth0  proto kernel  scope link  src 10.0.2.15
172.17.8.0/24 dev eth1  proto kernel  scope link  src 172.17.8.104
vagrant@node1:~$ █
```

Figure 2-10. *Get the IP address of node1*

6. Open another terminal and login to **node2** using the vagrant ssh command.

   vagrant ssh node2 -- -A

7. To know the IP address of **node2**, execute the ip route command. Notice the highlighted IP address in Figure 2-11. That's the IP of our **node2** machine.

```
vagrant@node2:~$ ip route
default via 10.0.2.2 dev eth0
10.0.2.0/24 dev eth0  proto kernel  scope link  src 10.0.2.15
172.17.8.0/24 dev eth1  proto kernel  scope link  src 172.17.8.105
vagrant@node2:~$
```

Figure 2-11. Get the IP address of node2

Configuring Communication Between the node1 and node2

We are now done creating our HA node machines. Let us configure them to talk with each other.

1. Execute the ping command to check if node1 and node2 can ping each other. Figure 2-12 shows a ping test from node1 to node2.

```
vagrant@node1:~$ ping -c 3 172.17.8.105
PING 172.17.8.105 (172.17.8.105) 56(84) bytes of data.
64 bytes from 172.17.8.105: icmp_seq=1 ttl=64 time=0.645 ms
64 bytes from 172.17.8.105: icmp_seq=2 ttl=64 time=0.675 ms
64 bytes from 172.17.8.105: icmp_seq=3 ttl=64 time=0.534 ms

--- 172.17.8.105 ping statistics ---
3 packets transmitted, 3 received, 0% packet loss, time 2002ms
rtt min/avg/max/mdev = 0.534/0.618/0.675/0.060 ms
vagrant@node1:~$
```

Figure 2-12. Ping test

2. Repeat the above step by pinging **node1** from **node2**.

3. Now check if the machines (node1 and node2) can communicate using their hostnames. If you have a DNS server, add additional entries for the two machines. Otherwise, you'll need to add the machine's hostname to /etc/hosts on both nodes. Figure 2-13, depicts the content of my **/etc/hosts** file on **node1**.

```
vagrant@node1:~$ cat /etc/hosts
127.0.0.1        node1    node1
127.0.0.1 localhost
::1 ip6-localhost ip6-loopback
fe00::0 ip6-localnet
ff00::0 ip6-mcastprefix
ff02::1 ip6-allnodes
ff02::2 ip6-allrouters
ff02::3 ip6-allhosts
vagrant@node1:~$
```

Figure 2-13. List the content of /etc/hosts file on node1

3. Open the **/etc/hosts** file and add the following entries to it.

    ```
    172.17.8.104    node1    node1
    172.17.8.105    node2    node2
    ```

4. Finally the **/etc/hosts** file on **node1** should look like Figure 2-14.

```
vagrant@node1:~$ cat /etc/hosts
127.0.0.1       node1   node1
172.17.8.104    node1   node1
172.17.8.105    node2   node2
127.0.0.1 localhost
::1 ip6-localhost ip6-loopback
fe00::0 ip6-localnet
ff00::0 ip6-mcastprefix
ff02::1 ip6-allnodes
ff02::2 ip6-allrouters
ff02::3 ip6-allhosts
vagrant@node1:~$ ▮
```

Figure 2-14. *Content of /etc/hosts file on node1 after updating*

5. Similarly, modify the **/etc/hosts** file on **node2** by adding the same lines mentioned in step 3. Finally, the **/etc/hosts** file on **node2** should look as shown in Figure 2-15.

```
vagrant@node2:~$ sudo cat /etc/hosts
127.0.0.1       node2   node2
172.17.8.104    node1   node1
172.17.8.105    node2   node2
127.0.0.1 localhost
::1 ip6-localhost ip6-loopback
fe00::0 ip6-localnet
ff00::0 ip6-mcastprefix
ff02::1 ip6-allnodes
ff02::2 ip6-allrouters
ff02::3 ip6-allhosts
vagrant@node2:~$ ▮
```

Figure 2-15. *Content of /etc/hosts file on node2 after updating*

6. Now check if node1 and node2 are able to communicate using their hostnames. Figure 2-16 is a ping test from node1 to node2.

```
vagrant@node1:~$ ping -c 3 node2
PING node2 (172.17.8.105) 56(84) bytes of data.
64 bytes from node2 (172.17.8.105): icmp_seq=1 ttl=64 time=0.779 ms
64 bytes from node2 (172.17.8.105): icmp_seq=2 ttl=64 time=0.662 ms
64 bytes from node2 (172.17.8.105): icmp_seq=3 ttl=64 time=0.666 ms

--- node2 ping statistics ---
3 packets transmitted, 3 received, 0% packet loss, time 2001ms
rtt min/avg/max/mdev = 0.662/0.702/0.779/0.058 ms
vagrant@node1:~$ ▮
```

Figure 2-16. *Ping test using hostnames*

7. Repeat the above step by pinging **node1** from **node2**.

Configuring ssh Key

SSH is a convenient and secure way to copy files and perform commands remotely. We will create a key without a password (using the -N option).

1. On **node1**, create a new key using the following command. The output of the command is depicted in Figure 2-17.

   ```
   ssh-keygen -t dsa -f ~/.ssh/id_dsa -N ""
   ```

```
vagrant@node1:~$ ssh-keygen -t dsa -f ~/.ssh/id_dsa -N ""
Generating public/private dsa key pair.
Your identification has been saved in /home/vagrant/.ssh/id_dsa.
Your public key has been saved in /home/vagrant/.ssh/id_dsa.pub.
The key fingerprint is:
5c:33:4e:7f:ae:b6:77:cd:a4:b7:a1:a7:f6:3f:2c:84 vagrant@node1
The key's randomart image is:
+--[ DSA 1024]----+
|                 |
|                 |
|        =        |
|     . + +       |
|      S . o .    |
|       E +  .    |
|        . o=.    |
|         .+++*   |
|         .+====| |
+-----------------+
vagrant@node1:~$ █
```

Figure 2-17. *Generate ssh key*

2. Copy the key to the authorized keys folder using the following command.

   ```
   cp ~/.ssh/id_dsa.pub ~/.ssh/authorized_keys
   ```

3. Install the key on the other node using the following command. The output of the command is depicted in Figure 2-18.

   ```
   scp -r ~/.ssh node2:
   ```

```
vagrant@node1:~$ scp -r ~/.ssh node2:
The authenticity of host 'node2 (172.17.8.105)' can't be established.
ECDSA key fingerprint is 10:bb:c8:f8:22:e9:ea:71:d0:b0:b5:1b:30:f7:c0:62.
Are you sure you want to continue connecting (yes/no)? yes
Warning: Permanently added 'node2' (ECDSA) to the list of known hosts.
vagrant@node2's password:
id_dsa                         100%  668     0.7KB/s   00:00
known_hosts                    100%  444     0.4KB/s   00:00
id_dsa.pub                     100%  603     0.6KB/s   00:00
authorized_keys                100%  603     0.6KB/s   00:00
vagrant@node1:~$ █
```

Figure 2-18. *Install key on node2 from node1 using scp command*

4. Test that you can now run commands remotely on node2 from node1, without being prompted. As shown in Figure 2-19.

```
vagrant@node1:~$ ssh node2 -- hostname
node2
vagrant@node1:~$ ▮
```

Figure 2-19. *Run commands on node2 from node1 using ssh*

Configuring Time Zone

For our HA setup to work properly It's important that both nodes are under the same time zone.

1. On both nodes (node1 and node2), use the following command to open a time zone selector.

```
sudo dpkg-reconfigure tzdata
```

2. You will be presented with a list of options to choose from. Follow the directions that appear on the screen. For example, I have chosen Asia/Kolkata, as shown in Figure 2-20.

```
vagrant@node1:~$ sudo dpkg-reconfigure tzdata

Current default time zone: 'Asia/Kolkata'
Local time is now:      Mon Oct  3 23:13:44 IST 2016.
Universal Time is now:  Mon Oct  3 17:43:44 UTC 2016.

vagrant@node1:~$ ▮
```

Figure 2-20. *Set the time zone*

3. Then install the **ntp** package using the following command. **ntp** is used to synchronize clocks over a network.

```
sudo apt-get -y install ntp
```

Configuring the Firewall

Corosync uses UDP transport between ports 5404 and 5406. If you are running a firewall, ensure that communication on those ports is allowed between the servers. Execute the following commands on both the nodes (node1 and node2).

```
sudo iptables -A INPUT  -i eth1 -p udp -m multiport --dports 5404,5405,5406 -m conntrack
--ctstate NEW,ESTABLISHED -j ACCEPT

sudo iptables -A OUTPUT  -o eth1 -p udp -m multiport --sports 5404,5405,5406 -m conntrack
--ctstate ESTABLISHED -j ACCEPT
```

Installing Apache Tomcat Server

In this section we will install Tomcat 8 on both the nodes (node1 and node2). Before you begin, make sure you are logged in as a root user or as a non-root user with sudo privileges.

■ **Note**   Perform the steps mentioned in the following sections on both the nodes (node1 and node2).

Installing Java

Tomcat requires Java to be installed on the server.

1.   Update your apt-get package index using the following command.

```
sudo apt-get update
```

2.   Then install the Java Development Kit (JDK) package using the following command.

```
sudo apt-get install default-jdk
```

Creating a Tomcat User

For security purposes, Tomcat should be run as an unprivileged user. We will create a new user and group that will run the Tomcat service.

1.   First, create a new tomcat group using the following command.

```
sudo groupadd tomcat
```

2.   Now, create a new tomcat user using the following command.

```
sudo useradd -s /bin/false -g tomcat -d /opt/tomcat tomcat
```

■ **Note**   `-s /bin/false` is used so that nobody can log into the account. `-d /opt/tomcat` is used as this will be the location where we will install Tomcat.

Installing Apache Tomcat Server

1.   Find the latest version of Tomcat 8 from the apache tomcat website: `https://tomcat.apache.org/` and get the link address of "tar.gz" as shown in Figure 2-21.

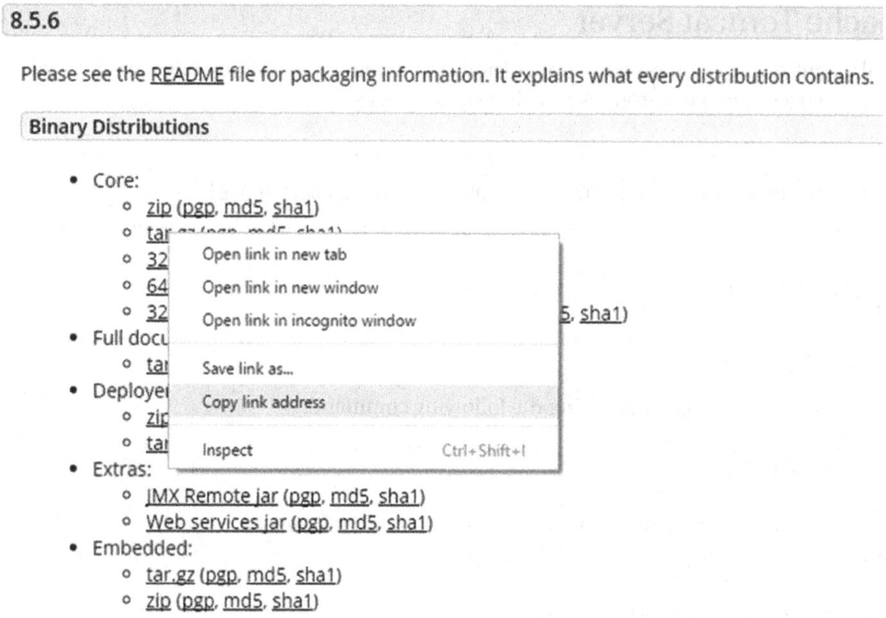

8.5.6

Please see the README file for packaging information. It explains what every distribution contains.

Binary Distributions

- Core:
  - zip (pgp, md5, sha1)
  - tar.gz (pgp, md5, sha1)
  - 32
  - 64
  - 32   5, sha1)
- Full docu
  - tar
- Deploye
  - zip
  - tar
- Extras:
  - JMX Remote jar (pgp, md5, sha1)
  - Web services jar (pgp, md5, sha1)
- Embedded:
  - tar.gz (pgp, md5, sha1)
  - zip (pgp, md5, sha1)

| Open link in new tab |
| Open link in new window |
| Open link in incognito window |
| Save link as... |
| Copy link address |
| Inspect   Ctrl+Shift+I |

Figure 2-21. *Get the tar.gz link address*

2. Change to the **/tmp** directory on your server. This is a good place to download temporary items.

   ```
   cd /tmp
   ```

3. Use wget to download the link that you copied from the Tomcat website.

   ```
   wget http://redrockdigimark.com/apachemirror/tomcat/tomcat-8/v8.5.5/
   bin/apache-tomcat-8.5.5.tar.gz
   ```

4. We will install Tomcat inside the **/opt/tomcat** directory. Create the directory, and then extract the archive to it with these commands.

   ```
   sudo mkdir /opt/tomcat
   ```

   ```
   sudo tar xzvf apache-tomcat-8*tar.gz -C /opt/tomcat --strip-components=1
   ```

■ **Note**   I have used Apache Tomcat 8.5.5. However, you can use any later stable version available.

For the purpose of installing Jenkins, Apache Tomcat Server 5.0 or greater is more than sufficient.

Updating Permissions

The tomcat user that we set up needs to have access to the Tomcat installation.

1. Change to the directory where we unpacked the Tomcat installation.

    ```
    cd /opt/tomcat
    ```

2. Give the tomcat group ownership over the entire installation directory.

    ```
    sudo chgrp -R tomcat /opt/tomcat
    ```

3. Next, give the tomcat group read access to the **conf** directory and all of its contents, and execute access to the directory itself.

    ```
    sudo chmod -R g+r conf
    ```

    ```
    sudo chmod g+x conf
    ```

4. Make the tomcat user the owner of the **webapps**, **work**, **temp**, and **logs** directories.

    ```
    sudo chown -R tomcat webapps/ work/ temp/ logs/
    ```

Adjusting the Firewall and Test the Tomcat Server

Before we start Tomcat, we need to adjust the firewall to allow our requests to get to the service. Tomcat uses port 8080 to accept requests.

1. Allow traffic to that port by typing the following command.

    ```
    sudo ufw allow 8080
    ```

2. Now run the **startup.sh** script to start Tomcat. It's present inside **/opt/tomcat/ bin** directory.

    ```
    cd /opt/tomcat/bin
    ```

    ```
    ./startup.sh
    ```

3. You can now access the default Tomcat dashboard on both the nodes by using the address: http://172.17.8.104:8080 for node1 and http://172.17.8.105:8080 for node2.

4. You will be able to see the default Tomcat dashboard on both the nodes. However, if you click the links for the Manager App, you will be denied access.

Configuring Tomcat Web Management Interface

In order to use the manager web app that comes with Tomcat, we must add a login to our Tomcat server.

1. First shut down Tomcat if it's running, using the **shutdown.sh** script present inside the **/opt/tomcat/bin** directory.

   ```
   cd /opt/tomcat/bin

   ./shutdown.sh
   ```

2. Open the **tomcat-users.xml** file for editing.

   ```
   sudo nano /opt/tomcat/conf/tomcat-users.xml
   ```

3. After opening the file, delete everything between <tomcat-users> </tomcat-users>.

4. Now, add a user who can access the manager-gui and admin-gui (web apps that come with Tomcat). You can do so by defining a user as shown below.

   ```
   <tomcat-users . . .>
       <user username="admin" password="password" roles="manager-
       gui,admin-gui"/>
   </tomcat-users>
   ```

5. Type **Ctrl+x** and then **Y** to save and exit the file.

   By default, newer versions of Tomcat restrict access to the Manager and Host Manager apps to connections coming from outside the Tomcat Server. Since we are accessing the Tomcat dashboard page from a remote machine (a machine that is other than the Tomcat Server), you will probably want to remove or alter this restriction. To change the IP address restrictions on these, open the **context. xml** files one by one.

6. For the Manager app. Do the following:

   ```
   sudo nano /opt/tomcat/webapps/manager/META-INF/context.xml
   ```

7. For the Host Manager app., do the following:

   ```
   sudo nano /opt/tomcat/webapps/host-manager/META-INF/context.xml
   ```

8. Inside these files, comment (disable) the IP address restriction to allow connections from anywhere.

   ```
   <Context antiResourceLocking="false" privileged="true" >
     <!--<Valve className="org.apache.catalina.valves.RemoteAddrValve"
           allow="127\.\d+\.\d+\.\d+|::1|0:0:0:0:0:0:0:1" />-->
   </Context>
   ```

9. Alternatively, if you would like to allow access only to the connections coming from a specific IP address or set of IP addresses then you can add your IP address to the list. Shown below is an example where the Tomcat dashboard is allowed to be accessed from the 172.17.8.101 IP address.

```
<Context antiResourceLocking="false" privileged="true" >
   <Valve className="org.apache.catalina.valves.RemoteAddrValve"
          allow="172.17.8.101" />
</Context>
```

10. Type **Ctrl+x** and then **Y** to save and exit the file.

11. Execute the **startup.sh** script to start Tomcat.

```
cd /opt/tomcat/bin

./startup.sh
```

12. Access the web management interface again in a web browser using the URL: http://172.17.8.104:8080 for node1 and http://172.17.8.105:8080 for node2.

Installing Jenkins as a Service on Apache Tomcat Server

Installing Jenkins as a service on Apache Tomcat Server is simple. You can choose to use Jenkins along with other services already present on the Apache Tomcat Server or you can use the Apache server solely for Jenkins.

■ **Note** Perform the steps mentioned in the following section on both the nodes (node1 and node2).

---

1. Go to the primary node (node1) and move to the **/tmp** directory.

```
cd /tmp
```

2. Use the wget command to download the **jenkins.war** file.

```
sudo wget http://mirrors.jenkins-ci.org/war-stable/latest/jenkins.war
```

■ **Note** Following are the links to download Jenkins:

Latest LTS Release: http://mirrors.jenkins-ci.org/war-stable/latest/jenkins.war

Latest Weekly Release: http://mirrors.jenkins-ci.org/war/latest/jenkins.war

---

3. Or you can also download **jenkins.war** from the Jenkins website, as shown in Figure 2-22.

Figure 2-22. *Jenkins download page*

4. By clicking on the **Download Jenkins** button you will be presented with an option to download the LTS Release and the Weekly Release.

5. Choose the LTS Release by clicking on the 2.19.1.war link. As shown in Figure 2-23, do not click on the drop-down menu. Clicking on the drop-down button will provide you with the stand-alone package for various Operating Systems.

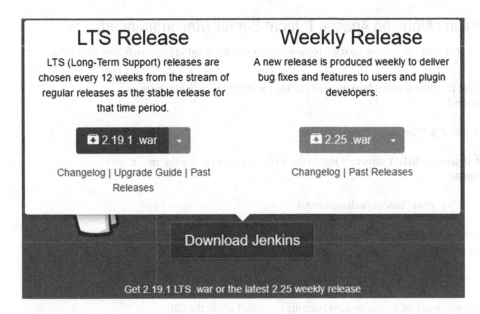

Figure 2-23. *Download the latest LTS release*

Installing Jenkins Along with Other Services on Apache Tomcat Server (Not Recommended)

Organizations can follow the current approach if they do not wish to have an individual server for Jenkins Master alone. But, what if they want to host it along with other services that are already running on their Apache Tomcat Servers?

1. Simply move the downloaded **jenkins.war** file from the **/tmp** folder to the **webapps** folder, which is present inside the installation directory of your Apache Tomcat Server. In our case it's **/opt/tomcat/webapps**.

   ```
   sudo cp /tmp/jenkins.war /opt/tomcat/webapps/
   ```

2. You will notice that a folder **jenkins** automatically gets created, the moment you move the **jenkins.war** package to the webapps folder (assuming that the Tomcat Server is running). See Figure 2-24.

```
vagrant@node1:~$ sudo ls -lrt /opt/tomcat/webapps/
total 68144
drwxr-x---  3 root root     4096 Oct  6 00:47 ROOT
drwxr-x--- 14 root root     4096 Oct  6 00:47 docs
drwxr-x---  6 root root     4096 Oct  6 00:47 examples
drwxr-x---  5 root root     4096 Oct  6 00:47 host-manager
drwxr-x---  5 root root     4096 Oct  6 00:47 manager
-rw-r--r--  1 root root 69754011 Oct  6 23:42 jenkins.war
drwxr-x--- 10 root root     4096 Oct  6 23:57 jenkins
vagrant@node1:~$ 
```

Figure 2-24. *List the content of webapps directory*

3. And that's all you need to do. In this way one can access Jenkins running on node1 using the URL http://172.17.8.104:8080/jenkins.

Installing Jenkins Alone on Apache Tomcat Server (Recommended)

On the other hand, if you chose to have Apache Tomcat Server solely for using Jenkins, follow the below steps:

1. Rename the downloaded **jenkins.war** package to **ROOT.war** using the move command.

   ```
   move /tmp/jenkins.war /tmp/ROOT.war
   ```

2. Next, delete the **ROOT** directory inside the webapps folder using the rm -r command.

   ```
   sudo rm -r /opt/tomcat/webapps/ROOT
   ```

3. Now move the **ROOT.war** (renamed) package to the **webapps** folder using the move command.

   ```
   sudo move /tmp/ROOT.war /opt/tomcat/webapps/
   ```

4. In this way, one can access Jenkins running on node1 using the URL `http://172.17.8.104:8080/` without any additional path. Apparently the Apache Server is now a Jenkins Server.

■ **Note**   It's always recommended to have a dedicated Web Server solely for Jenkins.

Deleting the content inside the webapps folder (leaving behind the ROOT directory and ROOT.war), and then moving the jenkins.war file to the webapps folder, is also sufficient to make Apache Tomcat Server solely for Jenkins use. The step of renaming jenkins.war to ROOT.war and then moving it to webapps folder is only necessary, if you want to make `http://localhost:8080/` as the standard URL for Jenkins.

Setting Up the Jenkins Home Path

Before we start using Jenkins, there is one important thing to configure, the JENKINS_HOME path. This is the location where all of the Jenkins configurations, Logs, and Builds are stored. Everything that you create and configure on the Jenkins dashboard is stored here.

In our case by default the JENKINS_HOME is set to **/root/.jenkins/**. We need to make it something more accessible, something like **/opt/jenkins/**.

1. Make sure to stop the Apache Tomcat Server.

2. Open the **/opt/tomcat/conf/context.xml** file for editing.

   ```
   sudo nano /opt/tomcat/conf/context.xml
   ```

3. Add the following line between <Context></Context>.

   ```
   <Environment name="JENKINS_HOME" value="/opt/jenkins" type="java.lang.String"/>
   ```

4. Type **Ctrl+x** and then **Y** to save and exit the file.

5. Now start the Apache Tomcat Server.

6. You will now be able to access Jenkins running on node1 using the following address, **https://172.17.8.104:8080/jenkins** or **https://172.17.8.104:8080/** depending on your configuration. Figure 2-25 and Figure 2-26, show the Jenkins startup page on node1 and node2 respectively.

Figure 2-25. *Jenkins running on node1*

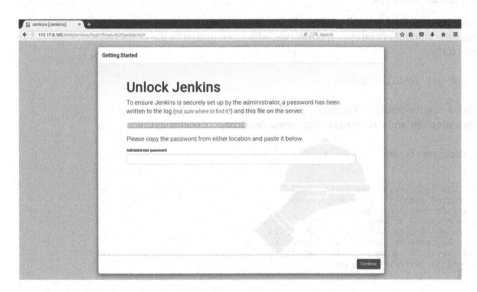

Figure 2-26. *Jenkins running on node2*

7. Now, bring down the Apache Tomcat Server on both the nodes (node1 and node2).

Installing the Cluster Software

1. On both the nodes (node1 and node2), install Corosync and Pacemaker using the apt-get command.

   ```
   sudo apt-get install pacemaker
   ```

■ **Note** Corosync is installed as a dependency of the Pacemaker package.

Perform the steps mentioned in the following section on both the nodes (node1 and node2).

Configuring Corosync

Corosync and Pacemaker are now installed but they need to be configured. Corosync must be configured so that our servers can behave as a cluster.

■ **Note** Perform the steps mentioned in the following section on both the nodes (node1 and node2), except for the "Creating Cluster Authorization Key" subsection, which is performed only on node1.

Creating Cluster Authorization Key

In order to allow the nodes (node1 and node2) to join a cluster, Corosync requires that each node possesses an identical cluster authorization key.

1. On **node1**, install the **haveged** package. This software package allows us to easily increase the amount of entropy on our server, which is required by the **corosync-keygen** script.

   ```
   sudo apt-get install haveged
   ```

2. On node1, run the corosync-keygen script. This will generate a 128-byte cluster authorization key, and write it to **/etc/corosync/authkey**. As shown in Figure 2-27.

   ```
   sudo corosync-keygen
   ```

```
vagrant@node1:~$ sudo corosync-keygen
Corosync Cluster Engine Authentication key generator.
Gathering 1024 bits for key from /dev/random.
Press keys on your keyboard to generate entropy.
Press keys on your keyboard to generate entropy (bits = 632).
Press keys on your keyboard to generate entropy (bits = 920).
Press keys on your keyboard to generate entropy (bits = 1000).
Writing corosync key to /etc/corosync/authkey.
vagrant@node1:~$ ▮
```

Figure 2-27. *Generate 128-byte cluster authorization key*

3. Now that we no longer need the haveged package, let's remove it from the **node1**.

```
sudo apt-get remove --purge haveged
```

```
sudo apt-get clean
```

4. From **node1**, copy the authkey to **node2** using the following command.

```
sudo scp /etc/corosync/authkey vagrant@node2:/tmp
```

5. Now ssh to **node2** from **node1**, and execute the following command.

```
sudo mv /tmp/authkey /etc/corosync
```

```
sudo chown root: /etc/corosync/authkey
```

```
sudo chmod 400 /etc/corosync/authkey
```

6. Now both the nodes should have an identical authorization key in the **/etc/ corosync/authkey** file.

Configuring Corosync Cluster

In order to get our desired cluster up and running, we must set these up.

1. On both the nodes (node1 and node2), open the **corosync.conf** file for editing.

```
sudo nano /etc/corosync/corosync.conf
```

2. Replace the contents of **corosync.conf** with the following code. Make sure to change the highlighted code accordingly.

```
# Please read the openais.conf.5 manual page
totem {
                version: 2
                cluster_name: HA cluster for Jenkins
                transport: udpu

        # How long before declaring a token lost (ms)
        token: 3000

        # How many token retransmits before forming a new configuration
        token_retransmits_before_loss_const: 10

        # How long to wait for join messages in the membership protocol (ms)
        join: 60

        # How long to wait for consensus to be achieved before starting
        a new round of membership configuration (ms)
        consensus: 3600
```

```
            # Turn off the virtual synchrony filter
            vsftype: none

            # Number of messages that may be sent by one processor on
            receipt of the token
            max_messages: 20

            # Limit generated nodeids to 31-bits (positive signed integers)
            clear_node_high_bit: yes

            # Disable encryption
            secauth: off

            # How many threads to use for encryption/decryption
            threads: 0

            # Optionally assign a fixed node id (integer)
            # nodeid: 1234

            # This specifies the mode of redundant ring, which may be none,
            active, or passive.
            rrp_mode: none

            interface {
                    # The following values need to be set based on your
                    environment
                    ringnumber: 0
                    bindnetaddr: 172.17.8.104
                    mcastaddr: 226.94.1.1
                    mcastport: 5405
            }
    }

    amf {
            mode: disabled
    }

    quorum {
            # Quorum for the Pacemaker Cluster Resource Manager
            provider: corosync_votequorum
            expected_votes: 1
    }

    aisexec {
            user:    root
            group:   root
    }

    nodelist {
      node {
        ring0_addr: 172.17.8.104
```

```
        name: primary
        nodeid: 1
    }
    node {
        ring0_addr: 172.17.8.105
        name: secondary
        nodeid: 2
    }
}

logging {
        fileline: off
        to_stderr: yes
        to_logfile: yes
        logfile: /var/log/corosync/corosync.log
        to_syslog: yes
        syslog_facility: daemon
        debug: off
        timestamp: on
        logger_subsys {
                subsys: AMF
                debug: off
                tags: enter|leave|trace1|trace2|trace3|trace4|trace6
        }
}
```

3. The **totem** section defines how the cluster members should communicate with each other. In our setup, the important settings include **transport: udpu** (specifies unicast mode) and bindnetaddr: **172.17.8.104** for **node1** and **bindnetaddr: 172.17.8.105** for **node2** (specifies which network address Corosync should bind to).

4. The **quorum** section defines that this is a two-node cluster, so only a single node is required for quorum (expected_votes: 1). This setting will allow our two-node cluster to elect a coordinator (DC), which is the node that controls the cluster at any given time.

5. The **nodelist** section defines the nodes in the cluster, and how each node can be reached. Here, we configure both our primary and secondary nodes, and specify that they can be reached via their respective private IP addresses.

6. The logging section defines that the Corosync logs should be written to **/var/log/ corosync/corosync.log**. You can change this to any location (directory) of your choice.

7. Type **Ctrl+x** and then **Y** to save and exit the file.

8. On both the nodes (node1 and node2), create the **pcmk** file in the Corosync service directory.

```
sudo nano /etc/corosync/service.d/pcmk
```

9. Then add the Pacemaker service to the file, as shown below.

```
service {
  name: pacemaker
  ver: 1
}
```

10. Type **Ctrl+x** and then **Y** to save and exit the file.

11. By default, the Corosync service is disabled. On both the nodes (node1 and node2), enable the Corosync service by editing the **/etc/default/corosync** file.

```
sudo nano /etc/default/corosync
```

12. Inside the file, change the value of START to yes. Note this is case sensitive.

```
START=yes
```

13. Type **Ctrl+x** and then **Y** to save and exit the file.

14. Now we can start the Corosync service. On both the nodes, start Corosync using the following command. You should get an output similiar to the one shown in Figure 2-28.

```
sudo service corosync start
```

```
vagrant@node1:~$ sudo service corosync start
 * Starting corosync daemon corosync                                    [ OK ]
vagrant@node1:~$ ▮
```

Figure 2-28. *Start the Corosync service*

15. Once Corosync is running on both the nodes, they should be clustered together. We can verify this by running the following command. The response should be something similiar to Figure 2-29.

```
sudo corosync-cmapctl | grep members
```

```
vagrant@node1:~$ sudo corosync-cmapctl | grep members
runtime.totem.pg.mrp.srp.members.1.config_version (u64) = 0
runtime.totem.pg.mrp.srp.members.1.ip (str) = r(0) ip(172.17.8.104)
runtime.totem.pg.mrp.srp.members.1.join_count (u32) = 1
runtime.totem.pg.mrp.srp.members.1.status (str) = joined
runtime.totem.pg.mrp.srp.members.2.config_version (u64) = 0
runtime.totem.pg.mrp.srp.members.2.ip (str) = r(0) ip(172.17.8.105)
runtime.totem.pg.mrp.srp.members.2.join_count (u32) = 1
runtime.totem.pg.mrp.srp.members.2.status (str) = joined
vagrant@node1:~$ ▮
```

Figure 2-29. *Verify the Corosync cluster members*

16. If you do not see the members listed, use the following command to restart Corosync.

```
sudo service corosync restart
```

Starting and Configuring Pacemaker

Pacemaker is now ready to be started. The Pacemaker service requires Corosync to be running, and it's disabled by default.

1. On both the nodes, enable Pacemaker to start on system boot using the following commands.

   ```
   sudo update-rc.d pacemaker defaults 20 01
   ```

2. We have set Pacemaker's start priority to 20. It is important to specify a start priority that is higher than Corosync (which is 19 by default), so that Pacemaker starts after Corosync.

3. Start Pacemaker using the following command as depicted in Figure 2-30.

   ```
   sudo service pacemaker start
   ```

```
vagrant@node1:~$ sudo service pacemaker start
Starting Pacemaker Cluster Manager: [ OK ]
vagrant@node1:~$ █
```

Figure 2-30. *Start the Pacemaker service*

4. To check the Pacemaker version execute the following command as depicted in Figure 2-31.

   ```
   pacemakerd --version
   ```

```
vagrant@node1:~$ pacemakerd --version
Pacemaker 1.1.10
Written by Andrew Beekhof
vagrant@node1:~$ █
```

Figure 2-31. *Get the pacemaker version*

5. To interact with Pacemaker, we will use the **crm** utility. Check the cluster status using the following command. See the output of the command as depicted in Figure 2-32.

   ```
   sudo crm status
   ```

```
vagrant@node1:~$ sudo crm status
Last updated: Tue Oct  4 00:45:17 2016
Last change: Tue Oct  4 00:43:44 2016 via crmd on secondary
Stack: corosync
Current DC: secondary (2) - partition with quorum
Version: 1.1.10-42f2063
2 Nodes configured
0 Resources configured


Online: [ primary secondary ]
vagrant@node1:~$ █
```

Figure 2-32. *crm status*

■ **Note**   To get more information on the crm commands, visit the following link: `http://crmsh.nongnu.org/crm.8.html`

All crm commands can be run from either node, as it automatically synchronizes all cluster-related changes across all member nodes.

In the above output notice the Current DC (Designated Coordinator) value. It should be set to either primary (1) or secondary (2). There are 2 Nodes and 0 Resources at the moment. Both the nodes are online.

6. You can also use the crm_mon utility to get real-time updates of the status of each node, and where each resource is running.

    ```
    sudo crm_mon
    ```

7. The output of this command looks identical to the output of crm status except it runs continuously.

8. If you want to quit, press **Ctrl-C**.

Configuring Cluster Properties

1. For a two-node cluster we do not need STONITH enabled. Execute the following command to disable STONITH.

    ```
    sudo crm configure property stonith-enabled=false
    ```

■ **Note**   STONITH is used to remove faulty nodes—because we are setting up a two-node cluster we don't need it.

---

2. We would also like to disable quorum-related messages in the logs. To do that, execute the following command. Again, this setting only applies to 2-node clusters.

    ```
    sudo crm configure property no-quorum-policy=ignore
    ```

3. To verify your Pacemaker configuration, run the following command.

    ```
    sudo crm configure show
    ```

Figure 2-33, depicts all of your active Pacemaker settings. Currently, this will only include two nodes, and the STONITH and quorum properties you just set.

```
vagrant@node1:~$ sudo crm configure show
node $id="1" primary
node $id="2" secondary
property $id="cib-bootstrap-options" \
        dc-version="1.1.10-42f2063" \
        cluster-infrastructure="corosync" \
        stonith-enabled="false" \
        no-quorum-policy="ignore"
vagrant@node1:~$
```

Figure 2-33. *Cluster configuration*

Create a Floating IP Resource Agent

Pacemaker and Corosync are running and configured; now we need to add resources for it to manage. Resources are services that the cluster is responsible for making highly available. In Pacemaker, adding a resource requires the use of a resource agent. The resource agent acts as an interface to the service that will be managed. Pacemaker ships with several resource agents for common services, and allows custom resource agents to be added.

■ **Note**   To get the list of available resource agents visit the link: `http://www.linux-ha.org/wiki/ Resource_Agents`

In our setup, we want to make sure that the service provided by our Tomcat Server, primary and secondary, is highly available in an active/passive setup, which means that we need a way to ensure that our Floating IP is always pointing to a server that is available.

Our first resource will be a unique IP address that the cluster can bring up on either node (node1 and node2). Regardless of where any cluster service(s) are running, end users need a consistent address to contact them. We will choose 172.17.8.200 as the floating address, and naming it as **ClusterIP** and tell the cluster to check whether it is running every 30 seconds.

1.   To do so execute the following command.

```
sudo crm configure primitive ClusterIP ocf:heartbeat:IPaddr2 params
ip=172.17.8.200 cidr_netmask=32 op monitor interval=30s
```

■ **Note**   ocf:heartbeat:IPaddr2 is the resource agent for ClusterIP

---

2.   Check the status of your cluster using the `crm status` command, and you should see that the ClusterIP resource is started on one of your nodes. As shown in Figure 2-34.

```
vagrant@node1:~$ sudo crm status
Last updated: Tue Oct  4 23:44:24 2016
Last change: Tue Oct  4 23:44:15 2016 via cibadmin on primary
Stack: corosync
Current DC: primary (1) - partition with quorum
Version: 1.1.10-42f2063
2 Nodes configured
1 Resources configured


Online: [ primary secondary ]

 ClusterIP      (ocf::heartbeat:IPaddr2):       Started primary
vagrant@node1:~$ ■
```

Figure 2-34. *ClusterIP resource running on one of the nodes*

Creating a Tomcat Resource Agent

Similarly we need to create a Tomcat resource agent that will start, stop, and monitor our Apache Tomcat Server (Jenkins service).

1. Get the java home path using the following command as depicted in Figure 2-35:

   ```
   sudo update-java-alternatives -l
   ```

```
vagrant@node1:~$ sudo update-java-alternatives -l
java-1.7.0-openjdk-amd64 1071 /usr/lib/jvm/java-1.7.0-openjdk-amd64
vagrant@node1:~$ ■
```

Figure 2-35. *Get the java home path*

2. Make sure tomcat is not running.

3. Execute the following command to create a tomcat resource.

   ```
   sudo crm configure primitive ApacheTomcat ocf:heartbeat:tomcat params
   java_home="/usr/lib/jvm/java-1.7.0-openjdk-amd64/jre" catalina_home=
   "/opt/tomcat" op start timeout=60s op stop timeout=120s op status
   timeout=60s interval=30s op monitor timeout=30s interval=10s
   ```

■ **Note**   "java_home" should be set to the path where java is installed. "catalina_home" is the installation directory of Tomcat. The op (operations) values are extremely important; failing to set then can result in failures.

ocf:heartbeat:tomcat is the resource agent for ApacheTomcat.

---

4. Check the status of your cluster using the crm status command. You should see that the **ApacheTomcat** resource is started on one of your nodes, as shown in Figure 2-36.

```
vagrant@node1:~$ sudo crm status
Last updated: Tue Oct  4 23:47:50 2016
Last change: Tue Oct  4 23:47:41 2016 via cibadmin on primary
Stack: corosync
Current DC: primary (1) - partition with quorum
Version: 1.1.10-42f2063
2 Nodes configured
2 Resources configured


Online: [ primary secondary ]

 ClusterIP      (ocf::heartbeat:IPaddr2):       Started primary
 ApacheTomcat   (ocf::heartbeat:tomcat):        Started secondary
vagrant@node1:~$ █
```

Figure 2-36. *ApacheTomcat resource running on one of the nodes*

■ **Note**   Notice that the ApacheTomcat resource isn't running on the same node as our ClusterIP resource.

Ensuring ClusterIP and Apache Tomcat Run on the Same Node

Now, we need to tell the cluster to run Apache Tomcat on the host that ClusterIP is running on. To do this, we will use a **colocation constraint**. The important part of the colocation constraint is indicated by using a score of INFINITY. The INFINITY score means that if ClusterIP is not active anywhere, ApacheTomcat will not be permitted to run.

1. To create a colocation constraint for ApacheTomcat and ClusterIP, execute the following command.

    ```
    sudo crm configure colocation ApacheTomcat-with-ClusterIP INFINITY:
    ApacheTomcat ClusterIP
    ```

2. Check the status of your cluster using the `crm status` command. You should see that the ApacheTomcat resource is now running on the primary node (node1). See Figure 2-37.

```
vagrant@node1:~$ sudo crm status
Last updated: Tue Oct  4 23:58:18 2016
Last change: Tue Oct  4 23:50:56 2016 via cibadmin on primary
Stack: corosync
Current DC: primary (1) - partition with quorum
Version: 1.1.10-42f2063
2 Nodes configured
2 Resources configured


Online: [ primary secondary ]

 ClusterIP      (ocf::heartbeat:IPaddr2):       Started primary
 ApacheTomcat   (ocf::heartbeat:tomcat):        Started primary
vagrant@node1:~$ █
```

Figure 2-37. *Apache Tomcat running along with ClusterIP on the primary node*

Ensuring ClusterIP Starts Before Apache Tomcat

We need to make sure ClusterIP ad Apache Tomcat not only runs on the same node, but ClusterIP starts before Apache Tomcat. A colocation constraint only ensures that the resources run together, but not the order in which they start and stop.

To achieve order, we will use ordering constraint. By default, all order constraints are mandatory, which means that the recovery of ClusterIP will also trigger the recovery of Apache Tomcat.

1. To create an ordering constraint. Execute the following command.

```
sudo crm configure order ApacheTomcat-after-ClusterIP mandatory:
ClusterIP ApacheTomcat
```

Replicating Jenkins Home Directory Using DRBD

In the event of primary node failure, the Jenkins Server running on node1 will be started on the secondary node (node2). When this happens we would also like to make sure that the Jenkins Sever on node2 gets access to the same configuration and data (Jenkins home directory content) that was created and used by Jenkins Server running on node1. To do this we can either choose to use a NAS (Network-Attached-Storage) or we can choose a reliable and cost-effective solution DRBD.

Install the DRBD Packages

1. Execute the following command to install DRBD. Do this on both the nodes.

```
sudo apt install drbd8-utils
```

Preparing Partitions

The first step in setting up DRBD is to prepare the partitions to be used as DRBD devices. We are assuming that we have an additional disk (sdb) on both the nodes (node1 and node2) that are of same sizes. We will create two partition tables (sdb1 and sdb2) of 20 GB each for the DRBD devices (drbd1 and drbd2).

1. Using the command below, list the disks that you have. Figure 2-38 depicts the additional disk (sdb) on node1.

```
sudo lsblk
```

```
vagrant@node1:~$ sudo lsblk
NAME    MAJ:MIN RM SIZE RO TYPE MOUNTPOINT
sda       8:0    0  40G  0 disk
└─sda1    8:1    0  40G  0 part /
sdb       8:16   0  40G  0 disk
vagrant@node1:~$
```

Figure 2-38. *List the disks*

2. To create the first primary partition, execute the following command.

```
sudo fdisk /dev/sdb
```

3. You will get the following output. With a prompt `Command (m for help):` asking for an input.

   ```
   Device contains neither a valid DOS partition table, nor Sun, SGI or
   OSF disklabel
   Building a new DOS disklabel with disk identifier 0x4527506d.
   Changes will remain in memory only, until you decide to write them.
   After that, of course, the previous content won't be recoverable.
   Warning: invalid flag 0x0000 of partition table 4 will be corrected by
   w(rite)
   Command (m for help):
   ```

■ **Note** Following are the valid inputs (case insensitive) that can be given as a value for `Command (m for help):`

p print the partition table

n create a new partition

d delete a partition

q quit without saving changes

w write the new partition table and exit

---

4. Type "P" to list the current partition table. The output will be empty as shown in Figure 2-39.

```
Command (m for help): P

Disk /dev/sdb: 42.9 GB, 42949672960 bytes
255 heads, 63 sectors/track, 5221 cylinders, total 83886080 sectors
Units = sectors of 1 * 512 = 512 bytes
Sector size (logical/physical): 512 bytes / 512 bytes
I/O size (minimum/optimal): 512 bytes / 512 bytes
Disk identifier: 0x12e7dc3d

   Device Boot      Start         End      Blocks   Id  System
```

Figure 2-39. *List the existing partition table on /dev/sdb*

5. Next, select "N" (to create a new partition), then P (to choose a primary partition), then 1 (this is our first primary partition), then press Enter to select the default value for the First sector, and lastly enter then +20480M for Last sector and press Enter, as shown in Figure 2-40.

```
Command (m for help): N
Partition type:
   p   primary (0 primary, 0 extended, 4 free)
   e   extended
Select (default p): P
Partition number (1-4, default 1): 1
First sector (2048-83886079, default 2048):
Using default value 2048
Last sector, +sectors or +size{K,M,G} (2048-83886079, default 83886079): +20480M
```

Figure 2-40. *Create a new primary partition*

6. Select "P" to list the partition tables. From the Figure 2-41, you can see the recently created primary partition **/dev/sdb1**.

```
Command (m for help): P

Disk /dev/sdb: 42.9 GB, 42949672960 bytes
255 heads, 63 sectors/track, 5221 cylinders, total 83886080 sectors
Units = sectors of 1 * 512 = 512 bytes
Sector size (logical/physical): 512 bytes / 512 bytes
I/O size (minimum/optimal): 512 bytes / 512 bytes
Disk identifier: 0x12e7dc3d

   Device Boot      Start         End      Blocks   Id  System
/dev/sdb1            2048    41945087    20971520   83  Linux
```

Figure 2-41. *List the partition table on /dev/sdb*

7. Again, select "N" (to create a new partition), then P (to choose a primary partition), then 2 (this is our second primary partition), then press Enter to select the default value for the First sector, and lastly press Enter to select the default value for the Last sector, as shown in Figure 2-42.

```
Command (m for help): n
Partition type:
   p   primary (1 primary, 0 extended, 3 free)
   e   extended
Select (default p): p
Partition number (1-4, default 2): 2
First sector (41945088-83886079, default 41945088):
Using default value 41945088
Last sector, +sectors or +size{K,M,G} (41945088-83886079, default 83886079):
Using default value 83886079
```

Figure 2-42. *Create a new primary partition*

8. Lastly press "W" to save the configuration. See Figure 2-43.

```
Command (m for help): w
The partition table has been altered!

Calling ioctl() to re-read partition table.
Syncing disks.
```

Figure 2-43. *Save the partition settings done on /dev/sdb*

9.   Select "P" to list the partition tables. From Figure 2-44, you can see the recently created primary partition **/dev/sdb1 and /dev/sdb2.**

```
Command (m for help): p

Disk /dev/sdb: 42.9 GB, 42949672960 bytes
255 heads, 63 sectors/track, 5221 cylinders, total 83886080 sectors
Units = sectors of 1 * 512 = 512 bytes
Sector size (logical/physical): 512 bytes / 512 bytes
I/O size (minimum/optimal): 512 bytes / 512 bytes
Disk identifier: 0x12e7dc3d

   Device Boot      Start         End      Blocks   Id  System
/dev/sdb1            2048    41945087    20971520   83  Linux
/dev/sdb2        41945088    83886079    20970496   83  Linux
```

Figure 2-44. *List the partition table on /dev/sdb*

10.   Now again list the disks that you have using the **lsblk** command. You can see the two new partition sdb1 and sdb2, as shown in Figure 2-45.

```
sudo lsblk
```

```
vagrant@node1:~$ sudo lsblk
NAME    MAJ:MIN RM SIZE RO TYPE MOUNTPOINT
sda       8:0    0  40G  0 disk
└─sda1    8:1    0  40G  0 part /
sdb       8:16   0  40G  0 disk
├─sdb1    8:17   0  20G  0 part
└─sdb2    8:18   0  20G  0 part
vagrant@node1:~$
```

Figure 2-45. *List the disks and partitions on node1*

11.   Repeat all the above steps on node2 as well. Use the same name and size for the partition.

Configuring DRBD

Simply run the following commands on both the nodes (node1 and node2).

1.   Create a file **data.res** under **/etc/drbd.d/** directory.

```
sudo nano /etc/drbd.d/data.res
```

2.   Add the code below to the new file.

```
resource data {
 protocol C;
 volume 0 {
    device /dev/drbd1;
    disk /dev/sdb1;
    meta-disk internal;
 }
```

```
volume 1 {
    device /dev/drbd2;
    disk /dev/sdb2;
    meta-disk internal;
}
syncer {
 verify-alg sha1;
}
net {
 allow-two-primaries;
}
on node1 {
 address  172.17.8.104:7789;
}
on node2 {
 address  172.17.8.105:7789;
}
}
```

3. We will configure DRBD to use port 7789, so allow that port from each host to the other.

```
sudo ufw allow 7789
```

Initializing DRBD

Now that we have configured DRBD, let us try to run it. In the following section we will create a local metadata for the DRBD resource and ensure that the DRBD kernel module is loaded. Then we will bring up the DRBD resource.

1. Perform the following steps on primary node (node1). You should see a similiar output, as shown in Figure 2-46.

```
sudo drbdadm create-md data
```

```
vagrant@node1:~$ sudo drbdadm create-md data
Writing meta data...
initializing activity log
NOT initializing bitmap
New drbd meta data block successfully created.
Writing meta data...
initializing activity log
NOT initializing bitmap
New drbd meta data block successfully created.
```

Figure 2-46. *Create metadata for the DRBD resource*

2. Next, execute the following commands in order.

```
sudo apt-get install linux-image-extra-virtual
```

```
sudo depmod -a
```

```
sudo modprobe drbd
```

3. Now, execute the following command to start the DRBD resource.

    ```
    sudo drbdadm up data
    ```

4. We can confirm DRBD's status on this node (node1) using the following command.

    ```
    cat /proc/drbd
    ```

    In Figure 2-47, you can see **ds: Inconsistent/Inconsistent**. This is because we have not yet initialized the data.

    And because we have not yet initialized DRBD on the second node, the partner node's status is marked as **Unknown**.

```
vagrant@node1:~$ cat /proc/drbd
version: 8.4.3 (api:1/proto:86-101)
srcversion: 6551AD2C98F533733BE558C

 1: cs:WFConnection ro:Secondary/Unknown ds:Inconsistent/Inconsistent C r-----
    ns:0 nr:0 dw:0 dr:0 al:0 bm:0 lo:0 pe:0 ua:0 ap:0 ep:1 wo:f oos:20970844
 2: cs:WFConnection ro:Secondary/Unknown ds:Inconsistent/Inconsistent C r-----
    ns:0 nr:0 dw:0 dr:0 al:0 bm:0 lo:0 pe:0 ua:0 ap:0 ep:1 wo:f oos:20969820
vagrant@node1:~$ ▉
```

Figure 2-47. Sync status

5. Now, repeat step 1, 2, and 3 on **node2**.

6. After executing the steps successfully on node2, give the following command on node1 to check the sync status.

    ```
    cat /proc/drbd
    ```

    From Figure 2-48, we can see that the state has changed to **cs:Connected**, which means the two DRBD nodes are communicating. We can also see that both the nodes are in Secondary role with Inconsistent data.

```
vagrant@node1:~$ cat /proc/drbd
version: 8.4.3 (api:1/proto:86-101)
srcversion: 6551AD2C98F533733BE558C

 1: cs:Connected ro:Secondary/Secondary ds:Inconsistent/Inconsistent C r-----
    ns:0 nr:0 dw:0 dr:0 al:0 bm:0 lo:0 pe:0 ua:0 ap:0 ep:1 wo:f oos:20970844
 2: cs:Connected ro:Secondary/Secondary ds:Inconsistent/Inconsistent C r-----
    ns:0 nr:0 dw:0 dr:0 al:0 bm:0 lo:0 pe:0 ua:0 ap:0 ep:1 wo:f oos:20969820
vagrant@node1:~$ ▉
```

Figure 2-48. Sync status

7. To make the data consistent, we need to tell DRBD about the node that should be having the correct data. To do so, execute the following command to make node1 as the primary node with correct data.

    ```
    sudo drbdadm primary --force data
    ```

8. If we check the status immediately, we'll see something like this.

    `cat /proc/drbd`

    In Figure 2-49, we can see that that the node (node1) has the Primary role and
    the partner node has the Secondary role. Also the data on node1 is up to date
    and the partner node's data is still Inconsistent with a progress bar showing how
    far along the partner node is in sync.

```
vagrant@node1:~$ cat /proc/drbd
version: 8.4.3 (api:1/proto:86-101)
srcversion: 6551AD2C98F533733BE558C

 1: cs:SyncSource ro:Primary/Secondary ds:UpToDate/Inconsistent C r-----
    ns:50176 nr:0 dw:0 dr:50904 al:0 bm:3 lo:0 pe:0 ua:0 ap:0 ep:1 wo:f oos:2092
0668
        [>....................] sync'ed:  0.3% (20428/20476)Mfinish: 0:20:45 spe
ed: 16,724 (16,724) K/sec
 2: cs:SyncSource ro:Primary/Secondary ds:UpToDate/Inconsistent C r-----
    ns:7168 nr:0 dw:0 dr:7896 al:0 bm:0 lo:0 pe:0 ua:0 ap:0 ep:1 wo:f oos:209626
52
        [>....................] sync'ed:  0.1% (20468/20476)Mfinish: 2:25:34 spe
ed: 2,388 (2,388) K/sec
vagrant@node1:~$ ▮
```

Figure 2-49. *Sync status*

9. Executing the following command, and after a while, you'll see something as
    shown in Figure 2-50.

    `cat /proc/drbd`

```
vagrant@node1:~$ cat /proc/drbd
version: 8.4.3 (api:1/proto:86-101)
srcversion: 6551AD2C98F533733BE558C

 1: cs:Connected ro:Primary/Secondary ds:UpToDate/UpToDate C r-----
    ns:20970844 nr:0 dw:0 dr:20971572 al:0 bm:1280 lo:0 pe:0 ua:0 ap:0 ep:1 wo:f
 oos:0
 2: cs:Connected ro:Primary/Secondary ds:UpToDate/UpToDate C r-----
    ns:20969820 nr:0 dw:0 dr:20970548 al:0 bm:1280 lo:0 pe:0 ua:0 ap:0 ep:1 wo:f
 oos:0
vagrant@node1:~$ ▮
```

Figure 2-50. *Sync status*

Both sets of data are now up to date, and we can proceed to creating and
populating a file system for our Apache Tomcat and Jenkins.

Populating the DRBD Disk

On the node with the primary role (node1), create two file systems on the DRBD device **/dev/drbd1** and
/dev/drbd2 respectively.

■ **Note**   Perform the activities of this subsection only on the primary node (node1).

---

1. Execute the following command to create a file system on **/dev/drbd1**. As shown in Figure 2-51.

    ```
    sudo mkfs.ext3 /dev/drbd1
    ```

```
vagrant@node1:~$ sudo mkfs.ext3 /dev/drbd1
mke2fs 1.42.9 (4-Feb-2014)
Filesystem label=
OS type: Linux
Block size=4096 (log=2)
Fragment size=4096 (log=2)
Stride=0 blocks, Stripe width=0 blocks
2621440 inodes, 10485175 blocks
524258 blocks (5.00%) reserved for the super user
First data block=0
Maximum filesystem blocks=4294967296
320 block groups
32768 blocks per group, 32768 fragments per group
8192 inodes per group
Superblock backups stored on blocks:
        32768, 98304, 163840, 229376, 294912, 819200, 884736, 1605632, 2654208,
        4096000, 7962624

Allocating group tables: done
Writing inode tables: done
Creating journal (32768 blocks): done
Writing superblocks and filesystem accounting information: done

vagrant@node1:~$ 
```

Figure 2-51. *Create filesystem on /dev/drbd1*

2. Similarly, execute the following command to create a filesystem on **/dev/drbd2**.

    ```
    sudo mkfs.ext3 /dev/drbd2
    ```

3. To list the filesystem that we recently created, execute the **lsblk** command. From the Figure 2-52, we can see the list of filesystems.

    ```
    sudo lsblk
    ```

```
vagrant@node1:~$ sudo lsblk
NAME    MAJ:MIN RM SIZE RO TYPE MOUNTPOINT
sda       8:0    0  40G  0 disk
└─sda1    8:1    0  40G  0 part /
sdb       8:16   0  40G  0 disk
├─sdb1    8:17   0  20G  0 part
└─sdb2    8:18   0  20G  0 part
drbd1   147:1    0  20G  0 disk
drbd2   147:2    0  20G  0 disk
vagrant@node1:~$ 
```

Figure 2-52. *List the filesystem*

■ **Note** In this example, we created an ext3 filesystem with no special options. In a production environment, you should choose a filesystem type and options that are suitable for your application.

---

4. Mount the newly created filesystems and populate it with the contents of **/opt/tomcat/webapps** and **/opt/jenkins**.

5. To do so, execute the following command to mount the **/dev/drbd1** filesystem to **/mnt** first.

```
mount /dev/drbd1 /mnt
```

6. Move to the **/mnt** directory and copy the contents of the webapps folder to it using the following commands.

```
cd /mnt
```

```
sudo cp -R /opt/tomcat/webapps/. /mnt
```

7. After copying the files, list the content of the **/mnt** directory, as shown in Figure 2-53.

```
vagrant@node1:/mnt$ ls -lrt
total 68216
drwxr-x---  5 root root      4096 Oct  7 15:05 manager
drwxr-x---  6 root root      4096 Oct  7 15:05 examples
drwxr-x--- 14 root root      4096 Oct  7 15:05 docs
-rw-r--r--  1 root root  69754011 Oct  7 15:05 jenkins.war
drwxr-x--- 10 root root      4096 Oct  7 15:05 jenkins
drwxr-x---  5 root root      4096 Oct  7 15:05 host-manager
drwxr-x---  3 root root      4096 Oct  7 15:05 ROOT
```

Figure 2-53. List the contents of /mnt directory

8. Now unmount the **/dev/drbd1** filesystem.

```
sudo umount /dev/drbd1
```

9. Similarly, execute the following command to mount the **/dev/drbd2** filesystem to **/mnt**.

```
sudo mount /dev/drbd2 /mnt
```

10. Move to the /mnt directory and copy the contents of **/opt/jenkins** folder to it using the following commands.

```
cd /mnt
```

```
sudo cp -R /opt/jenkins/. /mnt
```

11. After copying the files, list the content of the **/mnt** directory, as shown in Figure 2-54.

```
vagrant@node1:/mnt$ ls -lrt
total 60
drwxr-x--- 3 root root 4096 Oct  7 15:10 users
drwxr-x--- 2 root root 4096 Oct  7 15:10 userContent
drwx------ 4 root root 4096 Oct  7 15:10 secrets
-rw-r----- 1 root root    0 Oct  7 15:10 secret.key.not-so-secret
-rw-r----- 1 root root  129 Oct  7 15:10 queue.xml.bak
drwxr-x--- 2 root root 4096 Oct  7 15:10 nodes
-rw-r----- 1 root root  907 Oct  7 15:10 nodeMonitors.xml
drwxr-x--- 3 root root 4096 Oct  7 15:10 logs
drwxr-x--- 2 root root 4096 Oct  7 15:10 jobs
-rw-r----- 1 root root    6 Oct  7 15:10 jenkins.install.UpgradeWizard.state
-rw------- 1 root root 1712 Oct  7 15:10 identity.key.enc
-rw-r----- 1 root root  159 Oct  7 15:10 hudson.model.UpdateCenter.xml
-rw-r----- 1 root root 1592 Oct  7 15:10 config.xml
drwxr-x--- 2 root root 4096 Oct  7 15:10 updates
-rw-r----- 1 root root   64 Oct  7 15:10 secret.key
drwxr-x--- 2 root root 4096 Oct  7 15:10 plugins
```

Figure 2-54. List the contents of /mnt directory

12. Now unmount the **/dev/drbd2** filesystem.

```
sudo umount /dev/drbd2
```

Creating a Cluster Resource for the DRBD Device

Now just like ClusterIP and ApacheTomcat, we will create a cluster resource for the DRBD device, and an additional clone resource to allow the resource to run on both nodes at the same time.

1. To do so, execute the following commands in sequence.

```
sudo crm configure primitive Data ocf:linbit:drbd  params
drbd_resource=data op monitor interval=60s

sudo crm configure ms DataClone WebappsData params master-max=1
master-node-max=1 clone-max=2 clone-node-max=1 notify=true
```

2. Let's see the new configuration by executing the crm status command.

```
sudo crm status
```

From Figure 2-55, we can see that the DataClone (our DRBD device) is running as master (DRBD's primary role) on node1 and as a slave (DRBD's secondary role) on node2.

```
vagrant@node1:/$ sudo crm status
Last updated: Fri Oct  7 15:16:45 2016
Last change: Fri Oct  7 15:16:38 2016 via cibadmin on primary
Stack: corosync
Current DC: primary (1) - partition with quorum
Version: 1.1.10-42f2063
2 Nodes configured
4 Resources configured


Online: [ primary secondary ]

 ClusterIP      (ocf::heartbeat:IPaddr2):      Started primary
 ApacheTomcat   (ocf::heartbeat:tomcat):       Started primary
 Master/Slave Set: DataClone [Data]
     Masters: [ primary ]
     Slaves: [ secondary ]
```

Figure 2-55. *crm status*

Creating a Cluster Resource for the Filesystems

Now that we have a working DRBD device, let us mount its filesystems.

1. To create a cluster resource for the filesystem "/dev/drbd1", execute the
    following command.

    ```
    sudo crm configure primitive WebappsFS Filesystem params device=
    "/dev/drbd1" directory="/opt/tomcat/webapps" fstype="ext3" op start
    timeout=60s op stop timeout=60s op notify timeout=60s op monitor
    timeout=40s interval=20s
    ```

2. Let's see the new configuration by executing the crm status command.
    Figure 2-56 depicts out new configuration.

    ```
    sudo crm status
    ```

```
vagrant@node1:/$ sudo crm status
Last updated: Fri Oct  7 15:21:36 2016
Last change: Fri Oct  7 15:21:30 2016 via cibadmin on primary
Stack: corosync
Current DC: primary (1) - partition with quorum
Version: 1.1.10-42f2063
2 Nodes configured
5 Resources configured


Online: [ primary secondary ]

 ClusterIP      (ocf::heartbeat:IPaddr2):      Started primary
 ApacheTomcat   (ocf::heartbeat:tomcat):       Started primary
 Master/Slave Set: DataClone [Data]
     Masters: [ primary ]
     Slaves: [ secondary ]
 WebappsFS      (ocf::heartbeat:Filesystem):   Started primary
```

Figure 2-56. *crm status*

3. Similarly, create a cluster resource for the filesystem "/dev/drbd2," and execute the following command.

    ```
    sudo crm configure primitive JenkinsHomeFS Filesystem params device=
    "/dev/drbd2" directory="/opt/jenkins" fstype="ext3" op start timeout=60s
    op stop timeout=60s op notify timeout=60s op monitor timeout=40s
    interval=20s
    ```

4. Let's see the new configuration by executing the crm status command. See Figure 2-57.

    ```
    sudo crm status
    ```

```
vagrant@node1:/$ sudo crm status
Last updated: Fri Oct  7 15:23:32 2016
Last change: Fri Oct  7 15:22:54 2016 via cibadmin on primary
Stack: corosync
Current DC: primary (1) - partition with quorum
Version: 1.1.10-42f2063
2 Nodes configured
6 Resources configured


Online: [ primary secondary ]

 ClusterIP      (ocf::heartbeat:IPaddr2):       Started primary
 ApacheTomcat   (ocf::heartbeat:tomcat):        Started primary
 Master/Slave Set: DataClone [Data]
     Masters: [ primary ]
     Slaves: [ secondary ]
 WebappsFS      (ocf::heartbeat:Filesystem):    Started primary
 JenkinsHomeFS  (ocf::heartbeat:Filesystem):    Started primary
```

Figure 2-57. *crm status*

5. We will group the two filesystems. To do so, execute the following command:

    ```
    sudo crm configure group FileSystem WebappsFS JenkinsHomeFS
    ```

6. Let's see the new configuration by executing the crm status command. From Figure 2-58, you can see the two Filesystems WebappsFS and JenkinsHomeFS are grouped together as **FileSystem**.

    ```
    sudo crm status
    ```

```
vagrant@node1:/$ sudo crm status
Last updated: Fri Oct  7 15:26:49 2016
Last change: Fri Oct  7 15:26:22 2016 via cibadmin on primary
Stack: corosync
Current DC: primary (1) - partition with quorum
Version: 1.1.10-42f2063
2 Nodes configured
6 Resources configured


Online: [ primary secondary ]

 ClusterIP      (ocf::heartbeat:IPaddr2):      Started primary
 ApacheTomcat   (ocf::heartbeat:tomcat):       Started primary
 Master/Slave Set: DataClone [Data]
     Masters: [ primary ]
     Slaves: [ secondary ]
 Resource Group: FileSystem
     WebappsFS  (ocf::heartbeat:Filesystem):   Started primary
     JenkinsHomeFS      (ocf::heartbeat:Filesystem):   Started primary
```

Figure 2-58. *crm status*

7. We would like to run the Filesystems (WebappsFS and JenkinsHomeFS) on the same node where the DataClone (Master) is running. To do so, execute the following colocation constraint command.

   ```
   sudo crm configure colocation FileSystem-with-DataClone INFINITY:
   FileSystem DataClone:Master
   ```

8. Also, we would like to create an order in which the resources FileSystem (WebappsFS and JenkinsHomeFS) and DataClone start and stop. The Data resource should start first then it should be promoted as Master and then the resource FileSystem (WebappsFS and JenkinsHomeFS) should start. To do so, execute the following colocation constraint command.

   ```
   sudo crm configure order FileSystem-after-DataClone mandatory:
   DataClone:promote FileSystem:start
   ```

9. We also need to tell the cluster that ApacheTomcat needs to run on the same node as the FileSystem (WebappsFS and JenkinsHomeFS) and that it must be active before ApacheTomcat can start. To do so, execute the following colocation constraint command in sequence.

   ```
   sudo crm configure colocation ApacheTomcat-with-FileSystem INFINITY:
   ApacheTomcat FileSystem
   ```

   ```
   sudo crm configure order ApacheTomcat-after-FileSystem mandatory:
   FileSystem ApacheTomcat
   ```

Checking the Apache Tomcat Server

As per our configuration so far, Apache Tomcat Server should be running on node1. We should be able to access it on http://172.17.8.200:8080/jenkins.

1. Access the Apache Tomcat Server dashboard and from the dashboard click on the Manager App button to access the Tomcat Web Application Manager page. You might need to log in using the user "admin," which we created in the previous section.

2. Once you are on the Tomcat Web Application Manager page, scroll down to Server Information section. And you will see that we are currently accessing Apache Tomcat Server of node1. See Figure 2-59.

Server Information								
Tomcat Version	**JVM Version**	**JVM Vendor**	**OS Name**	**OS Version**	**OS Architecture**	**Hostname**	**IP Address**
Apache Tomcat/8.5.5	1.7.0_111-b01	Oracle Corporation	Linux	3.13.0-96-generic	amd64	node1	127.0.0.1

Figure 2-59. *Server Information from Tomcat Web Application Manager page*

3. From the active node (node1), give the following command to see the mount points.

```
df -h
```

From the Figure 2-60, you can see the drbd1 filesystem is mounted on **/opt/tomcat/webapps** and the drbd2 Filesystem is mounted on **/opt/jenkins**.

```
vagrant@node1:/$ df -h
Filesystem      Size  Used Avail Use% Mounted on
udev            484M   12K  484M   1% /dev
tmpfs           100M  404K   99M   1% /run
/dev/sda1        40G  2.4G   36G   7% /
none            4.0K     0  4.0K   0% /sys/fs/cgroup
none            5.0M  8.0K  5.0M   1% /run/lock
none            497M   53M  445M  11% /run/shm
none            100M     0  100M   0% /run/user
/dev/drbd1       20G  199M   19G   2% /opt/tomcat/webapps
/dev/drbd2       20G   46M   19G   1% /opt/jenkins
vagrant@node1:/$ 
```

Figure 2-60. *List the mount points*

Simulating a Failover

Now let us see if our HA setup for Jenkins using Pacemaker, Corosync, and DRBD works. We will access Jenkins running on the active node (node1) and do some basic setup that one usually does when using Jenkins for the first time. Then we will bring down node1 and check if all changes are intact as Jenkins comes up on node2.

1. Access the Jenkins Server using http://172.17.8.200:8080/jenkins/. As shown in Figure 2-61.

Figure 2-61. *Access the Jenkins Server using the ClusterIP*

2. We know that the Jenkins Server that we are right now accessing is running inside the Apache Tomcat Server, which is running on node1. Therefore, on node1 execute the following command. This will print out the content of the file initialAdminPassword. As shown in Figure 2-62.

```
sudo cat /opt/jenkins/secrets/initialAdminPassword
```

```
vagrant@node1:/$ sudo cat /opt/jenkins/secrets/initialAdminPassword
d3772195eed24b55af4d0e625b551a40
vagrant@node1:/$
```

Figure 2-62. *Get the Initial Admin Password key*

3. Copy the key and paste it inside the **Administrator password** field.

4. On the next screen you will be asked to choose either to go with the recommended plugins or to install the plugins of your own choice. Choose anything you like.

5. I have chosen to go with the suggested plugins. As depicted in Figure 2-63.

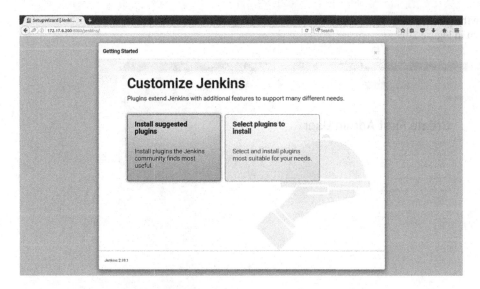

Figure 2-63. *Choose suggested plugins*

6. From Figure 2-64, you can see that the setup is installing all the required plugins suggested by the Jenkins community.

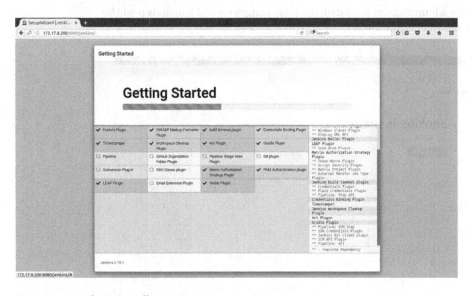

Figure 2-64. *Plugin installation in progress*

7. Once the plugins are installed, you will be asked to create an admin account, as shown in Figure 2-65.

Figure 2-65. *Creating the first admin user*

8. Once the admin account is created, the setup completes and Jenkins is ready for use as shown in Figure 2-66.

Figure 2-66. *Finishing the Jenkins setup*

9. By clicking on the **Start using Jenkins** button, you will be taken to the Jenkins Dashboard, as shown in Figure 2-67.

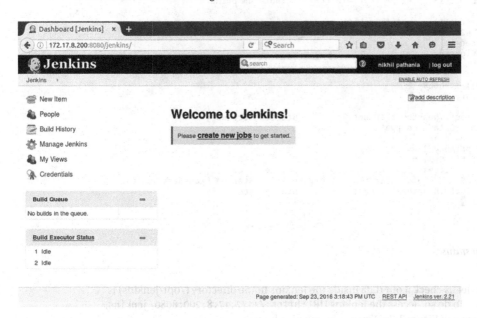

Figure 2-67. *The Jenkins Dashboard*

10. On the primary node (node1), execute the following command to check if there is a directory named **jenkins_admin** under **/opt/jenkins/users**. As shown in Figure 2-68.

```
vagrant@node1:/$ sudo ls -lrt /opt/jenkins/users/
total 4
drwxr-x--- 2 root root 4096 Oct  7 16:11 jenkins_admin
vagrant@node1:/$ 
```

Figure 2-68. *List the newly created admin user inside the Jenkins home directory*

11. Next, to simulate a failover, we will make the primary node (node1) on standby. Nodes that are in standby state continue to run Corosync and Pacemaker but are not allowed to run resources. Any resource found active on the standby node will be moved elsewhere. This feature is useful while performing system administration tasks.

12. Put the active node (node1) into standby mode using the following command, and observe the cluster move all the resources to the other node (node2). The node's status will change to indicate that it can no longer host resources.

    ```
    sudo crm node standby primary
    ```

13. Execute the crm status command to check the cluster status. You can see in a while that everything that was running on node1 (primary node) is moved to node2 (secondary node). See Figure 2-69.

```
vagrant@node2:~$ sudo crm status
Last updated: Thu Oct 13 21:46:30 2016
Last change: Thu Oct 13 21:42:28 2016 via crm_attribute on primary
Stack: corosync
Current DC: primary (1) - partition with quorum
Version: 1.1.10-42f2063
2 Nodes configured
6 Resources configured


Node primary (1): standby
Online: [ secondary ]

 ClusterIP       (ocf::heartbeat:IPaddr2):        Started secondary
 Master/Slave Set: DataClone [Data]
     Masters: [ secondary ]
     Stopped: [ primary ]
 Resource Group: FileSystem
     WebappsFS  (ocf::heartbeat:Filesystem):     Started secondary
     JenkinsHomeFS    (ocf::heartbeat:Filesystem):     Started secondary
 ApacheTomcat   (ocf::heartbeat:tomcat):         Started secondary
vagrant@node2:~$ ▉
```

Figure 2-69. *crm status*

14. Now, let us check if our data inside the Jenkins home directory (/opt/jenkins) is intact. To do so, access the Jenkins URL: `https://172.17.8.200:8080/jenkins`, as shown in Figure 2-70. You will be asked to log in.

Figure 2-70. *Jenkins login page*

15. Log in using the user that you created in the previous section.

16. If you are able to login using the same credentials, as shown in Figure 2-71, it means the data is intact.

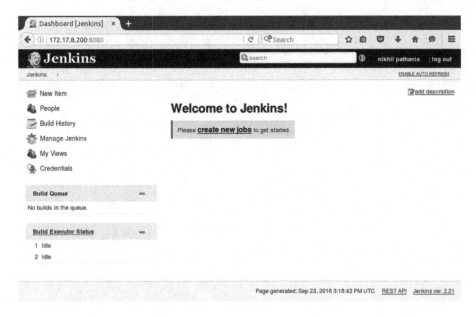

Figure 2-71. *The Jenkins Dashboard*

Summary

In the current chapter we learned to create a highly available (HA) setup for Jenkins using Pacemaker, Corosync, and DRBD. This was a classic approach to create a HA solution for Jenkins. In the next chapter we will take a modern approach to create a HA setup for Jenkins using CoreOS, Docker, and GlusterFS.

■ ■ ■

## CHAPTER 3

HA Jenkins Setup Using CoreOS, Docker, and GlusterFS

Highly available (Active/Passive) setup using Pacemaker, Corosync, and DRBD discussed in the previous chapter is a stable and proven solution. Nevertheless, in this chapter we are going to try something new and exclusive; we are going to build a highly available (HA) Jenkins Server using CoreOS, Docker, and GlusterFS. For the first time you'll see how the clustering feature of CoreOS is utilized to achieve a HA setup for Jenkins. We will start the chapter by discussing a HA design along with a few failover scenarios. This will give you clarity on how to proceed, and what to expect out of our HA setup. Next, you will learn to create and start a HA setup for Jenkins. Lastly, we will test our HA setup by simulating a few failover scenarios.

Designing a High Availability Setup for Jenkins

Failure could occur at the hardware level (machine shutdown/reboot/freeze), Application Server level (Application Server failure/reboot), or at the service level (the service itself fails to start). High Availability ensures that a service or a group of services is available continuously without any interruption. Every HA system comes with a **Failover** mechanism. This mechanism ensures that the controls of the primary system are transferred to a secondary system (replica of the primary system) if there are any failures on the primary system. To detect failures, every HA setup has a feature to check the health of the hardware and the applications that are being served. Figure 3-1 is a typical HA setup (Active/Passive).

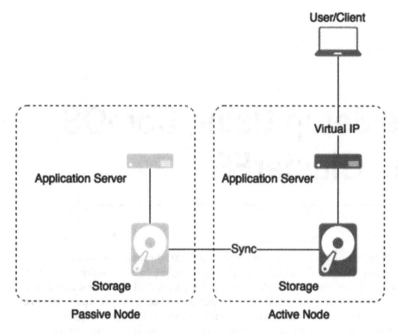

Figure 3-1. *A typical Active/Passive HA setup*

HA Setup for Jenkins

Figure 3-2 depicts how our HA setup for Jenkins will look. There are three CoreOS machines Host1, Host2, and Host3. Each CoreOS machine is running a GlusterFS Server(marked as G) inside a container. All the GlusterFS Servers are in sync, and each GlusterFS Server is aware of the other. There is also a Jenkins Server(marked as J) running inside a container on one of the Hosts.

The Jenkins Server is in communication with one of the GlusterFS Servers that is running on the same Host. This communication is possible, since the docker image that we are using to run the Jenkins Server also contains a GlusterFS client. The GlusterFS client is aware of all the three GlusterFS servers.

Whether it's a build or a configuration change, everything that happens on the Jenkins Server is stored inside the **jenkins_home** directory, thus making the data inside the **jenkins_home** redundant is of utter most importance. This is the reason why we are using Jenkins in collaboration with GlusterFS.

The Jenkins Server is accessible to the outside world using a virtual IP (Figure 3-2).

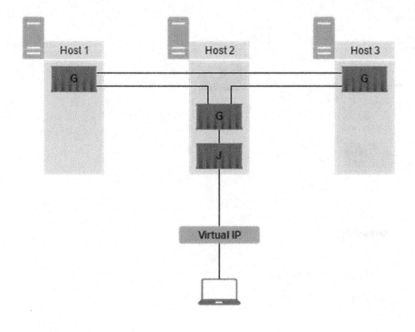

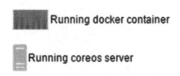

Running docker container

Running coreos server

Figure 3-2. *Jenkins HA setup*

Failover Scenarios

Let us understand how our HA setup should react to failures of various types. Shown in Figure 3-3 is a failover scenario in which the GlusterFS Server that is running on Host2 fails or is disconnected. In this situation the Jenkins Server, or shall we say the GlusterFS client, running on the Jenkins Server should automatically connect to any one of the remaining GlusterFS Servers running on Host1 or Host3.

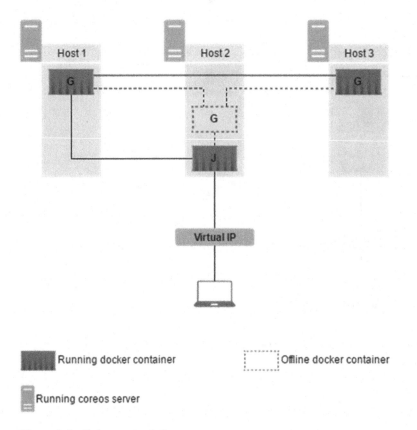

Figure 3-3. *Failover senario 1*

Shown in Figure 3-4 is another failover scenario wherein the CoreOS Host2 that is running the Jenkins Server and one of the GlusterFS servers fails or gets disconnected.

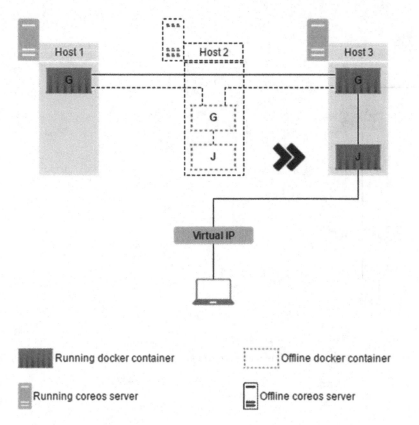

Running docker container

Offline docker container

Running coreos server

Offline coreos server

Figure 3-4. *Failover senario 2*

In such a situation the Jenkins Server should automatically start on any of the remaining CoreOS hosts, and it should connect with the GlusterFS server on that host. The failed GlusterFS Server need not start anywhere else as there are already other GlusterFS Servers running on the remaining CoreOS hosts.

The following scenario in Figure 3-5 is not that important. However, it is also a failure.

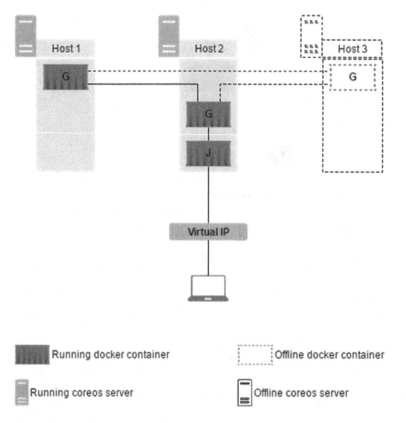

Figure 3-5. *Failover senario 3*

Creating a HA Cluster for Jenkins

In the following section we will realize the HA setup design discussed in the previous section; see Figure 3-2. *Jenkins HA setup*. We are going to use **Vagrant** along with **Oracle VirtualBox** to create the three CoreOS hosts. Once the CoreOS hosts (Host 1, Host 2, and Host 3) are ready, we will create unit files for Jenkins and GlusterFS respectively. The unit files for Jenkins, when executed, will start the Jenkins Server inside a docker container on one of the CoreOS host. Similarly, the unit file for GlusterFS, when executed, will start GlusterFS Servers inside a docker container on all the CoreOS hosts. These systemd units (Jenkins Server and GlusterFS Servers) will be managed using fleet.

■ **Note**   While writing this chapter, I have chosen a machine with Ubuntu 16.04 OS. You can perform the setup mentioned in the chapter on Windows 7/8/10 without any issues.

For simplicity I am using Vagrant along with Oracle VirtualBox to create the three CoreOS host machines. However, in reality you may choose to create the three CoreOS hosts on three bare metal machines or using a cloud platform like AWS.

Installing Vagrant

To install Vagrant on Ubuntu, follow the steps below. Make sure you perform these steps as a root or with an account having root privileges (sudo access).

1. Open up a terminal and type the following commands to download Vagrant.

   ```
   wget https://releases.hashicorp.com/vagrant/1.8.5/vagrant_1.8.5_x86_64.deb
   ```

   (or)

   You can also download the latest Vagrant package from the Vagrant website (Figure 3-6):
   `https://www.vagrantup.com/downloads.html`

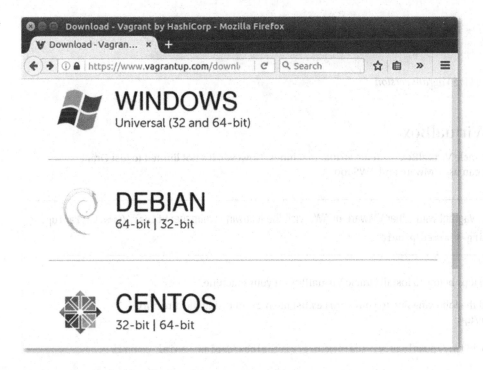

Figure 3-6. *Vagrant download webpage*

■ **Note**   Use the latest version of Vagrant and VirtualBox available. Using an older version of Vagrant with a newer version of VirtualBox or vice versa may result in issues while creating Vms.

---

2. After the download is complete you should see a **.deb** file.

3. Execute the following commands to install Vagrant using the downloaded package file. You may be prompted to provide a password.

```
sudo dpkg -i vagrant_1.8.5_x86_64.deb

sudo apt-get install -f
```

4. Once the installation is complete, check the installed version of Vagrant by executing the following command.

```
vagrant --version
```

5. You should see the Vagrant version as shown in Figure 3-7.

```
nikhil@dev01:~/Downloads$ vagrant --version
Vagrant 1.8.5
nikhil@dev01:~/Downloads$ ▮
```

Figure 3-7. *Checking Vagrant version*

Installing VirtualBox

Vagrant needs Oracle VirtualBox to create virtual machines. However, it's not limited to just Oracle VirtualBox; you can use VMware and AWS too.

■ **Note** To run Vagrant with either VMware or AWS visit the following webpage: https://www.vagrantup.com/docs/getting-started/providers.html

---

Follow the steps below to install Oracle VirtualBox on your machine.

1. Add the following line to your **sources.list** file present inside the directory **/etc/apt**:

```
deb http://download.virtualbox.org/virtualbox/debian xenial contrib
```

■ **Note** According to your Ubuntu distribution, replace 'xenial' by 'vivid', 'utopic', 'trusty', 'raring', 'quantal', 'precise', 'lucid', 'jessie', 'wheezy', or 'squeeze'.

---

2. Download and register the keys. The output of these commands should be similiar to as shown in Figure 3-8.

```
wget -q https://www.virtualbox.org/download/oracle_vbox_2016.asc -O- |
sudo apt-key add -

wget -q https://www.virtualbox.org/download/oracle_vbox.asc -O- | sudo
apt-key add -
```

```
nikhil@dev01:~$ sudo wget -q https://www.virtualbox.org/download/oracle_vbox_201
6.asc -O- | sudo apt-key add -
OK
nikhil@dev01:~$ sudo wget -q https://www.virtualbox.org/download/oracle_vbox.asc
 -O- | sudo apt-key add -
OK
nikhil@dev01:~$ ▮
```

Figure 3-8. *Download and register the VirtualBox keys*

3.   To install VirtualBox, execute the following commands.

     ```
     sudo apt-get update
     ```

     ```
     sudo apt-get install virtualbox-5.1
     ```

4.   Execute the following command to see the installed VirtualBox version, as shown in Figure 3-9.

     VBoxManage --version

```
nikhil@dev01:~$ VBoxManage --version
5.1.6r110634
nikhil@dev01:~$ ▮
```

Figure 3-9. *Check VirtualBox version*

■ **Note**   Ubuntu/Debian users might want to install the dkms package to ensure that the VirtualBox host kernel modules (vboxdrv, vboxnetflt, and vboxnetadp) are properly updated if the Linux kernel version changes during the next apt-get upgrade. For Debian it is available in Lenny backports and in the normal repository for Squeeze and later. The dkms package can be installed through the Synaptic Package manager or through the following command:

```
sudo apt-get install dkms
```

Creating the CoreOS Host Machines

In order to create the CoreOS hosts using Vagrant we need to download the Vagrantfile for CoreOS. A Vagrantfile is a manuscript that describes how to build a virtual machine. Follow the steps below to download the Vagrantfile for CoreOS.

1.   Make sure GIT is installed on your machine. If not, then install GIT using the following commands.

     ```
     sudo apt-get update
     ```

     ```
     sudo apt-get install git
     ```

2. Execute the following command to clone the **coreos-vagrant** repository from GitHub.

   ```
   git clone https://github.com/coreos/coreos-vagrant.git
   ```

3. Go to the directory **coreos-vagrant** and list the files inside it. See Figure 3-10.

   ```
   cd coreos-vagrant
   ```

   ```
   ls -lrt
   ```

```
nikhil@dev01:~/coreos-vagrant$ ls -lrt
total 52
-rw-rw-r-- 1 nikhil nikhil  4900 Sep 19 19:38 Vagrantfile
-rw-rw-r-- 1 nikhil nikhil  1349 Sep 19 19:38 user-data.sample
-rw-rw-r-- 1 nikhil nikhil  4150 Sep 19 19:38 README.md
-rw-rw-r-- 1 nikhil nikhil   126 Sep 19 19:38 NOTICE
-rw-rw-r-- 1 nikhil nikhil   104 Sep 19 19:38 MAINTAINERS
-rw-rw-r-- 1 nikhil nikhil 11325 Sep 19 19:38 LICENSE
-rw-rw-r-- 1 nikhil nikhil  1422 Sep 19 19:38 DCO
-rw-rw-r-- 1 nikhil nikhil  2448 Sep 19 19:38 CONTRIBUTING.md
-rw-rw-r-- 1 nikhil nikhil  3378 Sep 19 19:38 config.rb.sample
nikhil@dev01:~/coreos-vagrant$ █
```

Figure 3-10. *List the files inside the coreos-vagrant folder*

The files Vagrantfile, user-data.sample, and config.rb.sample need some modifications.

4. Rename the file **config.rb.sample** to **config.rb** and open it for editing.

5. Search for the variable **$num_instances** and change its value from **1** to **3**, as shown below.

   ```
   # Size of the CoreOS cluster created by Vagrant
   $num_instances=3
   ```

6. Search for the variable **$update_channel**, uncomment it, and change its value from **alpha** to **stable**, as shown below.

   ```
   # Official CoreOS channel from which updates should be downloaded
   $update_channel='stable'
   ```

7. Search for the variable **$expose_docker_tcp** and uncomment it, as shown below.

   ```
   $expose_docker_tcp=2375
   ```

8. Save and exit the file **config.rb**.

9. Now, rename the file **user-data.sample** to **user-data** and open it for editing.

10. Search for the variable **discovery:** and uncomment it.

    ```
    discovery: https://discovery.etcd.io/<token>
    ```

11. Provide the address **https://discovery.etcd.io/new?size=3** in your web browser and copy the response, as shown in Figure 3-11.

Figure 3-11. *Discovery token*

12. Substitute the token value in place of **<token>**, as shown below.

    https://discovery.etcd.io/7b2ba3d5c89938b886d2fa4d2ddda8de

13. Save and exit the file **user-data.**

Starting the Virtual Machines

Starting the VMs is simple.

1. Move to the coreos-vagrant directory and run the vagrant command to start the VMs.

    ```
    cd coreos-vagrant
    vagrant up
    ```

2. The **vagrant up** command should execute without any errors.

3. To check the status of the VMs, execute the command **vagrant status.** The output of the **vagrant status** command is shown in Figure 3-12.

```
nikhil@dev01:~/coreos-vagrant$ vagrant status
Current machine states:

core-01                   running (virtualbox)
core-02                   running (virtualbox)
core-03                   running (virtualbox)

This environment represents multiple VMs. The VMs are all listed
above with their current state. For more information about a specific
VM, run `vagrant status NAME`.
nikhil@dev01:~/coreos-vagrant$ 
```

Figure 3-12. *List the running VMs*

4. To log in to any one of the VMs use the **Vagrant ssh** command as shown in Figure 3-13.

```
vagrant ssh core-01 -- -A
```

```
nikhil@dev01:~/coreos-vagrant$ vagrant ssh core-01 -- -A
CoreOS stable (1122.2.0)
Last login: Mon Sep 19 15:13:36 2016 from 10.0.2.2
core@core-01 ~ $
```

Figure 3-13. *Log in to CoreOS host*

5. To know the IP address of our new VM, execute the **ip route** command. Notice the highlighted IP in Figure 3-14. That's the IP of our new **core-01** host.

```
core@core-01 ~ $ ip route
default via 10.0.2.2 dev eth0  proto dhcp  src 10.0.2.15  metric 1024
10.0.2.0/24 dev eth0  proto kernel  scope link  src 10.0.2.15
10.0.2.2 dev eth0  proto dhcp  scope link  src 10.0.2.15  metric 1024
10.1.0.0/16 dev flannel0  proto kernel  scope link  src 10.1.58.0
172.17.8.0/24 dev eth1  proto kernel  scope link  src 172.17.8.101
core@core-01 ~ $
```

Figure 3-14. *List the IP address of the new CoreOS host*

6. All the three CoreOS host machines are part of a cluster and are aware of each other. This can be confirmed by executing the following **fleetctl** command. See Figure 3-15.

```
fleetctl list-machines
```

```
core@core-01 ~ $ fleetctl list-machines
MACHINE        IP            METADATA
0e8187f9...    172.17.8.102  -
35c4295e...    172.17.8.101  -
b40a8da9...    172.17.8.103  -
core@core-01 ~ $
```

Figure 3-15. *List the machines using the fleetctl command*

7. To list the running units execute the **fleetctl list-units** command, as shown in Figure 3-16. Right now there are no units running on any of the coreos VMs, so the list is empty.

```
core@core-01 ~ $ fleetctl list-units
UNIT    MACHINE ACTIVE   SUB
core@core-01 ~ $
```

Figure 3-16. *List the units*

8. To see the docker version, execute the command **docker –version**, as shown in Figure 3-17.

```
core@core-01 ~ $ docker --version
Docker version 1.10.3, build 1f8f545
core@core-01 ~ $
```

Figure 3-17. *Print the docker version*

9. To list the network interfaces, execute the **ifconfig** command. Note the IP address from the Figure 3-18.

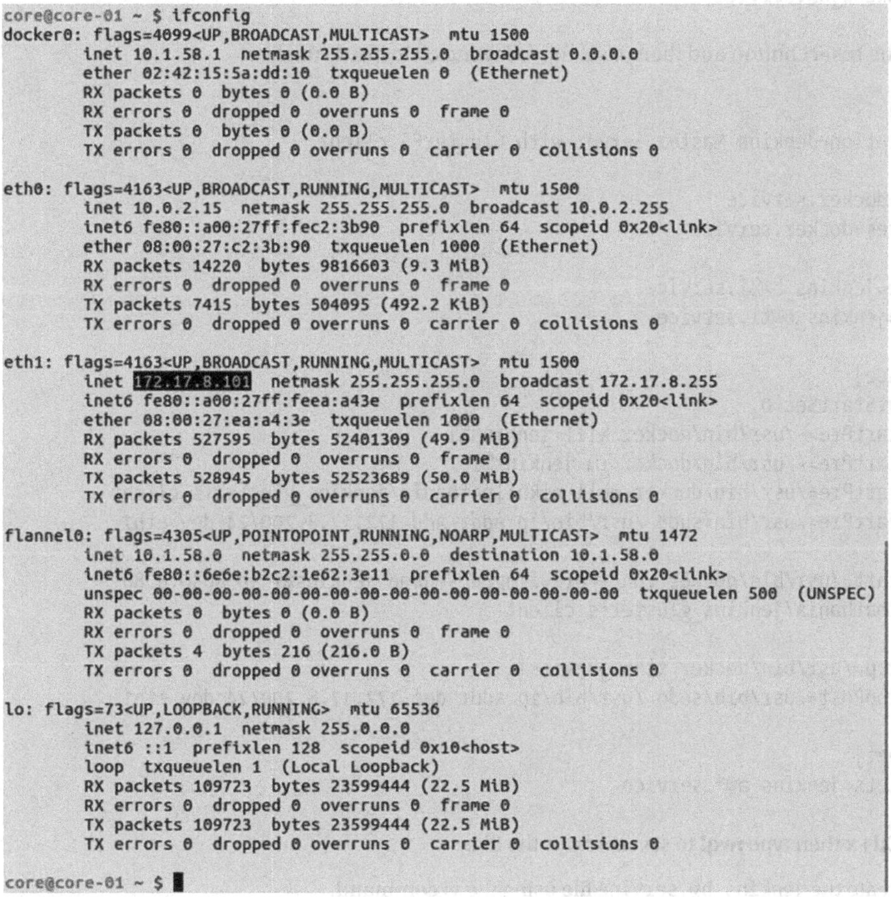

```
core@core-01 ~ $ ifconfig
docker0: flags=4099<UP,BROADCAST,MULTICAST>  mtu 1500
        inet 10.1.58.1  netmask 255.255.255.0  broadcast 0.0.0.0
        ether 02:42:15:5a:dd:10  txqueuelen 0  (Ethernet)
        RX packets 0  bytes 0 (0.0 B)
        RX errors 0  dropped 0  overruns 0  frame 0
        TX packets 0  bytes 0 (0.0 B)
        TX errors 0  dropped 0 overruns 0  carrier 0  collisions 0

eth0: flags=4163<UP,BROADCAST,RUNNING,MULTICAST>  mtu 1500
        inet 10.0.2.15  netmask 255.255.255.0  broadcast 10.0.2.255
        inet6 fe80::a00:27ff:fec2:3b90  prefixlen 64  scopeid 0x20<link>
        ether 08:00:27:c2:3b:90  txqueuelen 1000  (Ethernet)
        RX packets 14220  bytes 9816603 (9.3 MiB)
        RX errors 0  dropped 0  overruns 0  frame 0
        TX packets 7415  bytes 504095 (492.2 KiB)
        TX errors 0  dropped 0 overruns 0  carrier 0  collisions 0

eth1: flags=4163<UP,BROADCAST,RUNNING,MULTICAST>  mtu 1500
        inet 172.17.8.101  netmask 255.255.255.0  broadcast 172.17.8.255
        inet6 fe80::a00:27ff:feea:a43e  prefixlen 64  scopeid 0x20<link>
        ether 08:00:27:ea:a4:3e  txqueuelen 1000  (Ethernet)
        RX packets 527595  bytes 52401309 (49.9 MiB)
        RX errors 0  dropped 0  overruns 0  frame 0
        TX packets 528945  bytes 52523689 (50.0 MiB)
        TX errors 0  dropped 0 overruns 0  carrier 0  collisions 0

flannel0: flags=4305<UP,POINTOPOINT,RUNNING,NOARP,MULTICAST>  mtu 1472
        inet 10.1.58.0  netmask 255.255.0.0  destination 10.1.58.0
        inet6 fe80::6e6e:b2c2:1e62:3e11  prefixlen 64  scopeid 0x20<link>
        unspec 00-00-00-00-00-00-00-00-00-00-00-00-00-00-00-00  txqueuelen 500  (UNSPEC)
        RX packets 0  bytes 0 (0.0 B)
        RX errors 0  dropped 0  overruns 0  frame 0
        TX packets 4  bytes 216 (216.0 B)
        TX errors 0  dropped 0 overruns 0  carrier 0  collisions 0

lo: flags=73<UP,LOOPBACK,RUNNING>  mtu 65536
        inet 127.0.0.1  netmask 255.0.0.0
        inet6 ::1  prefixlen 128  scopeid 0x10<host>
        loop  txqueuelen 1  (Local Loopback)
        RX packets 109723  bytes 23599444 (22.5 MiB)
        RX errors 0  dropped 0  overruns 0  frame 0
        TX packets 109723  bytes 23599444 (22.5 MiB)
        TX errors 0  dropped 0 overruns 0  carrier 0  collisions 0

core@core-01 ~ $ █
```

Figure 3-18. *List the network interfaces*

Creating Unit Files

Unit files describe how to run and monitor a service and lots more. The service can be a script, a simple command, or a docker container.

Creating Unit Files for Jenkins Server

For the Jenkins Server we will create two unit files named, jenkins_a@.service and jenkins_b@.service. The first unit file will be used to run the Jenkins Server inside a docker container. The second unit will be used to make a configuration on the docker container created by the first unit file.

1. Log in to the **core-01** host using the command **vagrant ssh** command.

    ```
    vagrant ssh core-01 -- -A
    ```

2. The CoreOS is a lightweight Linux OS with minimalistic features. Hence, we have to manage with the VI editor. To create a file, execute the following command.

```
vi jenkins_a@.service
```

3. Press the **Insert** button and then paste the following code inside the file.

```
[Unit]
Description=Jenkins Master Server with GlusterFS client

After=docker.service
Requires=docker.service

Before=jenkins_b@%i.service
Wants=jenkins_b@%i.service

[Service]
TimeoutStartSec=0
ExecStartPre=-/usr/bin/docker kill jenkins%i
ExecStartPre=-/usr/bin/docker rm jenkins%i
ExecStartPre=/usr/bin/docker pull nikhilpathania/jenkins_glusterfs_client
ExecStartPre=/usr/bin/sudo /usr/bin/ip addr add 172.17.8.200/24 dev eth1

ExecStart=/usr/bin/docker run --privileged --name jenkins%i -p 8080:8080
nikhilpathania/jenkins_glusterfs_client

ExecStop=/usr/bin/docker stop jenkins%i
ExecStopPost=/usr/bin/sudo /usr/bin/ip addr del 172.17.8.200/24 dev eth1

[X-Fleet]
Conflicts=jenkins_a@*.service
```

4. Click **Ctl+x** then type **:wq!** to save and exit the file.

5. Now create the jenkins_b@.service file using the vi command.

```
vi jenkins_a@.service
```

6. Press the **Insert** button and then paste the below code inside the file.

```
[Unit]
Description=Mount /var/jenkins_home to /volume1

After=docker.service
Requires=docker.service

After=jenkins_a@%i.service
Requires=jenkins_a@%i.service
BindsTo=jenkins_a@1.service

[Service]
TimeoutStartSec=0
```

```
ExecStart=/usr/bin/docker exec -u root jenkins%i /bin/bash -c 'cp
-R /var/jenkins_home /var/jenkins_home_backup && mount.glusterfs
172.17.8.101:/volume1 /var/jenkins_home && if [ "$(ls -A /var/jenkins_
home)" ]; then echo "jenkins_home directory is in sync with GlusterFS
Server"; else cp -R /var/jenkins_home_backup/. /var/jenkins_home; fi &&
chown -R jenkins:jenkins /var/jenkins_home'

RestartSec=30
Restart=on-failure

[X-Fleet]
MachineOf=jenkins_a@%i.service
```

7. Click **Ctl+x** then type **:wq!** to save and exit the file.

Creating Unit Files for GlusterFS Server

For the GlusterFS Servers we will create a single files glusterfs_a@.service. The unit file will be used to run the GlusterFS Server inside a docker container on all the three CoreOS hosts.

1. Log in to the **core-01** host using the command **vagrant ssh** command.

    ```
    vagrant ssh core-01 -- -A
    ```

2. To create a file, execute the following command.

    ```
    vi glusterfs_a@.service
    ```

3. Press the **Insert** button and then paste the code below inside the file.

    ```
    [Unit]
    Description=Glusterfs Server

    After=docker.service
    Requires=docker.service

    Before=glusterfs_b@%i.service
    Wants=glusterfs_b@%i.service

    [Service]
    TimeoutStartSec=0
    ExecStartPre=-/usr/bin/docker kill glusterfs%i
    ExecStartPre=-/usr/bin/docker rm glusterfs%i
    ExecStartPre=/bin/bash -c 'if [[ $(docker images --format
    "{{.Repository}}" gluster/gluster-centos:latest) ]]; then echo
    "image gluster/gluster-centos:latest already exists"; else /usr/bin/
    docker pull gluster/gluster-centos:latest; fi'

    ExecStart=/usr/bin/docker run --privileged --name glusterfs%i
    --net=host -p 22:22 gluster/gluster-centos:latest
    ```

```
ExecStop=/usr/bin/docker stop glusterfs%i
ExecStopPost=-/usr/bin/docker rmi gluster/gluster-centos:last
ExecStopPost=/bin/bash -c '/usr/bin/docker tag gluster/gluster-
centos:latest gluster/gluster-centos:last && /usr/bin/docker rmi
gluster/gluster-centos:latest && /usr/bin/docker commit glusterfs%i
gluster/gluster-centos:latest'

[X-Fleet]
Conflicts=glusterfs_a@*.service
```

4. Click **Ctl+x** then type **:wq!** to save and exit the file.

5. List all the files that we have created using the ls command, as shown in Figure 3-19.

```
core@core-01 ~ $ ls -lrt
total 24
-rw-r--r--. 1 core core 699 Sep 20 13:36 jenkins_a@.service
-rw-r--r--. 1 core core 680 Sep 20 13:37 jenkins_b@.service
-rw-r--r--. 1 core core 962 Sep 21 17:14 glusterfs_a@.service
core@core-01 ~ $ █
```

Figure 3-19. *List the unit files*

Starting the Cluster

We are ready with our unit files. We will be using fleetctl commands to start our GlusterFS Server and Jenkins units. First we will start the GlusterFS Server on each of the CoreOS hosts. And then we will do a little configuration on one of the GlusterFS server. Then once all the GlusterFS servers are up and configured, we will start our Jenkins Server.

Starting the GlusterFS Servers

We are done creating the unit files for Jenkins as well as GlusterFS. Now let us start the GlusterFS service on each of the cluster nodes.

1. To start the GlusterFS servers, execute the following command, as shown in Figure 3-20.

   ```
   fleetctl start glusterfs_a@{1,2,3}.service
   ```

```
core@core-01 ~ $ fleetctl start glusterfs_a@{1,2,3}.service
Unit glusterfs_a@1.service inactive
Unit glusterfs_a@2.service inactive
Unit glusterfs_a@3.service inactive
Unit glusterfs_a@3.service launched on b40a8da9.../172.17.8.103
Unit glusterfs_a@2.service launched on 35c4295e.../172.17.8.101
Unit glusterfs_a@1.service launched on 0e8187f9.../172.17.8.102
core@core-01 ~ $ █
```

Figure 3-20. *Starting the GlusterFS Servers*

2. To check the status of the units that we just started do,

   ```
   fleetctl list-units
   ```

3. From Figure 3-21, we can see that the status of all three units is still **activating**. It will take some time (depending on you network speed) as fleet is downloading the GlusterFS docker image from the docker hub.

```
core@core-01 ~ $ fleetctl list-units
UNIT                    MACHINE                      ACTIVE        SUB
glusterfs_a@1.service   0e8187f9.../172.17.8.102     activating    start-pre
glusterfs_a@2.service   35c4295e.../172.17.8.101     activating    start-pre
glusterfs_a@3.service   b40a8da9.../172.17.8.103     activating    start-pre
core@core-01 ~ $ ▌
```

Figure 3-21. *List the Units*

4. To know what's happening behind the scene, execute the following command. You should get an output similar to the one shown in Figure 3-22.

```
fleetctl status glusterfs_a@2.service
```

```
● glusterfs_a@2.service - Glusterfs Server
   Loaded: loaded (/run/fleet/units/glusterfs_a@2.service; linked-runtime; vendor preset: disabled)
   Active: activating (start-pre) since Wed 2016-09-21 18:16:05 UTC; 6min ago
  Process: 4489 ExecStartPre=/usr/bin/docker rm glusterfs%i (code=exited, status=1/FAILURE)
  Process: 4482 ExecStartPre=/usr/bin/docker kill glusterfs%i (code=exited, status=1/FAILURE)
 Main PID: 2773 (code=exited, status=137);              : 4497 (bash)
    Tasks: 6
   CGroup: /system.slice/system-glusterfs_a.slice/glusterfs_a@2.service
           └─control
             ├─4497 /bin/bash -c if [[ $(docker images --format "{{.Repository}}" gluster/gluster-c
             └─4503 /usr/bin/docker pull gluster/gluster-centos:latest

Sep 21 18:16:10 core-01 bash[4497]: 1b781115d2eb: Waiting
Sep 21 18:16:10 core-01 bash[4497]: 0ec08d1764ed: Waiting
Sep 21 18:16:10 core-01 bash[4497]: e1d611ab84e9: Waiting
Sep 21 18:16:10 core-01 bash[4497]: beae858c2fc8: Waiting
Sep 21 18:16:10 core-01 bash[4497]: bb5dad06280b: Waiting
Sep 21 18:16:10 core-01 bash[4497]: 9bd8ccd030e1: Waiting
Sep 21 18:16:10 core-01 bash[4497]: 7d25ca733a91: Waiting
Sep 21 18:16:10 core-01 bash[4497]: 9576315e08a8: Waiting
Sep 21 18:16:14 core-01 bash[4497]: 1076f819c26d: Verifying Checksum
Sep 21 18:16:14 core-01 bash[4497]: 1076f819c26d: Download complete
~
lines 1-22/22 (END)
```

Figure 3-22. *Fleetctl status command*

5. You can also use the following command to get a live status about the unit.

```
fleetctl journal -f glusterfs_a@2.service
```

6. Or you can use the following command to list the last 50 lines from the log file that will give you some idea about the unit.

```
fleetctl journal –lines 50 glusterfs_a@2.service
```

7. Run the **fleetctl list-units** command again and now you can see all the GlusterFS Servers that have been started and are active. As shown in Figure 3-23.

```
core@core-01 ~ $ fleetctl list-units
UNIT                    MACHINE                      ACTIVE  SUB
glusterfs_a@1.service   0e8187f9.../172.17.8.102     active  running
glusterfs_a@2.service   35c4295e.../172.17.8.101     active  running
glusterfs_a@3.service   b40a8da9.../172.17.8.103     active  running
core@core-01 ~ $ 
```

Figure 3-23. *List the Units*

8. Run the **fleectl status glusterfs_a@2.service** command again. And you should see something as shown in Figure 3-24.

```
core@core-01 ~ $ fleetctl status glusterfs_a@2.service
● glusterfs_a@2.service - Glusterfs Server
   Loaded: loaded (/run/fleet/units/glusterfs_a@2.service; linked-runtime; vendo
   Active: active (running) since Wed 2016-09-21 18:51:35 UTC; 3min 15s ago
  Process: 4497 ExecStartPre=/bin/bash -c if [[ $(docker images --format "{{.Rep
  Process: 4489 ExecStartPre=/usr/bin/docker rm glusterfs%i (code=exited, status
  Process: 4482 ExecStartPre=/usr/bin/docker kill glusterfs%i (code=exited, stat
 Main PID: 4780 (docker)
    Tasks: 5
   CGroup: /system.slice/system-glusterfs_a.slice/glusterfs_a@2.service
           └─4780 /usr/bin/docker run --privileged --name glusterfs2 --net=host

Sep 21 18:51:31 core-01 bash[4497]: bb5dad06280b: Pull complete
Sep 21 18:51:33 core-01 bash[4497]: 9bd8ccd030e1: Pull complete
Sep 21 18:51:33 core-01 bash[4497]: 9bd8ccd030e1: Pull complete
Sep 21 18:51:33 core-01 bash[4497]: 7d25ca733a91: Pull complete
Sep 21 18:51:34 core-01 bash[4497]: 7d25ca733a91: Pull complete
Sep 21 18:51:34 core-01 bash[4497]: 9576315e08a8: Pull complete
Sep 21 18:51:35 core-01 bash[4497]: 9576315e08a8: Pull complete
Sep 21 18:51:35 core-01 bash[4497]: Digest: sha256:dfbfe9e563f5832711a1323e123b9
Sep 21 18:51:35 core-01 bash[4497]: Status: Downloaded newer image for gluster/g
Sep 21 18:51:35 core-01 systemd[1]: Started Glusterfs Server.
lines 1-21/21 (END)
```

Figure 3-24. *Fleetctl status command*

9. Give the following command to see the list of containers running on the core-01 host. From Figure 3-25, you can see a docker image named **gluster/gluster-ce ntos:latest**.

```
docker ps
```

```
core@core-01 ~ $ docker ps
CONTAINER ID IMAGE                         COMMAND             CREATED         STATUS          PORTS NAMES
b962e9811ae4 gluster/gluster-centos:latest "/usr/sbin/init" 7 minutes ago  Up 7 minutes          glusterfs2
core@core-01 ~ $ 
```

Figure 3-25. *List the docker containers*

Exercise:
Log in to the remaining CoreOs hosts and execute the above commands and check the output.

Configuring the GlusterFS Servers

Our GlusterFS service is up and running. We will now manually configure one among the three GlusterFS services.

1. Log in to the **core-01** host using the command **vagrant ssh** command.

    ```
    vagrant ssh core-01 -- -A
    ```

2. We will now access the GlusterFS Server named **glusterfs2,** which is running on **core-01** using the **docker exec** command. You will be logged in as a root user on the glusterfs2 Server, as shown in Figure 3-26.

    ```
    docker exec -it glusterfs2 /bin/bash
    ```

```
core@core-01 ~ $ docker exec -it glusterfs2 /bin/bash
[root@core-01 /]# 
```

Figure 3-26. *Access the GlusterFS Server container*

3. To probe the other GlusterFS Servers that are running on **core-02** and **core-03**, we will use the **gluster peer probe** command.

4. First probe the GlusterFS server running on **core-02**.

    ```
    gluster peer probe 172.17.8.102
    ```

5. This should return the following.

    ```
    peer probe: success.
    ```

6. Similarly probe the GlusterFS server running on **core-03**.

    ```
    gluster peer probe 172.17.8.103
    ```

7. Try probing the GlusterFS Server that you are currently inside.

    ```
    gluster peer probe 172.17.8.101
    ```

8. It should return the following.

    ```
    peer probe: success. Probe on localhost not needed
    ```

9. To get the status of peer probe, execute the command **gluster peer status**, as shown in Figure 3-27.

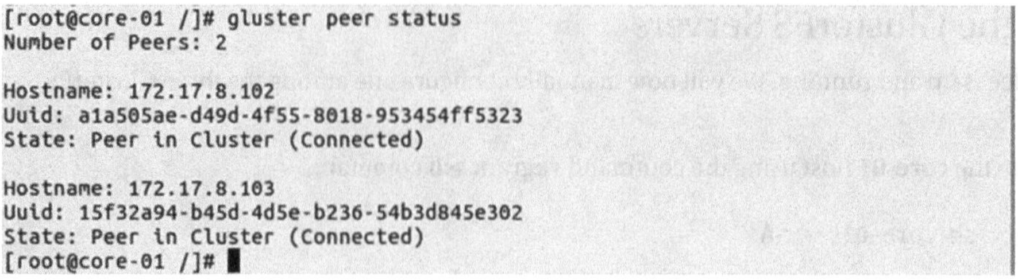

```
[root@core-01 /]# gluster peer status
Number of Peers: 2

Hostname: 172.17.8.102
Uuid: a1a505ae-d49d-4f55-8018-953454ff5323
State: Peer in Cluster (Connected)

Hostname: 172.17.8.103
Uuid: 15f32a94-b45d-4d5e-b236-54b3d845e302
State: Peer in Cluster (Connected)
[root@core-01 /]# ▓
```

Figure 3-27. *Gluster peer status*

10. We will now create a volume that will be replicated across the GlusterFS Servers. To do so, execute the following command.

    gluster volume create volume1 replica 3 transport tcp 172.17.8.101:/gluster 172.17.8.102:/gluster 172.17.8.103:/gluster force

11. You should see a similar output,

    volume create: volume1: success: please start the volume to access data

12. To start the volume, do the following:

    gluster volume start volume1

13. This should give an output,

    volume start: volume1: success

14. To see the volume status, execute the following command. You should see an output similar to the one shown in Figure 3-28.

    gluster volume info

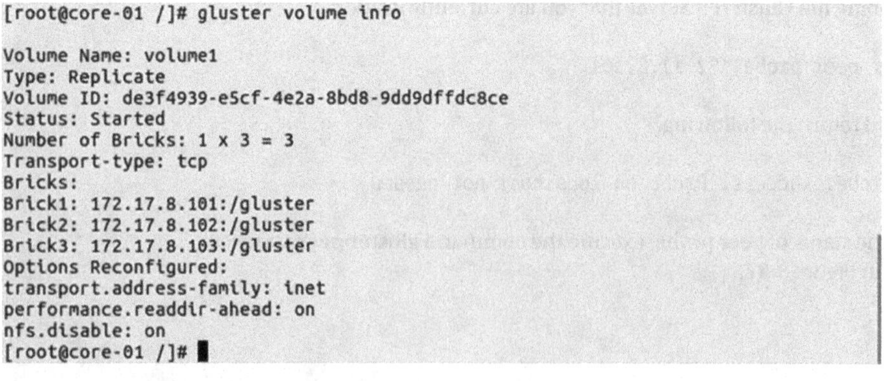

```
[root@core-01 /]# gluster volume info

Volume Name: volume1
Type: Replicate
Volume ID: de3f4939-e5cf-4e2a-8bd8-9dd9dffdc8ce
Status: Started
Number of Bricks: 1 x 3 = 3
Transport-type: tcp
Bricks:
Brick1: 172.17.8.101:/gluster
Brick2: 172.17.8.102:/gluster
Brick3: 172.17.8.103:/gluster
Options Reconfigured:
transport.address-family: inet
performance.readdir-ahead: on
nfs.disable: on
[root@core-01 /]# ▓
```

Figure 3-28. *Gluster volume info*

15. You can also give the following command. Figure 3-29 shows a different view of the volume status.

```
gluster volume status
```

```
[root@core-01 /]# gluster volume status
Status of volume: volume1
Gluster process                         TCP Port  RDMA Port  Online  Pid
------------------------------------------------------------------------
Brick 172.17.8.101:/gluster             49152     0          Y       369
Brick 172.17.8.102:/gluster             49152     0          Y       229
Brick 172.17.8.103:/gluster             49152     0          Y       221
Self-heal Daemon on localhost           N/A       N/A        Y       389
Self-heal Daemon on 172.17.8.103        N/A       N/A        Y       241
Self-heal Daemon on 172.17.8.102        N/A       N/A        Y       251

Task Status of Volume volume1
------------------------------------------------------------------------
There are no active volume tasks

[root@core-01 /]# █
```

Figure 3-29. *Gluster volume status*

16. Type **exit** to come out of the container.

Starting Jenkins Server

GlusterFS services are now running on all of the three nodes. Let us now start the Jenkins service using the unit file that we created earlier.

1. To start the Jenkins units, execute the following command. You should get the launch status on the unit as shown in Figure 3-30.

```
fleetctl start jenkins_a@1.service
```

```
core@core-01 ~ $ fleetctl start jenkins_a@1.service
Unit jenkins_a@1.service inactive
Unit jenkins_a@1.service launched on 0e8187f9.../172.17.8.102
core@core-01 ~ $ █
```

Figure 3-30. *Starting the Jenkins Server*

2. We can give the command **fleetctl list-units** to check the status of our units, as shown in Figure 3-31.

```
core@core-01 ~ $ fleetctl list-units
UNIT                  MACHINE                      ACTIVE      SUB
glusterfs_a@1.service 0e8187f9.../172.17.8.102     active      running
glusterfs_a@2.service 35c4295e.../172.17.8.101     active      running
glusterfs_a@3.service b40a8da9.../172.17.8.103     active      running
jenkins_a@1.service   0e8187f9.../172.17.8.102     activating  start-pre
core@core-01 ~ $ █
```

Figure 3-31. *List the units*

3. Open a new terminal and log in to the host where Jenkins is about to start, in our case it's **core-02**. See Figure 3-32.

    ```
    vagrant ssh core-02 -- -A
    ```

```
nikhil@dev01:~/coreos-vagrant$ vagrant ssh core-02 -- -A
CoreOS stable (1122.2.0)
Last login: Thu Sep 22 16:12:47 2016 from 10.0.2.2
core@core-02 ~ $
```

Figure 3-32. *Log in to CoreOS host running the Jenkins Server*

4. Check the status of Jenkins unit by executing the following command. You should see a similar output as shown in Figure 3-33.

    ```
    fleetctl status jenkins_a@1.service
    ```

```
core@core-02 ~ $ fleetctl status jenkins_a@1.service
● jenkins_a@1.service - Jenkins Master Server with GlusterFS client
   Loaded: loaded (/run/fleet/units/jenkins_a@1.service; linked-runtime; vendor
   Active: activating (start-pre) since Thu 2016-09-22 16:08:57 UTC; 5min ago
  Process: 2286 ExecStartPre=/usr/bin/docker rm jenkins%i (code=exited, status=1
  Process: 2279 ExecStartPre=/usr/bin/docker kill jenkins%i (code=exited, status
  Control: 2293 (docker)
    Tasks: 4
   CGroup: /system.slice/system-jenkins_a.slice/jenkins_a@1.service
           └─control
             └─2293 /usr/bin/docker pull nikhilpathania/jenkins_glusterfs_client

Sep 22 16:13:52 core-02 docker[2293]: 8b357fc28db9: Pull complete
Sep 22 16:13:52 core-02 docker[2293]: 8b357fc28db9: Pull complete
Sep 22 16:13:52 core-02 docker[2293]: 1a614fcb4b1b: Pull complete
Sep 22 16:13:52 core-02 docker[2293]: 1a614fcb4b1b: Pull complete
Sep 22 16:13:53 core-02 docker[2293]: 6db9b5f026fe: Verifying Checksum
Sep 22 16:13:53 core-02 docker[2293]: 6db9b5f026fe: Download complete
Sep 22 16:13:53 core-02 docker[2293]: 1fcd29499236: Pull complete
Sep 22 16:13:53 core-02 docker[2293]: 1fcd29499236: Pull complete
Sep 22 16:13:57 core-02 docker[2293]: 2af63ead7fda: Verifying Checksum
Sep 22 16:13:57 core-02 docker[2293]: 2af63ead7fda: Download complete
lines 1-21/21 (END)
```

Figure 3-33. *Fleetctl status command*

5. Or you can also try,

    ```
    fleetctl journal -lines 50 jenkins_a@1.service
    ```

    (Or)

    ```
    fleetctl journal -f jenkins_a@1.service
    ```

6. Keep checking the status of the units using the **fleetctl list-units** command unit until you see the Jenkins unit active and running, as shown in Figure 3-34.

```
core@core-02 ~ $ fleetctl list-units
UNIT                    MACHINE                    ACTIVE   SUB
glusterfs_a@1.service   0e8187f9.../172.17.8.102   active   running
glusterfs_a@2.service   35c4295e.../172.17.8.101   active   running
glusterfs_a@3.service   b40a8da9.../172.17.8.103   active   running
jenkins_a@1.service     0e8187f9.../172.17.8.102   active   running
core@core-02 ~ $ ▮
```

Figure 3-34. List the units

7. Once the Jenkins unit is up and running, check the detailed status by running the
    following command, as shown in Figure 3-35.

    ```
    fleetctl status jenkins_a@1.service
    ```

```
● jenkins_a@1.service - Jenkins Master Server with GlusterFS client
   Loaded: loaded (/run/fleet/units/jenkins_a@1.service; linked-runtime; vendor preset: disabled)
   Active: active (running) since Thu 2016-09-22 16:20:23 UTC; 4min 1s ago
  Process: 2565 ExecStartPre=/usr/bin/sudo /usr/bin/ip addr add 172.17.8.200/24 dev eth1 (code=exited, status=0/SUCCESS)
  Process: 2293 ExecStartPre=/usr/bin/docker pull nikhilpathania/jenkins_glusterfs_client (code=exited, status=0/SUCCESS)
  Process: 2286 ExecStartPre=/usr/bin/docker rm jenkins%i (code=exited, status=1/FAILURE)
  Process: 2279 ExecStartPre=/usr/bin/docker kill jenkins%i (code=exited, status=1/FAILURE)
 Main PID: 2589 (docker)
    Tasks: 5
   CGroup: /system.slice/system-jenkins_a.slice/jenkins_a@1.service
           └─2589 /usr/bin/docker run --privileged --name jenkins1 -p 8080:8080 -p 50000:50000 nikhilpathania/jenkins_glu

Sep 22 16:21:05 core-02 docker[2589]: Sep 22, 2016 4:21:04 PM hudson.model.DownloadService$Downloadable load
Sep 22 16:21:05 core-02 docker[2589]: INFO: Obtained the updated data file for hudson.tasks.Maven.MavenInstaller
Sep 22 16:21:05 core-02 docker[2589]: Sep 22, 2016 4:21:05 PM hudson.model.UpdateSite updateData
Sep 22 16:21:05 core-02 docker[2589]: INFO: Obtained the latest update center data file for UpdateSource default
Sep 22 16:21:05 core-02 docker[2589]: Sep 22, 2016 4:21:05 PM hudson.WebAppMain$3 run
Sep 22 16:21:05 core-02 docker[2589]: INFO: Jenkins is fully up and running
Sep 22 16:21:08 core-02 docker[2589]: Sep 22, 2016 4:21:08 PM hudson.model.DownloadService$Downloadable load
Sep 22 16:21:08 core-02 docker[2589]: INFO: Obtained the updated data file for hudson.tools.JDKInstaller
Sep 22 16:21:08 core-02 docker[2589]: Sep 22, 2016 4:21:08 PM hudson.model.AsyncPeriodicWork$1 run
Sep 22 16:21:08 core-02 docker[2589]: INFO: Finished Download metadata. 20,732 ms
~
lines 1-22/22 (END)
```

Figure 3-35. Fleetctl status command

8. Type **:q** to exit.

Configuring Jenkins Master

Our Jenkins service is up and running. Now we need to run the second unit file **jenkins_b@1.service**. This
unit file will configure the Jenkins service (**jenkins_a@1.service**).

1. To run jenkins_b@1.service, execute the following command, as shown in
    Figure 3-36.

    ```
    fleetctl start jenkins_b@1.service
    ```

```
core@core-01 ~ $ fleetctl start jenkins_b@1.service
Unit jenkins_b@1.service inactive
Unit jenkins_b@1.service launched on 0e8187f9.../172.17.8.102
core@core-01 ~ $ ▮
```

Figure 3-36. Starting the jenkins configuration unit file

2. This should not take much time to execute. Check the status by running **fleetctl
    list-units** command. You should see something as shown in Figure 3-37.

```
core@core-01 ~ $ fleetctl list-units
UNIT                    MACHINE                       ACTIVE   SUB
glusterfs_a@1.service   0e8187f9.../172.17.8.102      active   running
glusterfs_a@2.service   35c4295e.../172.17.8.101      active   running
glusterfs_a@3.service   b40a8da9.../172.17.8.103      active   running
jenkins_a@1.service     0e8187f9.../172.17.8.102      active   running
jenkins_b@1.service     0e8187f9.../172.17.8.102      active   running
core@core-01 ~ $ █
```

Figure 3-37. *List the units*

3. Lastly, you should see something similar to the one shown in Figure 3-38.

```
core@core-01 ~ $ fleetctl list-units
UNIT                    MACHINE                       ACTIVE     SUB
glusterfs_a@1.service   0e8187f9.../172.17.8.102      active     running
glusterfs_a@2.service   35c4295e.../172.17.8.101      active     running
glusterfs_a@3.service   b40a8da9.../172.17.8.103      active     running
jenkins_a@1.service     0e8187f9.../172.17.8.102      active     running
jenkins_b@1.service     0e8187f9.../172.17.8.102      inactive   dead
core@core-01 ~ $ █
```

Figure 3-38. *List the units*

4. We can check the status of the jenkins_b@1.service by giving the following command.

   ```
   fleetctl status jenkins_b@1.service
   ```

5. Quickly open a new terminal and log in to core-02 host by using the vagrant ssh command.

   ```
   vagrant ssh core-02 -- -A
   ```

6. Execute the following command to check the running containers, as shown in Figure 3-39.

   ```
   docker ps --format  "{{.Names}}"
   ```

```
core@core-02 ~ $ docker ps --format  "{{.Names}}"
jenkins1
glusterfs1
core@core-02 ~ $ █
```

Figure 3-39. *List the running containers*

7. You can see the jenkins1 container is running on core-02. Let us go inside the running container and have a look. From the core-02 machine execute the following command as shown in Figure 3-40.

   ```
   docker exec -it -u root jenkins1 /bin/bash
   ```

```
core@core-02 ~ $ docker exec -it -u root jenkins1 /bin/bash
root@cd16b6e6a0e9:/# █
```

Figure 3-40. *Access the Jenkins Server container*

8. Once inside the container execute the following commands to list the files inside the jenkins_home directory, as shown in Figure 3-41.

```
cd  /var/jenkins_home
```

```
ls -lrt
```

```
root@cd16b6e6a0e9:/var/jenkins_home# ls -lrt
total 47
drwxr-xr-x.  3 jenkins jenkins 4096 Sep 22 17:25 users
drwxr-xr-x.  2 jenkins jenkins 4096 Sep 22 17:25 userContent
drwxr-xr-x.  2 jenkins jenkins 4096 Sep 22 17:25 updates
drwx------.  4 jenkins jenkins 4096 Sep 22 17:25 secrets
-rw-r--r--.  1 jenkins jenkins    0 Sep 22 17:25 secret.key.not-so-secret
-rw-r--r--.  1 jenkins jenkins   64 Sep 22 17:25 secret.key
drwxr-xr-x.  2 jenkins jenkins 4096 Sep 22 17:25 plugins
drwxr-xr-x.  2 jenkins jenkins 4096 Sep 22 17:25 nodes
-rw-r--r--.  1 jenkins jenkins  907 Sep 22 17:25 nodeMonitors.xml
drwxr-xr-x.  3 jenkins jenkins 4096 Sep 22 17:25 logs
drwxr-xr-x.  2 jenkins jenkins 4096 Sep 22 17:25 jobs
-rw-r--r--.  1 jenkins jenkins    4 Sep 22 17:25 jenkins.install.UpgradeWizard.state
drwxr-xr-x.  2 jenkins jenkins 4096 Sep 22 17:25 init.groovy.d
-rw-------.  1 jenkins jenkins 1712 Sep 22 17:25 identity.key.enc
-rw-r--r--.  1 jenkins jenkins  159 Sep 22 17:25 hudson.model.UpdateCenter.xml
-rw-r--r--.  1 jenkins jenkins  102 Sep 22 17:25 copy_reference_file.log
-rw-r--r--.  1 jenkins jenkins 1592 Sep 22 17:25 config.xml
drwxr-xr-x. 10 jenkins jenkins 4096 Sep 22 17:25 war
root@cd16b6e6a0e9:/var/jenkins_home# █
```

Figure 3-41. *List the files inside the jenkins_home directory*

9. Execute the command **df -h** to check if the mount was a success, as highlighted in Figure 3-42.

```
root@cd16b6e6a0e9:/# df -h
Filesystem            Size  Used Avail Use% Mounted on
overlay                16G  2.3G   13G  16% /
tmpfs                 499M     0  499M   0% /dev
tmpfs                 499M     0  499M   0% /sys/fs/cgroup
172.17.8.102:/volume1  16G  2.3G   13G  16% /var/jenkins_home
/dev/sda9              16G  2.3G   13G  16% /etc/hosts
shm                    64M     0   64M   0% /dev/shm
root@cd16b6e6a0e9:/# █
```

Figure 3-42. *Check the mount status*

10. Our Jenkins is up and running. Let us access it in using the following address **http://172.17.8.200:8080/**. See Figure 3-43.

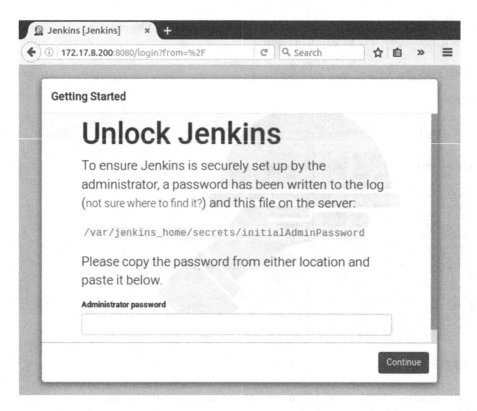

Figure 3-43. *Jenkins initial login page*

11. To get the password from the file **/var/jenkins_home/secrets/ initialAdminPassword**, execute the following command from the CoreOS host where the Jenkins Server container is running.

```
docker exec -u root jenkins1 /bin/bash -c 'cat /var/jenkins_home/secrets/
initialAdminPassword'
```

12. Doing this will fetch the password present inside the file **initialAdminPassword**. See Figure 3-44.

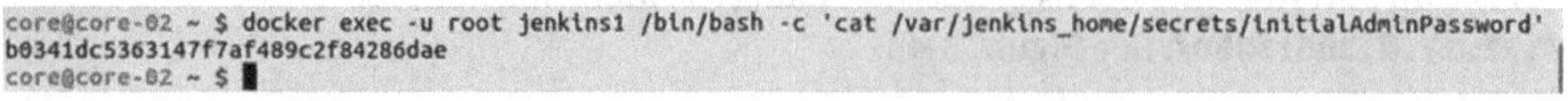

```
core@core-02 ~ $ docker exec -u root jenkins1 /bin/bash -c 'cat /var/jenkins_home/secrets/initialAdminPassword'
b0341dc5363147f7af489c2f84286dae
core@core-02 ~ $
```

Figure 3-44. *Fetch the initialAdminPassword*

13. After you provide the password, the next screen will ask you to select and install plugins, as shown in Figure 3-45.

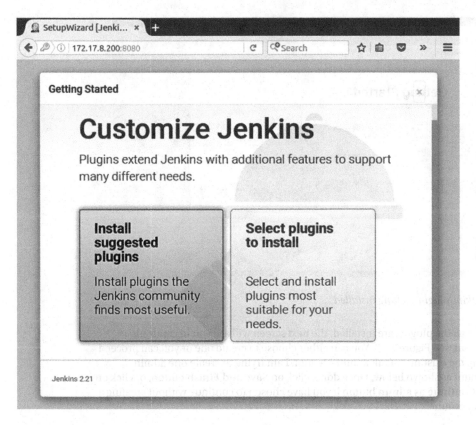

Figure 3-45. *Install plugins*

14. Choose any one of the options. I have chosen to install the plugins suggested by the Jenkins community. The next screen in Figure 3-46 will show you the progress of installation.

Figure 3-46. *Jenkins plugins getting installed*

15. Once all the plugins are installed, the next screen will ask you to create an account, see Figure 3-47. You can either choose to create one or you can proceed using the existing default admin account. I am trying to create one admin account as shown below. Once done, click on **Save and Finish** button, or click on the **Continue as admin** button if you have chosen to continue without creating a new account.

Figure 3-47. *Creating the first admin account*

16. Once done, Jenkins is ready for use. Click on the **Start using Jenkins** button, as shown in Figure 3-48.

Figure 3-48. *Jenkins installation complete*

17. Figure 3-49 shows a Jenkins dashboard.

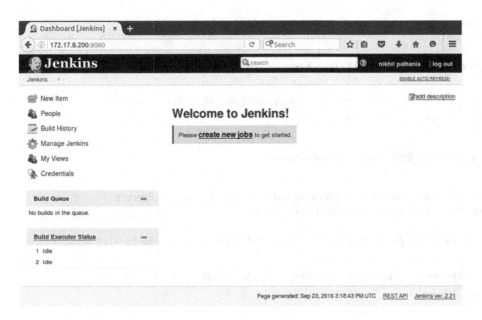

Figure 3-49. *Jenkins dashboard*

Simulating a Failover

We now have three machine core-01, core-02, and core-03. The status of our services is as shown below:

```
Jenkins    is running on core-02
Glusterfs2 is running on core-01
Glusterfs1 is running on core-02
Glusterfs3 is running on core-03
```

In the previous steps we created an admin user in Jenkins and installed a few basic Jenkins plugins while setting up Jenkins. All these changes will be stored inside the **jenkins_home** directory. Let us first see if these changes have been reflected across our glusterfs cluster of servers.

1. To do this, open three terminals and log in to each CoreOS hosts using the vagrant ssh command.

2. First we will see what's there inside our **/var/jenkins_home/users** directory. Execute the following command, as shown in Figure 3-50.

    ```
    docker exec -it jenkins1 /bin/bash -c 'cd /var/jenkins_home/users && ls -lrt'
    ```

```
core@core-02 ~ $ docker exec -it jenkins1 /bin/bash -c 'cd /var/jenkins_home/users && ls -lrt'
total 4
drwxr-xr-x. 2 jenkins jenkins 4096 Sep 23 17:06 jenkins_admin
core@core-02 ~ $
```

Figure 3-50. *List the Jenkins users*

3. Now on the same machine execute the command below, as shown in Figure 3-51.

    ```
    docker exec -it glusterfs1 /bin/bash -c 'cd /gluster/users && ls -lrt'
    ```

```
core@core-02 ~ docker exec -it glusterfs1 /bin/bash -c 'cd /gluster/users && ls -lrt'
total 8
drwxr-xr-x. 2 1000 1000 4096 Sep 23 17:06 jenkins_admin
core@core-02 ~ $
```

Figure 3-51. *Jenkins users reflecting on the gluster volume*

4. Switch to the terminal where you have logged in on core-01 machine. Execute the following command, as shown in Figure 3-52.

    ```
    docker exec -it glusterfs2 /bin/bash -c 'cd /gluster/users && ls -lrt'
    ```

```
core@core-01 ~ $ docker exec -it glusterfs2 /bin/bash -c 'cd /gluster/users && ls -lrt'
total 8
drwxr-xr-x. 2 1000 1000 4096 Sep 23 17:06 jenkins_admin
core@core-01 ~ $
```

Figure 3-52. *Jenkins users reflecting on the gluster volume*

5. Switch to the terminal where you have logged in on core-03 machine. Execute the following command, as shown in Figure 3-53.

```
docker exec -it glusterfs3 /bin/bash -c 'cd /gluster/users && ls -lrt'
```

```
core@core-03 ~ $ docker exec -it glusterfs3 /bin/bash -c 'cd /gluster/users && ls -lrt'
total 8
drwxr-xr-x. 2 1000 1000 4096 Sep 23 17:06 jenkins_admin
core@core-03 ~ $
```

Figure 3-53. Jenkins users reflecting on the gluster volume

Failover Scenario 1

GlusterFS service (glusterfs1) running on core-02 stops and Jenkins connects to another GlusterFS service running on some another node, keeping everything intact.

1. To do this, stop the glusterfs1 service on core-02 using fleetctl command as shown in Figure 3-54.

```
fleetctl stop glusterfs_a@1.service
```

```
core@core-02 ~ $ fleetctl stop glusterfs_a@1.service
Unit glusterfs_a@1.service loaded on 0e8187f9.../172.17.8.102
core@core-02 ~ $
```

Figure 3-54. Stop the glusterfs1 unit

2. To check the glusterfs1 service status, run the `fleetctl list-units` command as shown in Figure 3-55.

```
core@core-02 ~ $ fleetctl list-units
UNIT                    MACHINE                     ACTIVE      SUB
glusterfs_a@1.service   0e8187f9.../172.17.8.102    failed      failed
glusterfs_a@2.service   35c4295e.../172.17.8.101    active      running
glusterfs_a@3.service   b40a8da9.../172.17.8.103    active      running
jenkins_a@1.service     0e8187f9.../172.17.8.102    active      running
jenkins_b@1.service     0e8187f9.../172.17.8.102    inactive    dead
core@core-02 ~ $
```

Figure 3-55. List the units

3. Execute the following command to see if the container related to glusterfs1 service is still running, as shown in Figure 3-56.

```
docker ps -a –format='{{.Names}} {{.Status}}' or you simply give docker ps -a
```

```
core@core-02 ~ $ docker ps -a --format='{{.Names}} {{.Status}}'
glusterfs1 Exited (137) 7 minutes ago
jenkins1 Up 2 hours
core@core-02 ~ $
```

Figure 3-56. List the running containers

4. We can also check about glusterfs1 service from other glusterfs servers. Open a terminal and log in to core-01 using the vagrant ssh command.

5. Open the glusterfs2 container in an interactive mode using the below command.

```
docker exec -it glusterfs2 /bin/bash
```

6. Once inside the container, execute the following command, as shown in Figure 3-57.

```
glusterfs volume status
```

```
core@core-01 ~ $ docker exec -it glusterfs2 /bin/bash
[root@core-01 /]# gluster volume status
Status of volume: volume1
Gluster process                           TCP Port  RDMA Port  Online  Pid
------------------------------------------------------------------------------
Brick 172.17.8.101:/gluster               49152     0          Y       255
Brick 172.17.8.103:/gluster               49152     0          Y       199
Self-heal Daemon on localhost             N/A       N/A        Y       275
Self-heal Daemon on 172.17.8.103          N/A       N/A        Y       219

Task Status of Volume volume1
------------------------------------------------------------------------------
There are no active volume tasks

[root@core-01 /]# ▮
```

Figure 3-57. *Gluster volume status*

7. To check the gluster peer status execute the following command, as shown in Figure 3-58.

```
gluster peer status
```

```
[root@core-01 /]# gluster peer status
Number of Peers: 2

Hostname: 172.17.8.102
Uuid: 51c90bfa-4e1c-4531-adc1-2ac7de865646
State: Peer in Cluster (Disconnected)

Hostname: 172.17.8.103
Uuid: 695fb9e1-e939-4eb5-bf01-3e419029f32d
State: Peer in Cluster (Connected)
[root@core-01 /]#
```

Figure 3-58. *Gluster peer status*

8. Open Jenkins master server and you can see it's still up. However, the user session has expired. And you are taken to the login page.

9. Log in using the admin account that we created in the previous section, as shown in Figure 3-59.

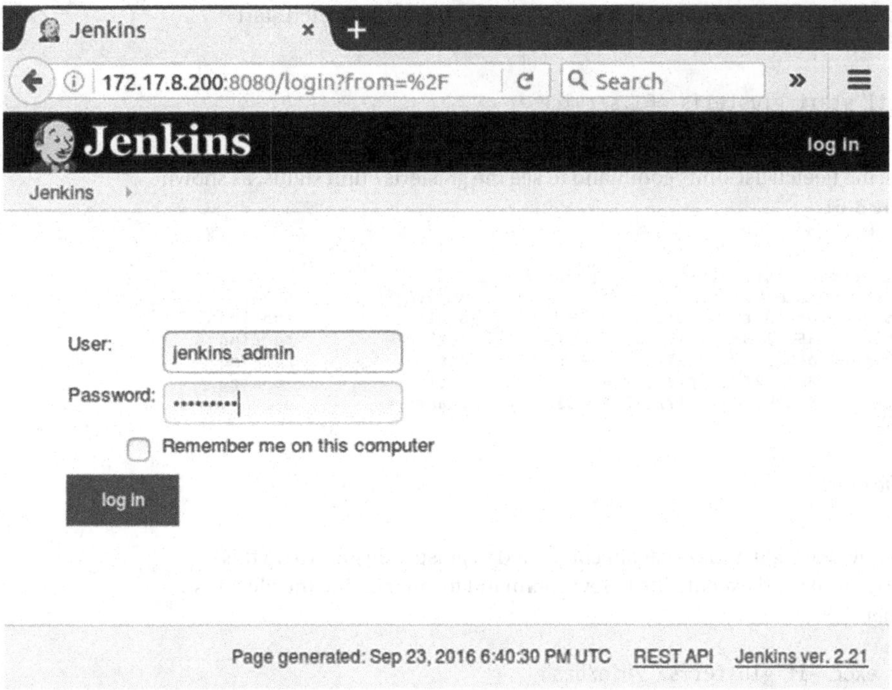

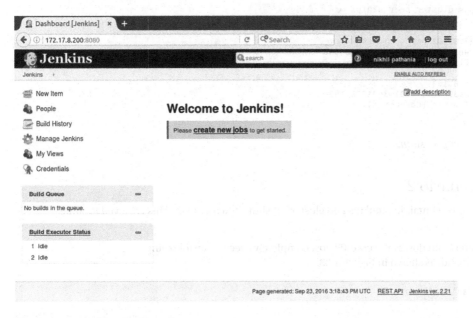

Figure 3-59. *Jenkins login screen*

10. If you are able to login successfully, you will see the Jenkins Dashboard as shown in Figure 3-60. This proves that the user account that we created in the previous section is still intact.

Figure 3-60. *Jenkins dashboard*

11. Now start the glusterfs1 container on core-02 again using the fleetctl start command as shown below.

```
fleetctl start glusterfs_a@1.service
```

12. Execute the fleetctl list-units command to see the glusterfs1 unit status, as shown in Figure 3-61.

```
core@core-01 ~ $ fleetctl list-units
UNIT                     MACHINE                  ACTIVE      SUB
glusterfs_a@1.service    0e8187f9.../172.17.8.102 active      running
glusterfs_a@2.service    35c4295e.../172.17.8.101 active      running
glusterfs_a@3.service    b40a8da9.../172.17.8.103 active      running
jenkins_a@1.service      0e8187f9.../172.17.8.102 active      running
jenkins_b@1.service      0e8187f9.../172.17.8.102 inactive    dead
core@core-01 ~ $ ▮
```

Figure 3-61. *List the units*

13. Lets us now see if glusterfs1 is again connected to gluster cluster. To do this, log in to core-02 and execute the below command to enter inside the glusterfs2 container.

```
docker exec -it glusterfs2 /bin/bash
```

14. From inside the glusterfs2 container execute the gluster command to get the peer status, as shown in Figure 3-62.

```
gluster peer status
```

```
[root@core-01 /]# gluster peer status
Number of Peers: 2

Hostname: 172.17.8.102
Uuid: 51c90bfa-4e1c-4531-adc1-2ac7de865646
State: Peer in Cluster (Connected)

Hostname: 172.17.8.103
Uuid: 695fb9e1-e939-4eb5-bf01-3e419029f32d
State: Peer in Cluster (Connected)
[root@core-01 /]#
```

Figure 3-62. *Gluster peer status*

Failover Scenario 2

The core-02 machine (containing Jenkins and glusterfs2) shuts down. And Jenkins is moved to some other host.

1. To stop (shut down) the core-02 host completely execute the following command, as shown in Figure 3-63.

```
vagrant halt core-02
```

```
nikhil@dev01:~/coreos-vagrant$ vagrant halt core-02
==> core-02: Attempting graceful shutdown of VM...
nikhil@dev01:~/coreos-vagrant$
```

Figure 3-63. *Shut down core-02 machine*

2. Log in to core-01 host and run the fleectl command to list the machines, as shown in Figure 3-64.

   ```
   fleetctl list-machines
   ```

```
core@core-01 ~ $ fleetctl list-machines
MACHINE        IP                METADATA
35c4295e...    172.17.8.101      -
b40a8da9...    172.17.8.103      -
core@core-01 ~ $
```

Figure 3-64. *List the machines using the fleetctl command*

3. Execute the **fleetctl list-units** command and you will see Jenkins is being started on core-01. Initially it might take time as the docker is downloading the Jenkins server image. See Figure 3-65.

```
core@core-01 ~ $ fleetctl list-units
UNIT                   MACHINE                      ACTIVE       SUB
glusterfs_a@2.service  35c4295e.../172.17.8.101     active       running
glusterfs_a@3.service  b40a8da9.../172.17.8.103     active       running
jenkins_a@1.service    35c4295e.../172.17.8.101     activating   start-pre
jenkins_b@1.service    35c4295e.../172.17.8.101     inactive     dead
core@core-01 ~ $
```

Figure 3-65. *List the units*

4. Keep executing the **fleetctl list-units** command until you see that the Jenkins unit is active and running, as shown in Figure 3-66.

```
core@core-01 ~ $ fleetctl list-units
UNIT                   MACHINE                      ACTIVE     SUB
glusterfs_a@2.service  35c4295e.../172.17.8.101     active     running
glusterfs_a@3.service  b40a8da9.../172.17.8.103     active     running
jenkins_a@1.service    35c4295e.../172.17.8.101     active     running
jenkins_b@1.service    35c4295e.../172.17.8.101     inactive   dead
core@core-01 ~ $
```

Figure 3-66. *List the units*

5. Now once everything is up, access the Jenkins master server.

6. You will see the login screen, log in using the admin user that we created earlier.

7. This time click on **Select plugins to install** option.

8. On the next screen you will see a list of plugins. The ones that are already installed are ticked. See Figure 3-67. This again confirms that our data inside the JENKINS_HOME directory is intact.

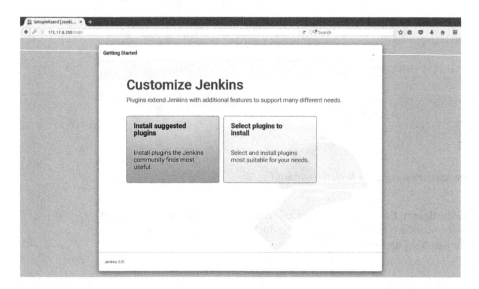

Figure 3-67. *Install plugins*

9. Choose nothing, by selecting the option **none**. And click on the **Install** button, as shown in Figure 3-68.

Figure 3-68. *Jenkins plugins getting installed*

Summary

In the current chapter we saw how the clustering feature of CoreOS can be used to create a highly available (HA) solution for Jenkins. We also saw the importance of GlusterFS in replicating the JENKINS_HOME data across the cluster nodes.

In the next chapter we will learn to set up Jenkins Master on Docker and Cloud solutions such as AWS.

CHAPTER 4

■ ■ ■

Setting Up Jenkins on Docker and Cloud

In the previous chapters we learned two different techniques of creating a highly available (HA) setup for Jenkins using various open source tools. These so-called methods of setting up Jenkins are progressive and intuitive in their approach, yet they are completely new. Keeping that in mind, in the current chapter we take the opportunity to explore some of the mainstream ways of setting up a Jenkins master. These are the following:

1. Jenkins on cloud (AWS).

2. Jenkins on Docker.

The underlying infrastructure of a Jenkins master can decide how scalable you can make your continuous Integration (CI) or continuous delivery (CD) solution.

Running Jenkins Inside a Docker Container

Jenkins can very well run inside a Docker container. It makes things even better when persistent volumes are used. When using persistent volumes, the data under the **jenkins_home** directory is stored inside a folder on the Docker host (data volumes), or it can also be mapped to a data container (data volume containers). In this way the container and the data (**jenkins_home**) become two separate but dependent entities. If the Docker container running Jenkins ceases to exist, a new Docker container can be immediately spawned and connected to the data volumes.

We can also use Docker to host Jenkins Slaves running as containers. Figure 4-1 depicts Jenkins Slaves running as containers on a Docker Host/Server. The Jenkins master may or may not be on Docker. The Docker Host/Server is in contact with the Jenkins master using a Plugin. In the following setup, Jenkins can spawn on demand Jenkins Slaves on the Docker Host/Server. We will learn about this setup with detail in **Chapter 6**.

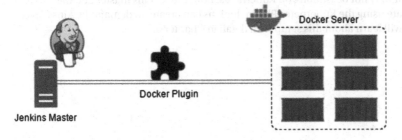

Figure 4-1. *Jenkins Master-slave setup on Docker using Docker Plugin*

© Nikhil Pathania 2017

N. Pathania, *Pro Continuous Delivery*, DOI 10.1007/978-1-4842-2913-2_4

A single Jenkins master may not be sufficient to handle a growing number of projects, in such cases the projects can be divided among multiple Jenkins masters, with each Jenkins master having its own set of Jenkins Slaves running on a Docker Host/Server, as shown in Figure 4-2.

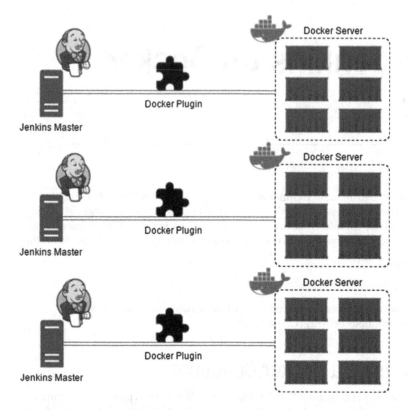

Figure 4-2. *Multiple Jenkins Master-slave setups on Docker using Docker Plugin*

However, using multiple Docker Servers can increase the maintenance overhead. Also, from Figure 4-2, you can see that there is a one-to-one connection between the Jenkins masters and the Docker Servers. This means if any of the Docker servers fails, a Jenkins master will completely lose all these build agents (Jenkins slaves). Also some Jenkins masters may overload their Docker Servers running build agents, while others at times may not build anything at all, keeping their Docker server idle.

Kubernetes seems to be a better solution to all the above issues. Figure 4-3 shows a Jenkins Master-Slave setup using Kubernetes. In the following setup, Kubernetes is responsible for managing multiple instances of Docker Hosts. Jenkins may or may not be running on Kubernetes. Both the Jenkins master and the Kubernetes cluster communicate using the Kubernetes Plugin. Jenkins can create on demand Jenkins Slaves on the Kubernetes cluster. We will learn about this setup with detail in Chapter 6.

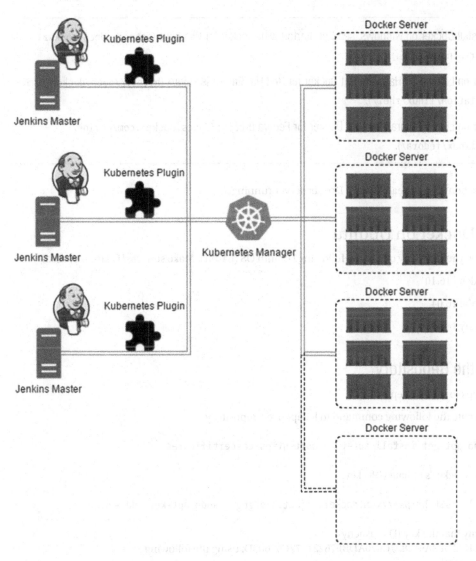

Figure 4-3. *Multiple Jenkins Master-slave setups on Docker using Kubernetes Plugin*

In the current section we will try to run Jenkins master inside a container on a Docker Host/Server.

For this exercise you need a Docker server. Installing Docker is simple. You can go through the following section, "Installing Docker on Ubuntu," to see the installation. For the other OS you can refer to the Notes.

■ **Note**   To install Docker on windows, see Get Started with Docker for Windows (`https://docs.docker.com/docker-for-windows/`).

To install Docker on Linux (Red Hat), see Get Docker for Red Hat Enterprise Linux (`https://docs.docker.com/engine/installation/linux/rhel/`).

To install Docker on Linux (Fedora), see Get Docker for Fedora (`https://docs.docker.com/engine/installation/linux/fedora/`).

Skip this section if you already have a Docker server running.

Installing Docker on Ubuntu

To install Docker, you need any one of the following Ubuntu OS (64-bit). Make sure *curl* is also installed.

- Yakkety 16.10
- Xenial 16.04
- Trusty 14.04

Setting Up the Repository

Follow these steps to set up a repository:

1. Execute the following command to let apt use a repository:

   ```
   sudo apt-get install apt-transport-https ca-certificates
   ```

2. Add Docker's official GPG key:

   ```
   curl -fsSL https://yum.dockerproject.org/gpg | sudo apt-key add -
   ```

3. Verify that the key ID is exactly 58118E89F3A912897C070ADBF76221572C52609D, using the following command.

   ```
   apt-key fingerprint 58118E89F3A912897C070ADBF76221572C52609D
   ```

   a. You should get an output as shown below.

   ```
   pub    4096R/2C52609D 2015-07-14
          Key fingerprint = 5811 8E89 F3A9 1289 7C07  0ADB F762 2157
          2C52 609D
   uid                    Docker Release Tool (releasedocker)
                          docker@docker.com
   ```

4. Use the following command to set up the stable repository to download Docker.

    ```
    sudo add-apt-repository "deb https://apt.dockerproject.org/repo/
    ubuntu-$(lsb_release -cs) main"
    ```

■ **Note**   It's recommended to always use the stable version of repository.

Installing Docker

After setting up the repository, do the following steps to install Docker:

1. Update the apt package index using the following command:

    ```
    sudo apt-get update
    ```

2. To install the latest version of Docker, do this:

    ```
    sudo apt-get -y install docker-engine
    ```

3. However, if you wish to install a specific version of Docker, do this:

    a. list the available versions, using the following command:

    ```
    apt-cache madison docker-engine
    ```

    b. The output should be something similar to as shown below:

    ```
    docker-engine | 1.16.0-0~trusty | https://apt.dockerproject.org/
    repo ubuntu-trusty/main amd64 Packages
    docker-engine | 1.13.3-0~trusty | https://apt.dockerproject.org/
    repo ubuntu-trusty/main amd64 Packages
    .
    .
    .
    ```

■ **Note**   The output of the above command depends on the type of repository configured in the previous section ("Setting Up the Repository").

---

4. Next, execute the following command to install the specific version of Docker.

    ```
    sudo apt-get -y install docker-engine=<VERSION_STRING>
    ```

■ **Note**   Example: sudo apt-get -y install docker-engine=1.16.0-0~trusty

---

5. The Docker service starts automatically. To verify if Docker is installed and running, do the following:

```
sudo docker run hello-world
```

6. If the above command runs without any errors, and you see a hello-world message, it means Docker is installed and running.

Install from a Package

For some reason, if you are unable to install Docker using the above repository method, you can download the *.deb* package.

1. Download the .deb package of your choice from *https://apt.dockerproject. org/repo/pool/main/d/docker-engine/*

2. To install the downloaded package do this:

```
sudo dpkg -i /<path to package>/<docker package>.deb
```

3. Verify your Docker installation by running the following command:

```
sudo docker run hello-world
```

4. You should see something as shown below:

```
Hello from Docker!
This message shows that your installation appears to be working correctly.
```

Creating a Jenkins Container

The steps demonstrated in the following section are performed on an Ubuntu machine running Docker server. Hereafter it is called as the **Docker host**. Running Jenkins inside a container is pretty straightforward.

1. Once you have Docker installed, run the following command to start a Docker container running Jenkins.

```
docker run -d -name <container instance name> -p 8080:8080
-p 50000:50000 jenkins
```

■ **Note** The above container runs a copy of the latest stable Jenkins LTS release. The Jenkins home directory inside the Docker container is /var/jenkins_home.

The above approach is not recommended as the data (plugins, jobs, configurations, etc.) inside the **jenkins_home** directory will cease to exist the moment you delete the container.

For the latest weekly releases, use the Docker image "jenkinsci/jenkins" instead of "Jenkins."

---

2. We won't be using the above command to run a Jenkins container. Instead, we will create a Jenkins container with its jenkins_home directory mapped to one of the directories on the **Docker host**.

3. To do this, create a directory named **jenkins_home_directory** on your Docker host using the following commands. As shown in Figure 4-4.

   ```
   mkdir jenkins_home_directory

   chmod 777 jenkins_home_directory
   ```

```
nikhil@dev01:~$ ls -lrt
total 84
-rw-r--r--  1 nikhil nikhil 8980 Aug 24 17:31 examples.desktop
drwxr-xr-x  2 nikhil nikhil 4096 Aug 24 17:53 Desktop
drwxr-xr-x  2 nikhil nikhil 4096 Aug 24 17:53 Videos
drwxr-xr-x  2 nikhil nikhil 4096 Aug 24 17:53 Templates
drwxr-xr-x  2 nikhil nikhil 4096 Aug 24 17:53 Public
drwxr-xr-x  2 nikhil nikhil 4096 Aug 24 17:53 Documents
drwxr-xr-x  2 nikhil nikhil 4096 Sep 19 17:58 Music
drwxr-xr-x  3 nikhil nikhil 4096 Jan 23 23:42 Downloads
drwxr-xr-x  2 nikhil nikhil 4096 Jan 23 23:55 Pictures
drwxrwxrwx  2 nikhil nikhil 4096 Jan 24 21:46 jenkins_home_directory
nikhil@dev01:~$
```

Figure 4-4. *Creating a directory on your docker host*

4. Now initiate a Jenkins container using the following command. See Figure 4-5.

   ```
   sudo docker run -d –name <container instance name> -p 8080:8080 -p
   50000:50000 -v /<path on Docker host>/jenkins_home_directory:/var/
   jenkins_home jenkins
   ```

```
nikhil@dev01:~$ sudo docker run -d --name jenkins_master -p 8080:8080 -p 50000:5
0000 -v /home/nikhil/jenkins_home_directory:/var/jenkins_home jenkins
acb2009b72fbd97bd96c24e8539125126983dd18f5b1692ee49c01b0fef6962c
nikhil@dev01:~$
```

Figure 4-5. *Docker command to run a jenkins container with a persistent volume*

5. From the Figure 4-5, we can see a Jenkins container getting created. The data inside the **jenkins_home** directory is in sync with the directory **jenkins_home_ directory** on the Docker host. It's a good way of backing up Jenkins data.

6. List the contents of jenkins_home_directory directory on the Docker host using the following commands.

   ```
   cd /<path on docker host>/jenkins_home_directory/

   ls -lrt
   ```

7. From the Figure 4-6, you can see the content of jenkins_home directory is listing inside the **jenkins_home_directory** on the Docker host.

```
nikhil@dev01:~/jenkins_home_directory$ ls -lrt
total 68
drwxr-xr-x  2 nikhil nikhil 4096 Jan 24 21:51 init.groovy.d
-rw-r--r--  1 nikhil nikhil  102 Jan 24 21:51 copy_reference_file.log
drwxr-xr-x 10 nikhil nikhil 4096 Jan 24 21:51 war
-rw-r--r--  1 nikhil nikhil    0 Jan 24 21:51 secret.key.not-so-secret
-rw-r--r--  1 nikhil nikhil   64 Jan 24 21:51 secret.key
drwxr-xr-x  2 nikhil nikhil 4096 Jan 24 21:51 plugins
drwxr-xr-x  2 nikhil nikhil 4096 Jan 24 21:51 jobs
drwxr-xr-x  2 nikhil nikhil 4096 Jan 24 21:51 nodes
-rw-r--r--  1 nikhil nikhil  159 Jan 24 21:51 hudson.model.UpdateCenter.xml
-rw-------  1 nikhil nikhil 1712 Jan 24 21:51 identity.key.enc
drwxr-xr-x  2 nikhil nikhil 4096 Jan 24 21:51 userContent
-rw-r--r--  1 nikhil nikhil  907 Jan 24 21:51 nodeMonitors.xml
drwxr-xr-x  3 nikhil nikhil 4096 Jan 24 21:51 logs
-rw-r--r--  1 nikhil nikhil    6 Jan 24 21:51 jenkins.install.UpgradeWizard.state
drwxr-xr-x  3 nikhil nikhil 4096 Jan 24 21:51 users
drwx------  4 nikhil nikhil 4096 Jan 24 21:51 secrets
-rw-r--r--  1 nikhil nikhil 1592 Jan 24 21:51 config.xml
drwxr-xr-x  2 nikhil nikhil 4096 Jan 24 21:51 updates
nikhil@dev01:~/jenkins_home_directory$ 
```

Figure 4-6. *Content of the jenkins_home_directory on docker host*

8. Execute the following command to work interactively with our new Jenkins container. This will expose the bash utility inside the Jenkins container.

    ```
    sudo docker exec -it <container instance name> /bin/bash
    ```

■ **Note** To login as root use the "-u root" parameter in the above command.

Example: sudo docker exec -it -u root <container instance name> /bin/bash

---

9. Once inside the container run the ip route command to know the IP address of the container, as shown in Figure 4-7.

    ```
    ip route
    ```

```
jenkins@acb2009b72fb:/$ ip route
default via 172.18.0.1 dev eth0
172.18.0.0/16 dev eth0  proto kernel  scope link  src 172.18.0.2
jenkins@acb2009b72fb:/$ 
```

Figure 4-7. *The ip route command*

10. Now that we know the IP address of our container running Jenkins, we can access Jenkins using the URL **http:<IP address of the container>:8080**, as shown in Figure 4-8.

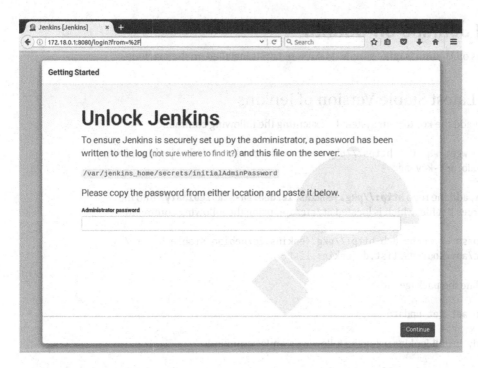

Figure 4-8. Jenkins login page

11. To get the password from the file **/var/jenkins_home/secrets/ initialAdminPassword**, execute the following command:

```
docker exec -u root <container instance name> /bin/bash -c 'cat /var/jenkins_home/secrets/initialAdminPassword'
```

12. This will print the password present inside the file initialAdminPassword.

13. Similarly one can also get the password from the jenkins_home_directory on the Docker host.

```
cat /<path on the Docker host>/jenkins_home_directory/secrets/ initialAdminPassword
```

■ **Note** Any changes inside the directory **jenkins_home_directory** on the Docker host will reflect inside the **jenkins_home** directory inside the container.

Installing Jenkins on Ubuntu

Installing Jenkins on Ubuntu is quite simple. Make sure Java is installed on the machine.

Install the Latest Stable Version of Jenkins

1. First add the key to your system by executing the following command:

    ```
    sudo wget -q -O - https://pkg.jenkins.io/debian-stable/jenkins.io.key
    | sudo apt-key add -
    ```

2. Now, add the repo **http://pkg.jenkins.io/debian-stablebinary/** into the
    sources.list file, which is located at /**etc**/**apt**, using the following command:

    ```
    sudo sh -c 'echo deb http://pkg.jenkins.io/debian-stable binary/ >
    /etc/apt/sources.list.d/jenkins.list'
    ```

3. Update the package index:

    ```
    sudo apt-get update
    ```

4. Lastly, install Jenkins using the following simple command:

    ```
    sudo apt-get install jenkins -y
    ```

Install the Latest Version of Jenkins

1. First add the key to your system by executing the following command:

    ```
    sudo wget -q -O - https://pkg.jenkins.io/debian/jenkins.io.key |
    sudo apt-key add -
    ```

2. Now, add the repo **http://pkg.jenkins.io/debianbinary/** into the **sources.list**
    file, which is located at /**etc**/**apt**, using the following command:

    ```
    sudo sh -c 'echo deb http://pkg.jenkins.io/debian binary/ >
    /etc/apt/sources.list.d/jenkins.list'
    ```

3. Update the package index:

    ```
    sudo apt-get update
    ```

4. Lastly, install Jenkins using the following simple command:

    ```
    sudo apt-get install jenkins -y
    ```

Once the Jenkins installation is successful, it will automatically run as a daemon service. By default
Jenkins runs on the port 8080. To access Jenkins, open the URL **http://<server IP address>:8080**.

Installing Jenkins on Fedora/Red Hat Linux

The Jenkins installation process on Red Hat Linux and Fedora is the same. To do these, open a terminal. Make sure Java is installed on the machine.

Installing the Latest Stable Version of Jenkins

1. If you prefer to install a stable version of Jenkins then issue the below-mentioned commands in sequence.

   ```
   sudo wget -O /etc/yum.repos.d/jenkins.repo https://pkg.jenkins.io/
   redhat-stable/jenkins.repo
   ```

   ```
   sudo rpm --import https://pkg.jenkins.io/redhat-stable/jenkins.io.key
   ```

   ```
   sudo yum install Jenkins
   ```

Installing the Latest Version of Jenkins

1. To install the latest version of Jenkins, issue the following command in sequence.

   ```
   sudo wget -O /etc/yum.repos.d/jenkins.repo https://pkg.jenkins.io/
   redhat/jenkins.repo
   ```

   ```
   sudo rpm --import https://pkg.jenkins.io/redhat/jenkins.io.key
   ```

   ```
   sudo yum install Jenkins
   ```

If for some reason you are unable to access Jenkins, check the firewall setting. This is because by default the firewall will block the ports. To enable them, execute the below commands. You might need admin privileges.

```
firewall-cmd --zone=public --add-port=8080/tcp –permanent
```

```
firewall-cmd --zone=public --add-service=http –permanent
```

```
firewall-cmd --reload
```

Once the Jenkins installation is successful, it will automatically run as a daemon service. By default Jenkins runs on the port 8080. To access Jenkins, open the URL **http://<server IP address>:8080**.

Installing Jenkins on Cloud (AWS)

Running Jenkins on a cloud platform (like AWS) requires setting up an instance of some capacity (CPU, memory, storage, and network) and choosing a right OS (AMI).

There are various types of instance available on AWS. Finding the best one for your Jenkins master mainly depends on how you plan to set up your Jenkins master-slave architecture. Given the tools and features in AWS, the Jenkins master-slave architecture would fall into one of the categories, as shown below:

Types of Jenkins Master-Slave Setups

Shown here is a very simple Jenkins master-slave setup. There is one Jenkins master running on an EC2 instance (M4.large) and the Jenkins slave instances are auto-spawned based on the build requirement. The advantage of using this strategy is that you need to maintain only one Jenkins master (maintenance includes updating Jenkins, updating plugins, managing logs, managing Jenkins master configuration, etc.). But as the number of projects grows beyond the capacity that a AWS instance can handle, you might need to rethink on the strategy.

Type of Cluster for Jenkins Slaves

We can configure Jenkins slaves on normal EC2 instances. These instances can be scaled horizontally depending on the number of builds that are running on a given Jenkins master. The EC2 instances can be auto-spawned using the Amazon EC2 Plugin for Jenkins (Figure 4-9).

Figure 4-9. Scalable Jenkins Slave cluster using EC2 Instances

Instead of using normal EC2 instances, we can go for the Docker way of doing builds. Amazon ECS provides a way to create a cluster of Docker containers for running builds, testing, etc. These Docker containers can be auto-spawned from Jenkins master using the Amazon EC2 Container Service Plugin for Jenkins. It gives the best of both worlds (Docker + Cloud) (see Figure 4-10).

Figure 4-10. Scalable Jenkins Slave cluster using ECS Instances

Jenkins can also auto-spawn a fleet of EC2 spot instances using the Amazon EC2 Fleet Plugin (Figure 4-11). Read more about the AWS Spot instances on https://aws.amazon.com/ec2/spot/.

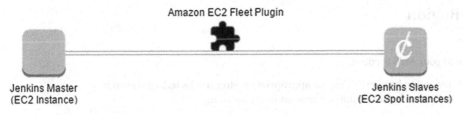

Amazon EC2 Fleet Plugin

Jenkins Master
(EC2 Instance)

Jenkins Slaves
(EC2 Spot instances)

Figure 4-11. *Scalable Jenkins Slave cluster using Spot Instances*

Finding the Best Instance Type for Your Jenkins Master

There is no right answer for this question. The only best way to find out is to benchmark your Jenkins master-slave setup discussed above. Only then we can know the right instance type for our Jenkins master and our Jenkins slaves. Nevertheless, depending on the characteristics of Jenkins master and the Jenkins slaves we can narrow down to what an instance should be like.

Assume that we perform all out builds on Jenkins slaves and nothing on the Jenkins master. Then, we can safely say that the Jenkins slaves should have a good amount of storage and decent amount of CPU.

The Jenkins master will mostly have frequent users visiting its dashboard; therefore we need an instance that has good network bandwidth and good CPU performance, keeping in mind the number of HTTP requests.

■ **Note** To learn more about AWS instance types, see **https://aws.amazon.com/ec2/instance-types/**.

Following is a benchmark example of Jenkins Master (from the AWS):

This is a benchmark of five different instance types: the T2.large, the M3.medium, and the M4.large, M4.XL, and M4.2XL. Each benchmark simulated traffic from 100 concurrent users loading multiple pages inside the Jenkins dashboard for a sustained period of 10 minutes.

Overall, we found the M4.large to be the best value for the performance. The average CPU utilization during load testing did not exceed 3%, with an average response time of 220 milliseconds. As expected, the XL and 2XL sizes performed well but at a lower cost per hour; therefore, the M4.large remains the best choice for our needs. The M3.medium, while a good choice for many applications, did not perform as well as the M4.large, and had an average CPU utilization of over 80% for the duration of the testing.

The T2.large performed well during the first few minutes of testing. However, because T2 instances offer burstable performance, 15 sustained an amount of high traffic from 100 users' depleted available CPU credits, and performance significantly decreased. Further testing with fewer users (i.e., 10 users) saw improved results. Thus, if you have a relatively small team and do not expect frequent or high-volume usage from your Jenkins master, the T2 family may be a good option for you.

In the following section we will launch a virtual application server using Amazon EC2 to host Jenkins master. You will need an AWS account. The exercise demonstrated in the current sections uses an EC2 instance from the AWS Free Tier limits.

Selecting a Region

Follow these steps:

1. Log in to your AWS account.

2. In the navigation bar, verify that the appropriate region is selected, as shown in Figure 4-12. I have chosen the one nearest to my location.

Figure 4-12. *Selecting region*

Creating a Security Group

Using security groups, you define and control access to your AWS instance. It acts more like a firewall. You can create multiple security groups in AWS. And an AWS instance can be mapped to more than one security group.

1. Open the Amazon EC2 console from the navigation bar, by clicking on the **Services ➤ EC2 (Compute)**, as shown in Figure 4-13.

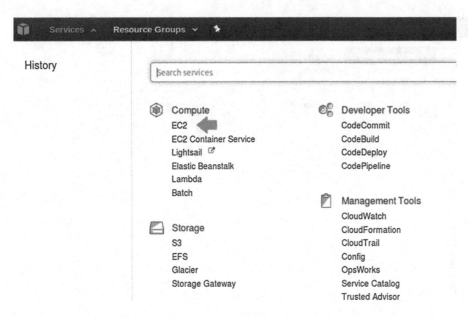

Figure 4-13. *Locating EC2 console*

■ **Note**   you can also open the EC2 console by accessing the following link: **https://console.aws.amazon. com/ec2/**.

---

2. On the left-hand side navigation bar, under **NETWORK & SECURITY** click on **Security Groups**, and then click on the **Create Security Group** button to create a new security group, as shown in Figure 4-14.

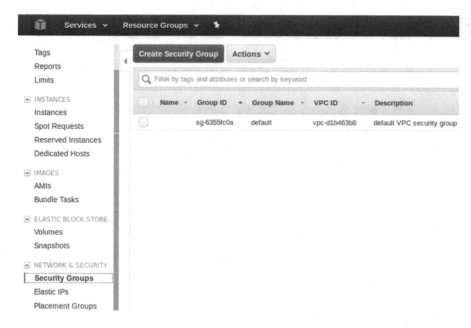

Figure 4-14. *Creating Security Group*

3. Enter a name in the **Security group name** field and add some description under the **Description** field. Choose the default value for the **VPC** field. As shown in Figure 4-15.

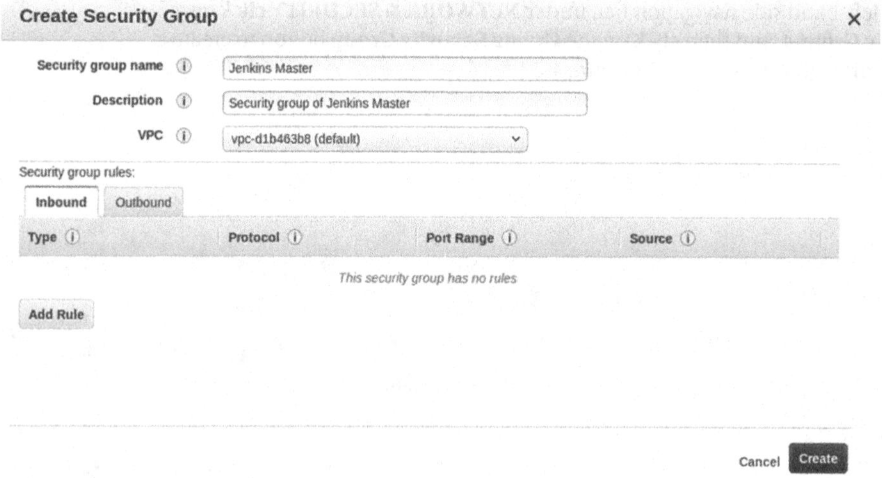

Figure 4-15. *Configuring Security Group*

4. Click the **Inbound** tab and then click on **Add Rule**. Choose *Type* as **SSH**. As shown in Figure 4-16.

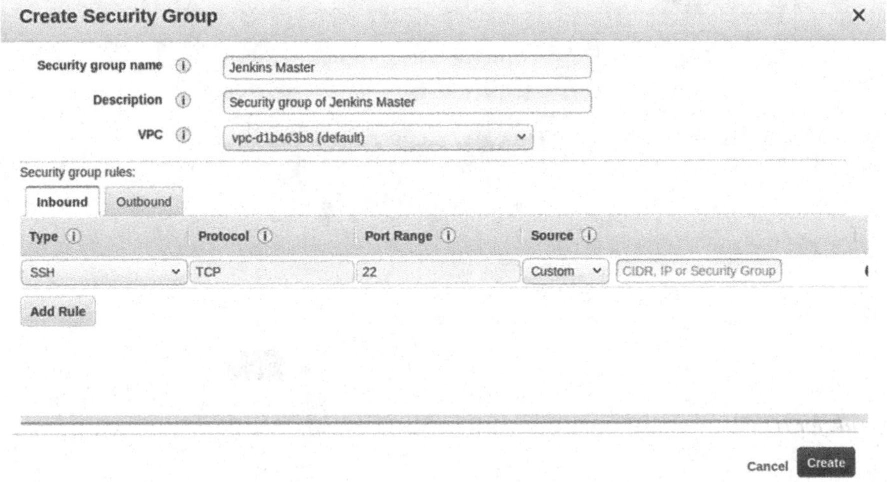

Create Security Group   ✕

Security group name ⓘ	Jenkins Master	
Description ⓘ	Security group of Jenkins Master	
VPC ⓘ	vpc-d1b463b8 (default) ˅	

Security group rules:

Inbound Outbound

Type ⓘ	Protocol ⓘ	Port Range ⓘ	Source ⓘ	
SSH ˅	TCP	22	Custom ˅	CIDR, IP or Security Group

Add Rule

Cancel **Create**

Figure 4-16. *Adding rule for SSH - Custom*

5. Under *Source* you have three options to choose from (**Custom**, **Anywhere,** and **My IP**).

    a. Select **Custom** and in the text box enter the public IP address range. Choose this option if you want to provide access to a range of IP address (a group of team members in your organization).

    b. Select **Anywhere**, and enter 0.0.0.0 if you want to give access to an SSH request coming from any IP address (not recommended), as shown in Figure 4-17.

SSH ˅	TCP	22	Anywhere ˅	0.0.0.0/0

Figure 4-17. *Adding rule for SSH - Anywhere*

    c. Select **My IP**, and AWS will automatically detect your IP. However, only the following IP will get SSH access to the AWS instance. As shown in Figure 4-18.

SSH ˅	TCP	22	My IP ˅	80.199.15.42/32

Figure 4-18. *Adding rule for SSH - My IP*

6. Next, click **Add Rule**, and then choose **HTTP** as *Type*. Under *Source* you have the same three options. Under *Source*, choose **Custom,** and give a range of IP addresses. You might want to give access to the Jenkins dashboard only to your team or your organization. As shown in Figure 4-19.

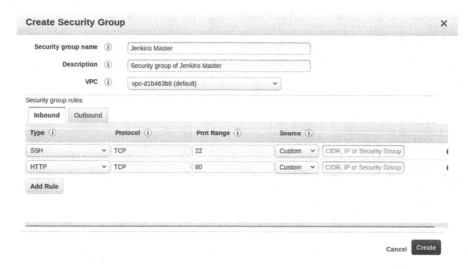

Figure 4-19. *Adding rule for HTTP*

7. Next, click **Add Rule** again, and then choose **Custom TCP Rule** as *Type*. Under **Port Range** enter **8080**. Under *Source*, choose **Custom,** and give a range of IP addresses. You might want to give access to the Jenkins dashboard only to your team or your organization. As shown in Figure 4-20.

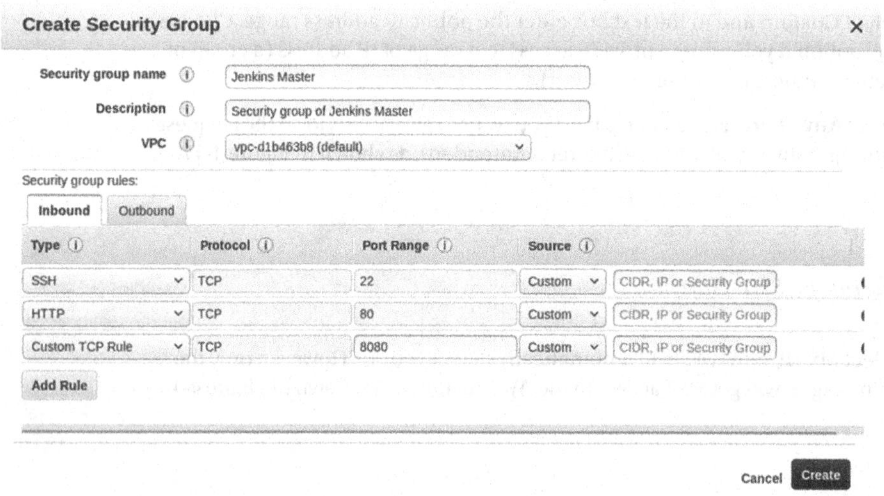

Figure 4-20. *Adding rule for TCP*

8. Next, click on the **Create** button.

Creating an EC2 Instance on AWS

1. On the left-hand navigation bar, under **INSTANCES** choose **Instances**, and then click **Launch Instance**. As shown in Figure 4-21.

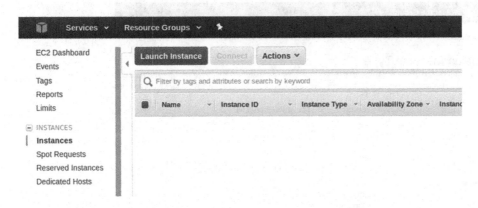

Figure 4-21. *Creating an instance*

2. On the **Choose an Amazon Machine Image (AMI)** page, select the AMI of your choice. In the following demonstration I have chosen an **Amazon Linux AMI** with HVM. As shown in Figure 4-22.

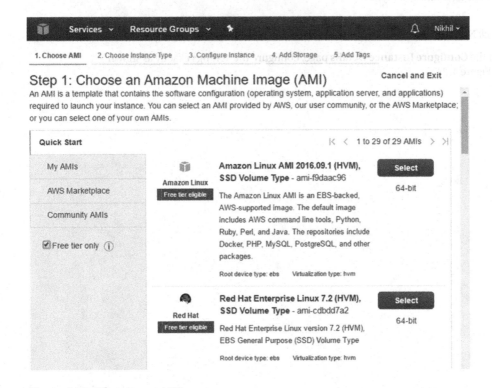

Figure 4-22. *Choosing an AMI*

3. On the **Choose an Instance Type** page, select the type of instance that you would like for your Jenkins master. In the following demonstration I have chosen an instance of type **t2.micro**. As shown in Figure 4-23.

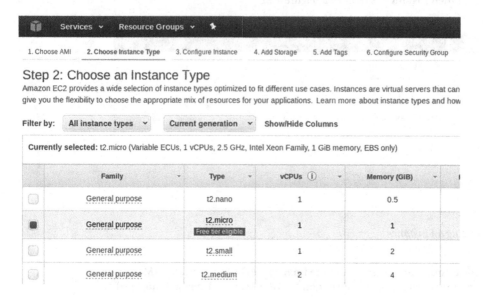

Figure 4-23. *Choosing an Instance type*

4. Click Next.

5. On the **Configure Instance Details** page, configure the settings exactly as shown in Figure 4-24.

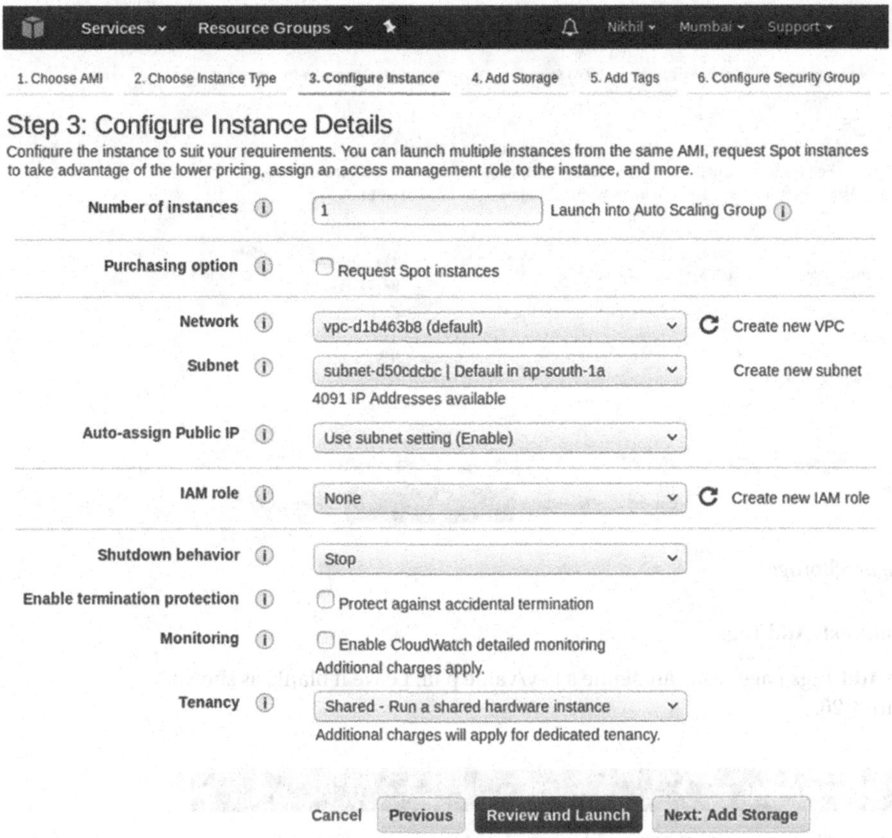

Figure 4-24. *Configure Instance details*

6. Click **Next: Add Storage**.

7. On the **Add Storage** page, choose the storage size under the field **Size (GiB)**. You can also add additional volumes by selecting **Add New Volume**. As shown in Figure 4-25.

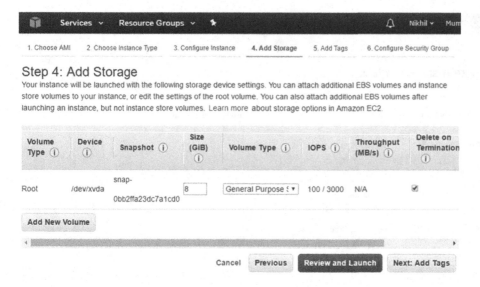

Figure 4-25. *Configure Storage*

8. Click on **Next: Add Tags**.

9. On the **Add Tags** page, you can define a key/value pair. Leave it blank, as shown in Figure 4-26.

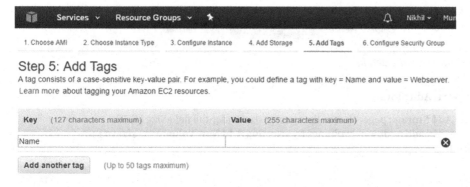

Figure 4-26. *Configure Tags*

10. Click on Next: **Configure Security Group**.

11. On the **Configure Security Group**, choose the **Select an existing security group** option. And from the resultant list, select the security group that we created in the previous section, as shown in Figure 4-27. Your values should look different from mine.

Figure 4-27. *Configure Security Group*

12. Next, click on **Review and Launch**.

13. On the **Review Instance Launch** page, review all your configurations. If you are satisfied, click on **Launch**.

14. You will be prompted to choose an existing key pair or create a new key pair. Since I have none, I choose to create a new key pair, as shown in Figure 4-28. This key pair will be used to SSH to the AWS instance.

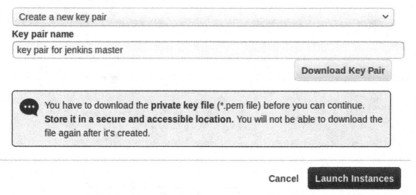

Figure 4-28. *Create a new key pair*

15. Give the newly created key pair a name, using the **Key pair name** section. Next download the key pair by clicking on the **Download Key Pair** button. See Figure 4-28.

16. Next, click **Launch Instances**. As you do, you will be presented with a **Launch Status** page. Click on the **View Instance** button.

17. Alternatively, you can view your instance from the left-hand navigation bar, by clicking **Instances**. Initially, the status of your instance will be in pending state and later it will change to running. As shown in Figure 4-29.

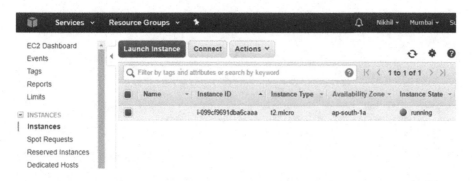

Figure 4-29. *Instance state*

18. Once it's running, you instance is ready for use.

Connecting to the AWS Instance

To connect to your instance you need the **Public DNS** or the **Public IP** of the instance. You will find these details on the Instance page, under the **Description** tab. See Figure 4-30.

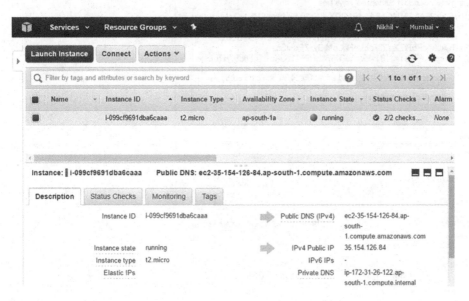

Figure 4-30. *Instance Details*

You will also need your key pair to connect to your instance using SSH.

Connecting to Your AWS Instance from Windows

Make sure you have **PuTTY** and **PuTTYgen** applications available on your machine. Follow the steps to connect to your instance using PuTTY.

1. The key pair file is a **.pem** file. PuTTY does not support the private key format (.pem). Hence, we will use PuTTYgen, to convert (.pem) keys to the required PuTTY format (.ppk).

2. Open **PuTTYgen** application. Follow Figure 4-31.

    a. From the menu, load the **.pem** file by clicking on **File ➤ Load private key**.

    b. Make sure you select the **Type of key to generate:** as **SSH-2 RSA**.

    c. Do not set any passphrase.

    d. Click on the **Save private key** button to download the **.ppk** file.

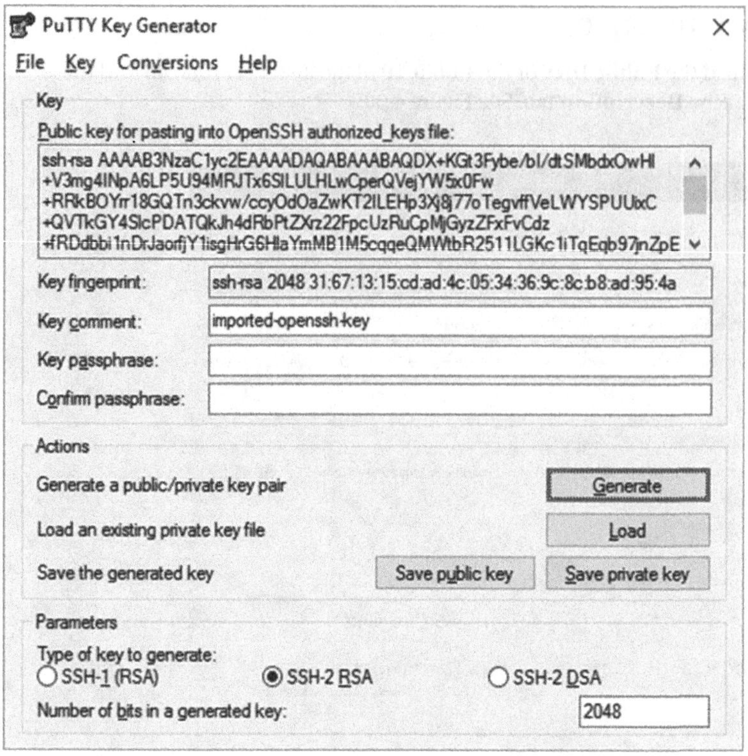

Figure 4-31. Converting .pem file to .ppk file

3. Now open the PuTTY application again. Follow Figure 4-32 and Figure 4-33.

    a. In the **Category** pane, go to **Connection ➤ SSH ➤ Auth**. Under **Authentication parameters** section click on the **Browse** button to select the **.ppk** file that we generated in the previous step.

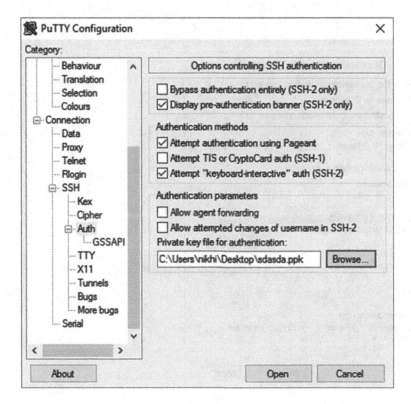

Figure 4-32. *Selecting the .ppk file*

    b.   In **Host Name (or IP address)** field, enter <username>@<Public DNS>.

    c.   Make sure to select the **Port** value as 22.

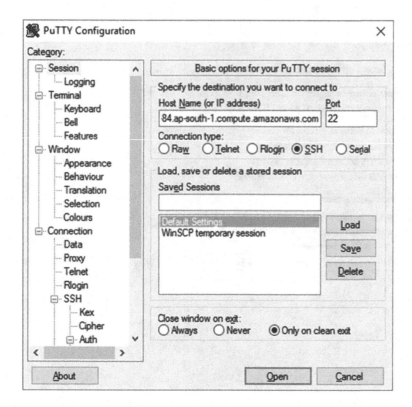

Figure 4-33. *Adding the hostname and port*

    d.   Click **Open** to access the AWS instance.

Connecting to Your AWS Instance from Linux Machine

Make sure you have the **.pem** file available with you on the machine from which you wish to access your AWS instance.

    1.   Run the following command to connect to your AWS instance, as shown in Figure 4-34.

```
ssh -i /path/my-key-pair.pem <username>@<Public DNS>
```

```
nikhil@dev01:~$ ssh -i /home/nikhil/Downloads/keypairforjenkinsmaster.pem ubuntu
@ec2-35-154-118-225.ap-south-1.compute.amazonaws.com
Welcome to Ubuntu 16.04.1 LTS (GNU/Linux 4.4.0-53-generic x86_64)

 * Documentation:  https://help.ubuntu.com
 * Management:     https://landscape.canonical.com
 * Support:        https://ubuntu.com/advantage

  Get cloud support with Ubuntu Advantage Cloud Guest:
    http://www.ubuntu.com/business/services/cloud

0 packages can be updated.
0 updates are security updates.


Last login: Mon Jan 23 22:40:19 2017 from 80.199.15.42
To run a command as administrator (user "root"), use "sudo <command>".
See "man sudo_root" for details.

ubuntu@ip-172-31-26-122:~$ █
```

Figure 4-34. *Connecting to aws instance using ssh*

Install the Latest Stable Version of Jenkins

Installing Jenkins from here is the same as installing Jenkins on any Ubuntu machine.

1. First add the key to your system by executing the following command:

    ```
    sudo wget -q -O - https://pkg.jenkins.io/debian-stable/jenkins.io.key
    | sudo apt-key add -
    ```

2. Now, add the repo **http://pkg.jenkins.io/debian-stablebinary/** into the
    sources.list file that is located at /**etc/apt**, using the following command:

    ```
    sudo sh -c 'echo deb http://pkg.jenkins.io/debian-stable binary/ >
    /etc/apt/sources.list.d/jenkins.list'
    ```

3. Update the package index:

    ```
    sudo apt-get update
    ```

4. Lastly, install Jenkins using the following simple command:

    ```
    sudo apt-get install jenkins -y
    ```

5. 4. You can now access Jenkins using the following URL **http://< Public
    DNS>:8080/**. Or using **http://< Public IP>:8080/**

Summary

In the current chapter we learned to install Jenkins Master on Docker, Cloud, and Bare Metal machines with Unix-like OS. Jenkins installation on Windows was skipped due to its shear simplicity.

In the next chapter we will learn in detail about the pipeline as code using Jenkins pipeline Job and Jenkins multibranch support using the multibranch pipeline Job.

CHAPTER 5

■■■■

Pipeline as a Code

Tired of creating and configuring Pipelines for your continuous integration (CI) and continuous delivery (CD) solution? *Pipeline as a Code* is the answer. The concept of *Pipeline as a Code* using Jenkinsfile or pipeline script is one of the newly introduced features in Jenkins (2.0). The current chapter is all about these new features in Jenkins, which are the following:

- Declarative Pipeline Syntax to model CI and CD pipelines, as a code.

- Support for multibranch Git and GitHub projects - to auto-spawn self-managed pipelines.

- Support for GitHub to automatically manage webhooks and more.

- Stage view - to make the pipeline progress and logs more intuitive.

In the current chapter, we will learn to use these new features with the help of a GitHub Maven project. To follow the example, you will need a GitHub account (public or private), and a Jenkins master (2.0) running on either Docker, AWS, or on a Linux/Windows machine.

Prerequisite

Before we create a pipeline inside Jenkins, we need to make sure that we have the following GitHub and Jenkins configurations ready:

1. A personal access token in GitHub.

2. An SSH key pair from the Jenkins master.

3. GitHub plugin for Jenkins, with the necessary configurations.

4. Maven, Git, and Java applications configured on Jenkins master.

5. Pipeline Maven Integration Plugin for Jenkins.

Let's see them one by one.

© Nikhil Pathania 2017
N. Pathania, *Pro Continuous Delivery*, DOI 10.1007/978-1-4842-2913-2_5

Creating a Personal Access Token in GitHub

A personal access token is just like a username and password. However, the difference lies in the fact that you can create as many personal access tokens as you want, each with a different set of permissions.

1. Sign In to your GitHub account.

2. Go to your GitHub account settings, as shown in Figure 5-1.

Figure 5-1. *GitHub account settings*

3. Navigate to **Developer settings ➤ Personal access tokens.** On the **Personal access tokens** page click on **Generate new token** button (Figure 5-2).

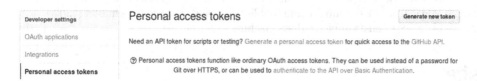

Figure 5-2. *Generate new token*

4. On the following page (Figure 5-3), do this:

   a. Add a name in the **Token description** field.

   b. Under **Select Scopes** field, pick **admin:org_hook** and **admin:repo_hook**.

   c. Click on the **Generate token** button to finish.

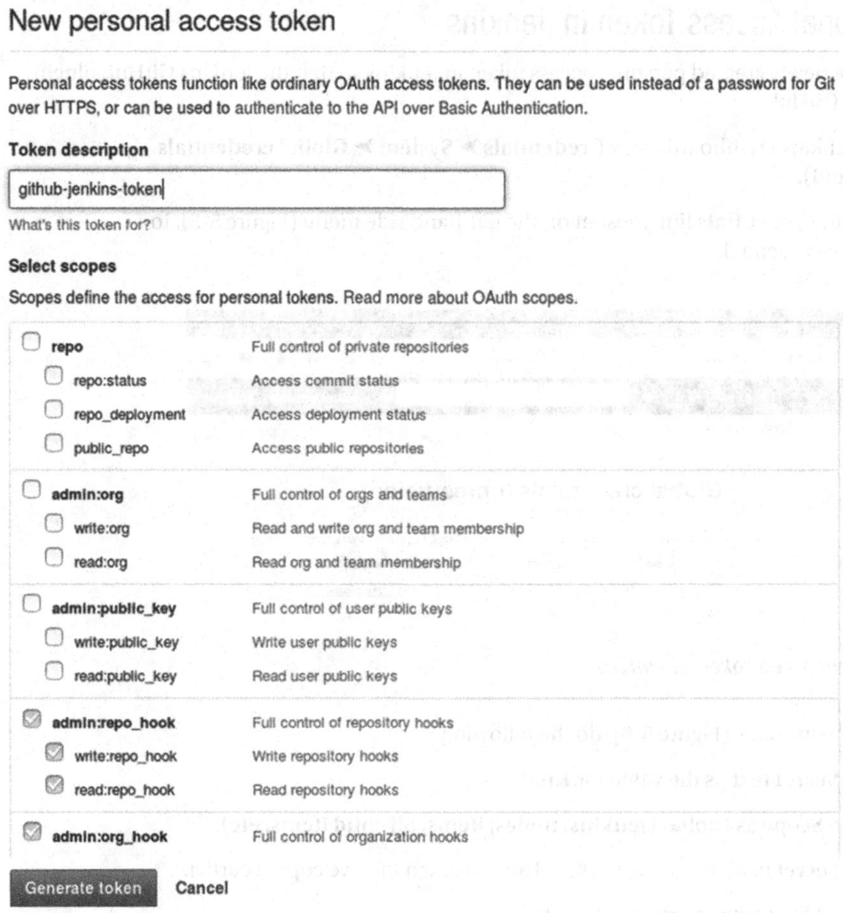

New personal access token

Personal access tokens function like ordinary OAuth access tokens. They can be used instead of a password for Git over HTTPS, or can be used to authenticate to the API over Basic Authentication.

Token description

    github-jenkins-token

What's this token for?

Select scopes

Scopes define the access for personal tokens. Read more about OAuth scopes.

☐ **repo**	Full control of private repositories	
☐ repo:status	Access commit status	
☐ repo_deployment	Access deployment status	
☐ public_repo	Access public repositories	
☐ **admin:org**	Full control of orgs and teams	
☐ write:org	Read and write org and team membership	
☐ read:org	Read org and team membership	
☐ **admin:public_key**	Full control of user public keys	
☐ write:public_key	Write user public keys	
☐ read:public_key	Read user public keys	
☑ **admin:repo_hook**	Full control of repository hooks	
☑ write:repo_hook	Write repository hooks	
☑ read:repo_hook	Read repository hooks	
☑ **admin:org_hook**	Full control of organization hooks	

    Generate token   Cancel

Figure 5-3. *Select scope*

5. You can see the new token under the **Personal access tokens** page (Figure 5-4). Save a copy of it by clicking on the small copy icon. We will need it later in the upcoming section.

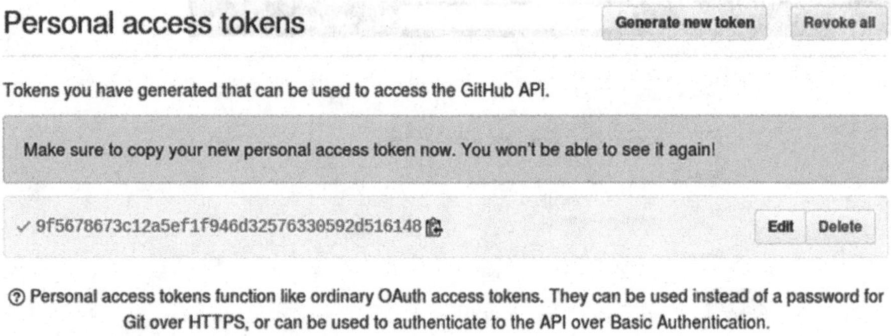

Personal access tokens

    Generate new token   Revoke all

Tokens you have generated that can be used to access the GitHub API.

Make sure to copy your new personal access token now. You won't be able to see it again!

✓ 9f5678673c12a5ef1f946d32576330592d516148 📋   Edit   Delete

⑦ Personal access tokens function like ordinary OAuth access tokens. They can be used instead of a password for Git over HTTPS, or can be used to authenticate to the API over Basic Authentication.

Figure 5-4. *Copy the new personal access token*

Adding the Personal Access Token in Jenkins

Now we need to add the newly created personal access token in Jenkins so that the Jenkins GitHub plugin can communicate with GitHub.

1. From the Jenkins Dashboard, click **Credentials ➤ System ➤ Global credentials (unrestricted).**

2. Click on **Add Credentials** link present on the left-hand side menu (Figure 5-5), to create a new credential.

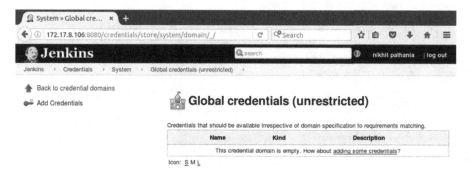

Figure 5-5. Add personal access token in Jenkins

3. On the following page (Figure 5-6), do the following:

   a. Select **Secret text** as the value for **Kind**.

   b. Choose **Scope** as **Global (Jenkins, nodes, items, all child items, etc).**

   c. In the **Secret** field, paste the personal access token that we copied earlier.

   d. In the ID field enter a meaningful ID.

   e. Add some description in the **Description** field.

   f. Click on the **OK** button when done.

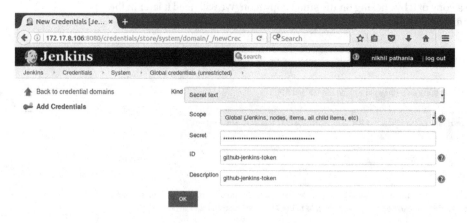

Figure 5-6. Create a secret text credential

4. You can see your newly created Secret text credential, which contains the GitHub personal access token, as shown in Figure 5-7.

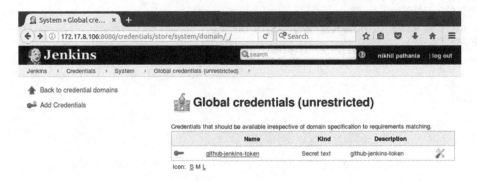

Figure 5-7. *A new Secret text credential*

Generating an SSH Key Pair

Jenkins pipeline needs an SSH key to clone the GitHub repository in order to build the code. The SSH key pair has to come from the Jenkins master server, since the underlying OS for Jenkins master can be a Windows or a Linux machine. We need to know the process to generate SSH key pairs on both of these OS.

Generate an SSH Key Pair on Ubuntu

Follow the below steps to generate an ssh key pair:

1. Open a Terminal and execute the following command, substituting in your email address (Figure 5-8).

```
ssh-keygen -t rsa -b 4096 -C "your e-mail id"
```

a. You will be prompted to "Enter a file in which to save the key." Press Enter, to accept the default file location.

■ **Note**   Make sure you do not have any existing key pair files with the default name. If so, choose a new name for the SSH key pair that we are creating.

---

b. At the next prompt, type a secure passphrase. You can choose not to enter any passphrase if you want.

```
vagrant@node3:~$ ssh-keygen -t rsa -b 4096 -C "nikhilpathania@gmail.com"
Generating public/private rsa key pair.
Enter file in which to save the key (/home/vagrant/.ssh/id_rsa):
Enter passphrase (empty for no passphrase):
Enter same passphrase again:
Your identification has been saved in /home/vagrant/.ssh/id_rsa.
Your public key has been saved in /home/vagrant/.ssh/id_rsa.pub.
The key fingerprint is:
08:d2:a8:01:20:d7:91:6c:b7:2a:61:77:d3:28:c2:1b nikhilpathania@gmail.com
The key's randomart image is:
+--[ RSA 4096]----+
|= .o.o           |
|o. o= .          |
|..o.o. +         |
| oE.o.=..        |
|.. * +..S        |
| o .             |
|   .             |
|                 |
|                 |
+-----------------+
vagrant@node3:~$ █
```

Figure 5-8. *Creating an SSH key pair*

2. This creates a new SSH key pair.

Adding your SSH private key to the ssh-agent

Adding the SSH private key to the ssh-agent makes it unnecessary for you to remember and enter your passphrase every time you use your key. You can skip this step if you haven't created a passphrase for your SSH key pair.

1. Start the ssh-agent if it's not already running using the below command. From the Figure 5-9, you can see a pid number.

   ```
   eval "$(ssh-agent -s)"
   ```

```
vagrant@node3:~$ eval "$(ssh-agent -s)"
Agent pid 1882
vagrant@node3:~$ █
```

Figure 5-9. *Starting the ssh-agent*

2. The SSH private key file is **id_rsa**. Add your SSH private key to the ssh-agent using the following command. You will be prompted to add your passphrase, as shown in Figure 5-10.

   ```
   ssh-add ~/.ssh/id_rsa
   ```

```
vagrant@node3:~$ ssh-add ~/.ssh/id_rsa
Enter passphrase for /home/vagrant/.ssh/id_rsa:
Identity added: /home/vagrant/.ssh/id_rsa (/home/vagrant/.ssh/id_rsa)
vagrant@node3:~$ █
```

Figure 5-10. *Adding the SSH private key to the ssh-agent*

Generate SSH Key Pair on Windows

Follow the below steps to generate an ssh key pair:

1. Open PuTTYgen.

    a. Under **Parameters ➤ Type of key to generate:** choose **SSH-2 RSA**.

    b. Next, click on the **Generate** button and hover your mouse over the blank space under the key section, as shown in (Figure 5-11).

***Figure 5-11.** Generating SSH key pair using puttygen*

    c. Once the key gets generated, add a passphrase in the **Key passphrase** field. Confirm the same by reentering the passphrase in the **Confirm passphrase** field (Figure 5-12). Creating a passphrase is, however, not mandatory.

    d. Download the public key and the private key by clicking on the **Save public key** and **Save private key** button (Figure 5-12).

151

Figure 5-12. *Saving the public and private key*

Copy the SSH Public Key to GitHub

Follow the below steps to copy the ssh public key to Github:

1. Log in to your GitHub account.

2. Navigate to **Settings ➤ Personal Settings ➤ SSH and GPG keys.**

3. On the **SSH keys** section click on the **New SSH key** button (Figure 5-13).

Figure 5-13. *Adding the public SSH key on Github*

4. On the following page (Figure 5-14), do the following:

    a. Add a name in the **Title** field.

    b. Paste your public key inside the **Key** field. (Be careful while entering the key.)

    c. Click on the **Add SSH key** button. You will be prompted to enter your GitHub account password.

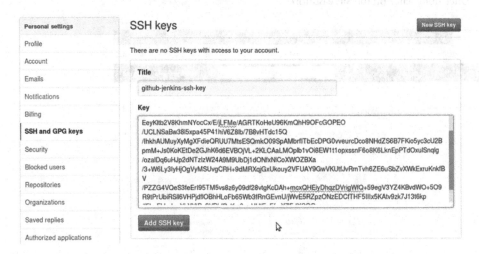

Figure 5-14. *Entering the SSH public key*

5. A new SSH key appears under **SSH keys** section, as shown in Figure 5-15.

Figure 5-15. *The new SSH key on GitHub*

Copy the SSH Private Key to Jenkins

Follow the below steps to copy the ssh private key pair to Jenkins:

1. From the Jenkins Dashboard, navigate to **Jenkins ➤ Credentials ➤ System ➤ Global credentials (unrestricted)**.

2. Click on the **Add Credentials** link on the left-hand side menu, to create a new credential (Figure 5-16).

    a. Choose **Kind** as **SSH Username with private key**.

    b. Add a username under the **Username** field. (This can be left blank.)

    c.   Under **Private key** field choose the **Enter directly** option and paste the private key in the text box. (Carefully paste the SSH private key.)

    d.   Enter the passphrase under the **Passphrase** field if you created one.

    e.   Add an ID under the **ID** field, and some description under the **Description** field.

    f.   Once done, click on the **Save** button.

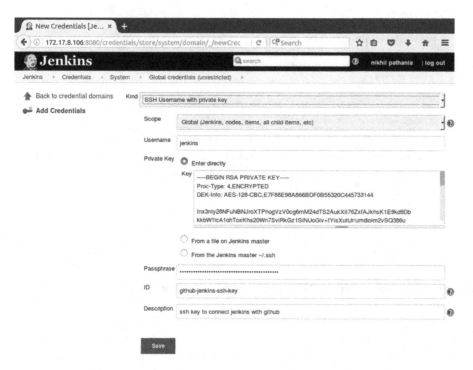

Figure 5-16. *Adding SSH private key in Jenkins*

3. The newly created SSH credentials are listed, as shown in Figure 5-17.

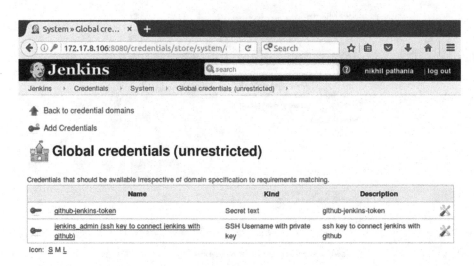

Figure 5-17. *List of credentials*

Configuring the GitHub Plugin

In order for Jenkins to communicate with GitHub account, we need to configure the GitHub plugin inside Jenkins.

1. From the Jenkins Dashboard, navigate to **Manage Jenkins ➤ Configure System**.

2. On the **Configure System** page scroll down until you see the **GitHub** section (Figure 5-18).

   a. Click on the **Add GitHub Server** button and choose **GitHub Server**.

   b. Choose the GitHub token (in our case it's **github-jenkins-token**) for the **Credentials** field.

   c. Leave the **Manage hooks** un-checked. (We will see this option later in the chapter.)

   d. You can test the connection between GitHub and Jenkins by clicking on the **Test connection** button.

   e. Leave the rest of the fields as they are. (We will see these options later in the chapter.)

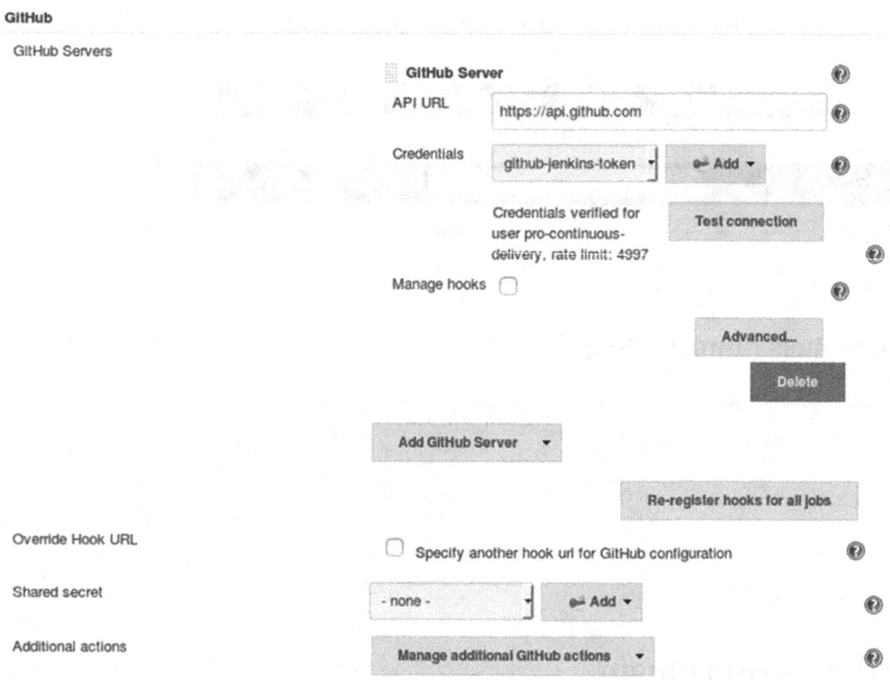

GitHub

GitHub Servers

GitHub Server

API URL https://api.github.com

Credentials github-jenkins-token ▾ 👤 Add ▾

Credentials verified for user pro-continuous-delivery, rate limit: 4997 Test connection

Manage hooks ☐

Advanced...

Delete

Add GitHub Server ▾

Re-register hooks for all jobs

Override Hook URL ☐ Specify another hook url for GitHub configuration

Shared secret - none - ▾ 👤 Add ▾

Additional actions Manage additional GitHub actions ▾

Figure 5-18. *Github plugin configuration in Jenkins*

Creating Webhooks in GitHub

In the following section we will learn to create webhooks in GitHub to automatically trigger a CI pipeline in Jenkins whenever there is a change on the version control system.

1. Log in to your GitHub account.

2. Open the GitHub repo that you would like to work on. Click on the **Settings** (tab).

    a. On the left-hand side menu, click on **Webhooks** (Figure 5-19).

    b. On the following page, click on **Add webhook** button to create a new webhook.

🗋 pro-continuous-delivery / **hello-world-example**   ⊙ Watch ▾ 0   ★ Star 0   ⑂ Fork 0

‹› Code   ⓘ Issues **0**   ⫝ Pull requests **0**   ⊞ Projects **0**   ▒ Wiki   ⤳ Pulse   ⊪ Graphs   ⚙ Settings

Options

Collaborators

Branches

Webhooks

Integrations & services

Deploy keys

Webhooks Add webhook

Webhooks allow external services to be notified when certain events happen within your repository. When the specified events happen, we'll send a POST request to each of the URLs you provide. Learn more in our Webhooks Guide.

Figure 5-19. *Create a new webhook in GitHub*

3.   Configure the new webhook as shown in Figure 5-20:

   a.   Under the **Payload URL** add your **Jenkins URL** followed by **github-webhook/**.

   b.   Choose the **Content** type as **application/json**.

   c.   For the **Which events would you like to trigger this webhook?** field, select **Send me everything**.

   d.   Once done click on **Add webhook** button.

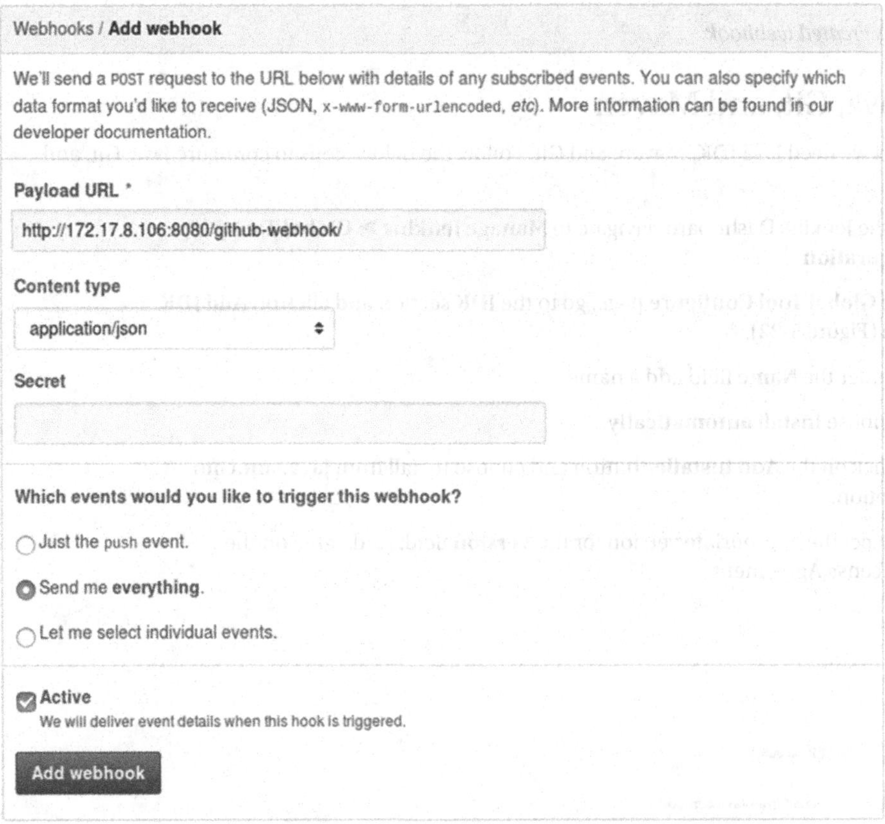

Webhooks / **Add webhook**

We'll send a POST request to the URL below with details of any subscribed events. You can also specify which data format you'd like to receive (JSON, x-www-form-urlencoded, *etc*). More information can be found in our developer documentation.

Payload URL *

    http://172.17.8.106:8080/github-webhook/

Content type

    application/json   ⬍

Secret

    [   ]

Which events would you like to trigger this webhook?

   ◯ Just the push event.

   ⦿ Send me **everything**.

   ◯ Let me select individual events.

   ☑ **Active**
      We will deliver event details when this hook is triggered.

   Add webhook

Figure 5-20. *Configure webhook*

157

4. You can see the newly created webhook, as shown in Figure 5-21.

Figure 5-21. *Newly created webhook*

Configure Java, Git, and Maven

To build our project we need Java JDK, Maven, and Git. Follow the below steps to configure Java, Git, and Maven:

1. From the Jenkins Dashboard navigate to **Manage Jenkins ➤ Global Tool Configuration**.

2. On the **Global Tool Configure** page, go to the **JDK** section and click on **Add JDK** button (Figure 5-22).

a. Under the **Name** field add a name.

b. Choose **Install automatically**.

c. Click on the **Add Installer** button and choose Install from **java.sun.com** option.

d. Select the appropriate version for the **Version** field. And agree on the License Agreement.

Figure 5-22. *Configuring Java*

■ **Note** You must have an Oracle account to use this method of installing Java. Enter your Oracle account details by clicking on the "Please enter your username/password" link.

---

3. Next, scroll down to the **Git** section (Figure 5-23).

    a. Add a name under the **Name** field.

    b. Under the **Path to Git executable** add **git**. (This assumes that you have installed Git on your Jenkins master.)

    c. Leave the **Install automatically** option un-checked.

Figure 5-23. *Configuring Git*

■ **Note** If you are using Git as the version control tool, make sure it is installed on the Jenkins master.

---

4. Next, scroll down to the **Maven** section (Figure 5-24).

    a. Click on **Add Maven** button.

    b. Add a name under the **Name** field.

    c. Choose the **Install automatically** option.

    d. Click on **Add Installer** button and choose **Install from Apache**.

    e. Choose the appropriate version for the **Version** field.

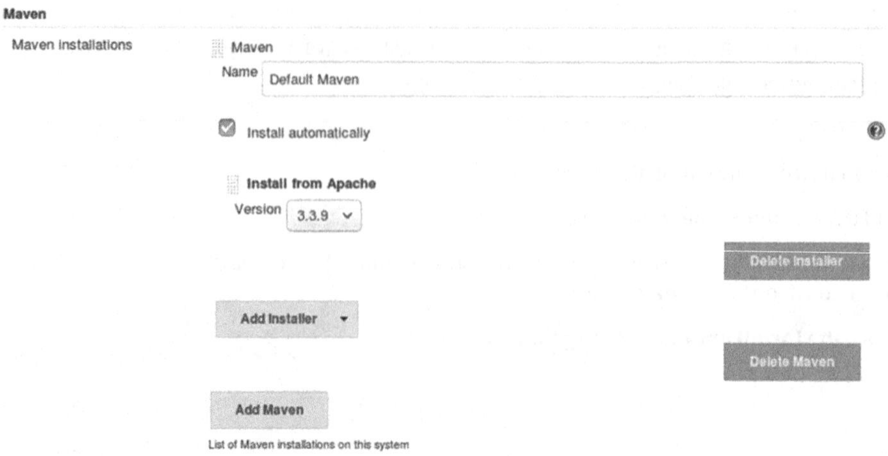

Maven

Maven installations ⠿ Maven

Name Default Maven

☑ Install automatically ❓

⠿ **Install from Apache**
Version 3.3.9 ∨

Delete Installer

Add Installer ▾

Delete Maven

Add Maven

List of Maven installations on this system

Figure 5-24. *Configuring Maven*

Install the Pipeline Maven Integration Plugin

Follow the below step to configure the pipeline maven integration plugin for Jenkins. The following plugin will allow us to use the Maven configuration inside out pipeline code.

1. From the Jenkins Dashboard click on **Manage Jenkins ➤ Plugin Manager ➤ Available (tab)**.

2. Type **Pipeline Maven Integration Plugin** inside the **Filter** field to search the respective plugin, as shown in Figure 5-25.

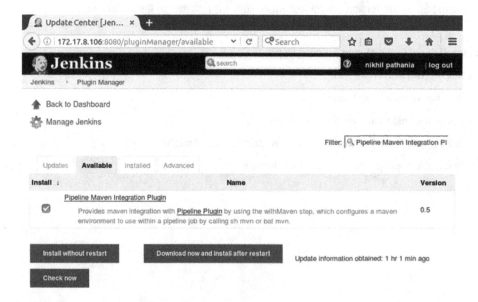

Figure 5-25. *Installing pipeline Maven integration plugin*

Using the Jenkins Pipeline Project

Let us create a Jenkins pipeline. In the example below I am using Jenkins 2.32.1, which is a stable release for Ubuntu. Our pipeline will download the code from GitHub repository and perform a build and unit test on it using Maven commands. Our pipeline will have two stages: first will be the **scm** stage, and the second will be the **build** stage.

Creating a Pipeline Project in Jenkins

Follow the steps to create a pipeline job inside Jenkins:

1. From the Jenkins Dashboard, click on the **New Item** link from the left-hand side menu.

2. On the following page (Figure 5-26), do the following:

   a. Name your pipeline by entering a name in the **Enter an item name** field.

   b. Choose Jenkins project type as **Pipeline** from the options.

   c. Click on the **OK** button.

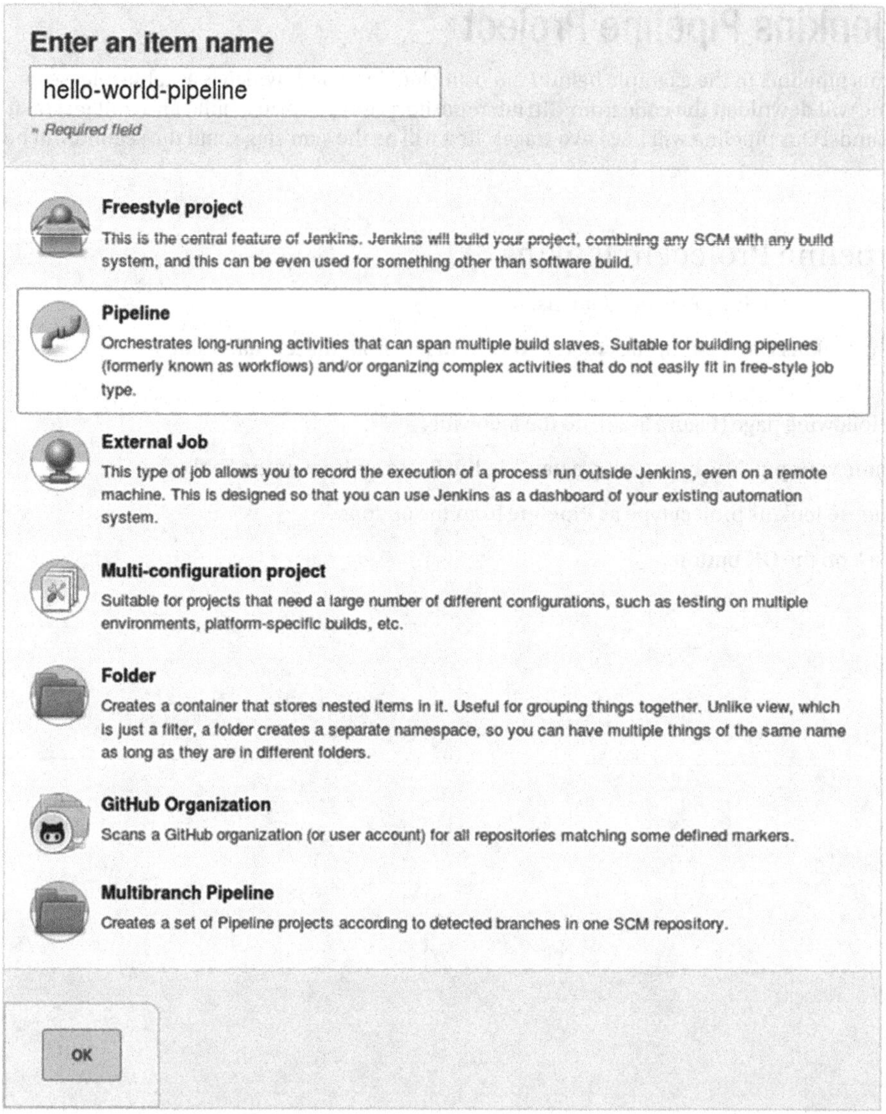

Enter an item name

hello-world-pipeline

~ Required field

Freestyle project

This is the central feature of Jenkins. Jenkins will build your project, combining any SCM with any build system, and this can be even used for something other than software build.

Pipeline

Orchestrates long-running activities that can span multiple build slaves. Suitable for building pipelines (formerly known as workflows) and/or organizing complex activities that do not easily fit in free-style job type.

External Job

This type of job allows you to record the execution of a process run outside Jenkins, even on a remote machine. This is designed so that you can use Jenkins as a dashboard of your existing automation system.

Multi-configuration project

Suitable for projects that need a large number of different configurations, such as testing on multiple environments, platform-specific builds, etc.

Folder

Creates a container that stores nested items in it. Useful for grouping things together. Unlike view, which is just a filter, a folder creates a separate namespace, so you can have multiple things of the same name as long as they are in different folders.

GitHub Organization

Scans a GitHub organization (or user account) for all repositories matching some defined markers.

Multibranch Pipeline

Creates a set of Pipeline projects according to detected branches in one SCM repository.

OK

Figure 5-26. *Creating a pipeline job*

3. On the pipeline configuration page, scroll down to the **Build Triggers** section. And choose the option **GitHub hook trigger for GITScm polling**, as shown in Figure 5-27.

Figure 5-27. *Choosing a build trigger*

4. Next, Scroll down to the **Pipeline** section and choose **Pipeline script** under the **Definition** field (Figure 5-28).

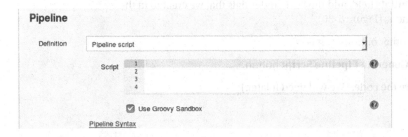

Figure 5-28. *Pipeline script*

5. Let's explore the **Pipeline Syntax** option. To do so, click on the **Pipeline Syntax** link which is right below the Script box.

The Pipeline Syntax Option in Jenkins

The Pipeline syntax utility is a very useful tool in Jenkins to convert Jenkins UI configurations to code. Let's see it in action.

1. The **Pipeline Syntax** utility will open in a new tab.

2. On the following page, go to the **Steps** section.

   a. For the **Sample Step** field, you will find a huge list of options.

   b. Choose **checkout: General SCM** option from the list. When you do so, the page refreshes with a new set of configurable items (Figure 5-30).

   c. Choose **Git** for the **SCM** field.

   d. Under **Repositories ➤ Repository URL**, add the GitHub repository's SSH link. You can find the SSH link for your repo on the GitHub repository page, as shown in Figure 5-29.

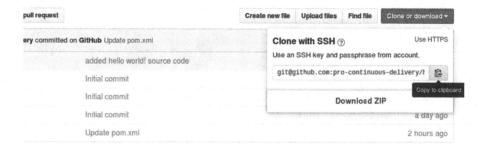

Figure 5-29. *Fetching the GitHub SSH URL*

    e.   Under **Credentials** field, add the SSH credentials that we created in the previous sections (Figure 5-30).

    f.   Leave all the other options as it is.

    g.   Click on the **Generate Pipeline Script** button.

    h.   Copy and save the code. (We will need it later.)

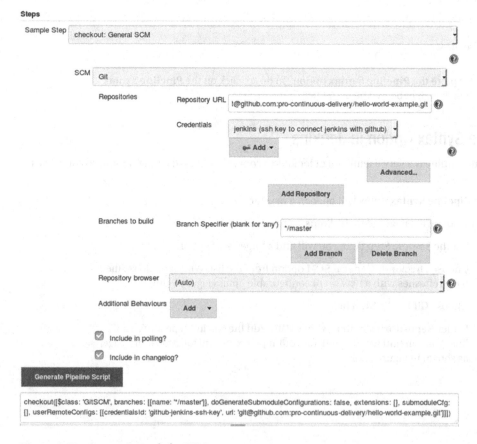

Figure 5-30. *Generating code for SCM*

3. Now, choose **node: Allocate node** from the list of options available under **Sample Step**. As you will see the page refreshes with the new set of configurable items (Figure 5-31).

   a. Add **master** under the **Label** field.

   b. Click on the **Generate Pipeline Script** button.

   c. Copy and save the code. (We will need it later.)

Steps

Sample Step	node: Allocate node	˅

Label: master

Label master is serviced by 1 node

Generate Pipeline Script

```
node('master') {
    // some block
}
```

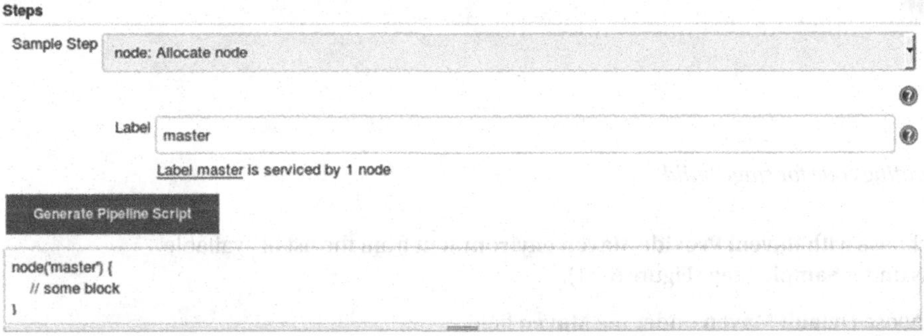

Figure 5-31. *Generating code for node*

4. Now, choose **stage: Stage** from the list of available options under **Sample Step** (Figure 5-32).

   a. Add **scm** under the **Stage Name** field.

   b. Click on the **Generate Pipeline Script** button.

   c. Copy and save the code. (We will need it later.).

Steps

Sample Step	stage: Stage	˅

Stage Name: scm

Generate Pipeline Script

```
stage('scm') {
    // some block
}
```

Figure 5-32. *Generating code for stage scm*

5. Create code for another stage named **build**, as shown in Figure 5-33. Copy the generated code.

Steps

Sample Step	stage: Stage

Stage Name build

`Generate Pipeline Script`

```
stage('build') {
    // some block
}
```

Figure 5-33. Generating code for stage build

6. Now, choose **withMaven: Provide Maven environment** from the list of available options under **Sample Step** (Figure 5-34).

   a. Choose **Default Maven** under the **Maven** field.

   b. Choose **Default Java** under the **JDK** field.

   c. Leave the rest of the fields as they are.

   d. Click on the **Generate Pipeline Script** button.

   e. Copy and save the code. (We will need it later.)

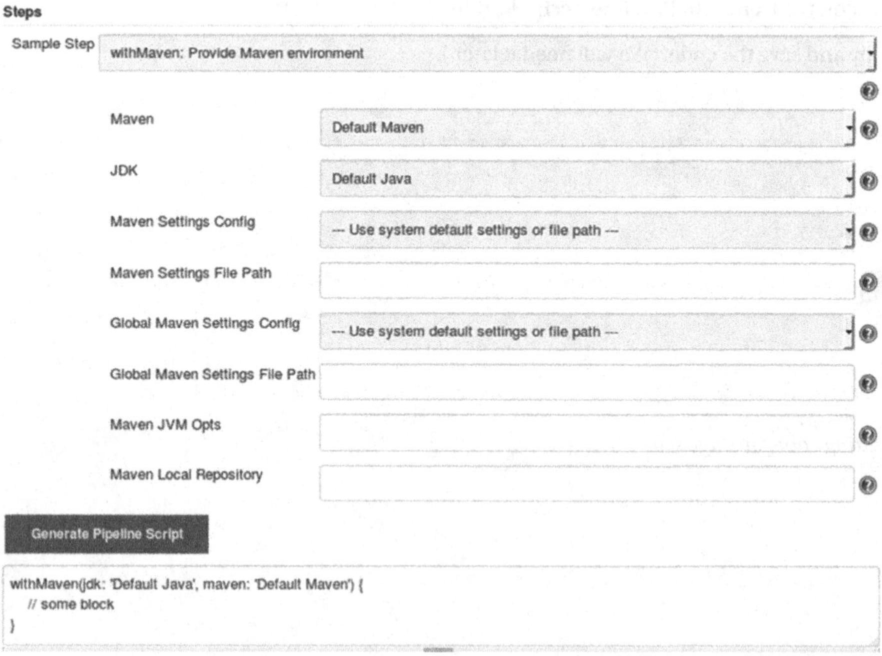

Steps

Sample Step	withMaven: Provide Maven environment

Maven	Default Maven
JDK	Default Java
Maven Settings Config	--- Use system default settings or file path ---
Maven Settings File Path	
Global Maven Settings Config	--- Use system default settings or file path ---
Global Maven Settings File Path	
Maven JVM Opts	
Maven Local Repository	

`Generate Pipeline Script`

```
withMaven(jdk: 'Default Java', maven: 'Default Maven') {
    // some block
}
```

Figure 5-34. Generating code for withMaven

■ **Note** To make **withMaven: Provide Maven environment** option available, in the Sample Step field we installed the **Pipeline Maven Integration Plugin** for Jenkins.

7. Now, choose **sh: Shell Script** from the list of available options under **Sample Step** (Figure 5-35).

    a. Inside the **Shell Script** field type the following code:

       `mvn clean install`

    b. Click on the **Generate Pipeline Script** button.

    c. Copy and save the code. (we will need it later).

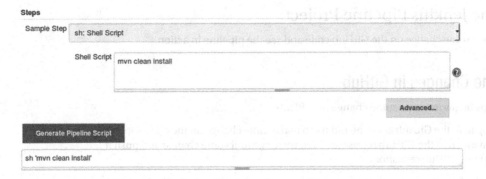

Figure 5-35. *Generating code for shell script*

8. The combined code that we have generated so far is as shown below:

```
node('master') {

stage('scm') {
    checkout([$class: 'GitSCM', branches: [[name: '*/master']],
doGenerateSubmoduleConfigurations: false, extensions: [], submoduleCfg: [],
userRemoteConfigs: [[credentialsId: 'github-jenkins-ssh-key', url:
'git@github.com:pro-continuous-delivery/hello-world-example.git']]])
}
stage('build') {
    withMaven(jdk: 'Default Java', maven: 'Default Maven') {
    sh 'mvn clean install'
}
}
}
```

9. Switch to the Jenkins Pipeline configuration page. And paste the above code under the **Script** field, as shown in Figure 5-36.

Figure 5-36. Pipeline script

Testing the Jenkins Pipeline Project

Let us now make some change on the GitHub code and see the pipeline in action.

Make Some Changes in GitHub

Follow the steps below to create some change on GitHub:

1. Log in to the GitHub account and try to make some change on the code. Or if you have cloned the GitHub repository then try to commit some change and push it to your GitHub repository.

2. In the following example, I am making some changes to the .pom file; I am doing this straight from the GitHub. See Figure 5-37.

Figure 5-37. Make some change on GitHub

3. As it can be seen below from Figure 5-38, I am committing the change to the master branch.

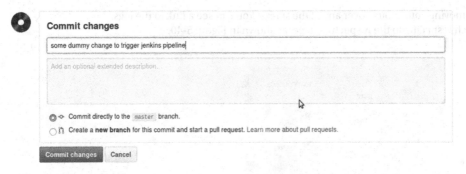

Figure 5-38. *Committing changes on GitHub*

Jenkins Pipeline Project in Action

The moment you commit or push a change on the GitHub repository, the Jenkins pipeline gets triggered.

1. To see this in action, from the Jenkins Dashboard quickly click on the pipeline project (in our example its hello-world-pipeline).

2. On the pipeline page you can see the **Stage View**, as shown in Figure 5-39.

Figure 5-39. *Pipeline in progress*

3. Try moving your mouse over any of the stages. You can see a link to the logs, which is specific to the respective stage, as shown in Figure 5-40.

Stage View

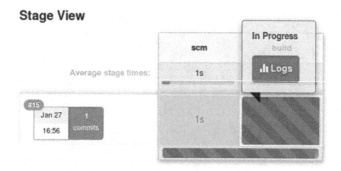

Figure 5-40. In-progress logs

4. Clicking on the logs will open a small window with the running logs inside it. Figure 5-41 shows a preview of what some of the running logs look like.

Figure 5-41. Stage logs

5. From the pipeline page, click on the **GitHub Hook Log** to check the GitHub Push details (Figure 5-42).

Last GitHub Push

```
Started on Jan 27, 2017 3:56:02 PM
Using strategy: Default
[poll] Last Built Revision: Revision 0f0107058b217e58340f10397d9d476a4f1ae465 (refs/remotes/origin/master)
using GIT_SSH to set credentials ssh key to connect jenkins with github
 > git ls-remote -h git@github.com:pro-continuous-delivery/hello-world-example.git # timeout=10
Found 1 remote heads on git@github.com:pro-continuous-delivery/hello-world-example.git
[poll] Latest remote head revision on refs/heads/master is: 67a27f64360081a383b46a6cc2270fdd35265986
Done. Took 2.9 sec
Changes found
```

Figure 5-42. *Github push details*

Using Jenkins Multibranch Pipeline Project

The Jenkins multibranch pipeline needs a Jenkinsfile for sure. All the pipeline steps and stages are configured (written) inside the Jenkinsfile. This Jenkinsfile is stored with the source code on your Version Control System (Git, GitHub, etc).

The Jenkins multibranch project configuration contains only the information about the GitHub or Git repository and nothing else. This multibranch pipeline is again dependent on webhooks.

Create Credentials for GitHub Account

We need to add the GitHub account credentials inside Jenkins, as the multibranch pipeline does not accept the SSH key pair authentication.

1. From the Jenkins dashboard click on **Credentials ➤ System ➤ Global credentials (unrestricted)**.

2. Click on the **Add Credentials** link from the left-hand side menu.

3. On the following page (Figure 5-43), do the following:

    a. Choose **Username and Password** under the **Kind** field.

    b. Add your GitHub account username under the **Username** field.

    c. Add your GitHub account password under **Password** field.

    d. Add some ID and description in the **ID** and **Description** fields respectively.

    e. Once done, click on the **OK** button.

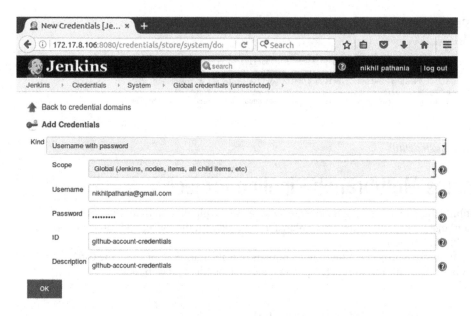

Figure 5-43. *Github account credentials in Jenkins*

Creating a Multibranch Pipeline Project

Follow the steps below to create a multibranch pipeline job in Jenkins:

1. From Jenkins Dashboard click **New Item**.

    a. Add a name to your new pipeline under the **Enter an item name** field (Figure 5-44).

    b. Choose **Multibranch Pipeline** from the project-type options and click the **OK** button.

Enter an item name

hello-world-multibranch-pipeline

» Required field

Freestyle project

This is the central feature of Jenkins. Jenkins will build your project, combining any SCM with any build system, and this can be even used for something other than software build.

Pipeline

Orchestrates long-running activities that can span multiple build slaves. Suitable for building pipelines (formerly known as workflows) and/or organizing complex activities that do not easily fit in free-style job type.

External Job

This type of job allows you to record the execution of a process run outside Jenkins, even on a remote machine. This is designed so that you can use Jenkins as a dashboard of your existing automation system.

Multi-configuration project

Suitable for projects that need a large number of different configurations, such as testing on multiple environments, platform-specific builds, etc.

Folder

Creates a container that stores nested items in it. Useful for grouping things together. Unlike view, which is just a filter, a folder creates a separate namespace, so you can have multiple things of the same name as long as they are in different folders.

GitHub Organization

Scans a GitHub organization (or user account) for all repositories matching some defined markers.

Multibranch Pipeline

Creates a set of Pipeline projects according to detected branches in one SCM repository.

if you want to create a new item from other existing, you can use this option:

Copy from   Type to autocomplete

OK

Figure 5-44. *Creating a multibranch pipeline job*

2. On the Job configuration page, scroll down until you see the **Branch Sources** section (Figure 5-45).

    a. Click on the **Add source** button and choose **GitHub**.

    b. Under the **Owner** field, add your GitHub account name.

    c. Under **Scan credentials** add the recently created GitHub account credentials in Jenkins.

    d. The Repository field will be automatically populated with the list of all the repositories that you have under your GitHub account. Choose the one that you want Jenkins to work on.

    e. Leave the rest of the options as is.

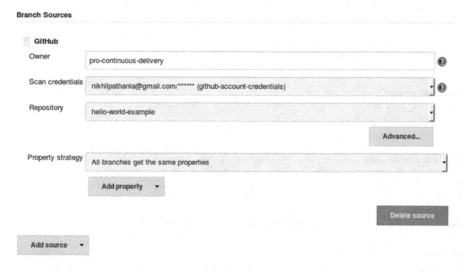

Figure 5-45. *Configuring Github repo*

3. Scroll down until you see **Build Configuration** section (Figure 5-46). Choose the **Mode** as **by Jenkinsfile**.

Figure 5-46. *Choose to build from Jenkinsfile*

4. Scroll down to the **Appearance** section (Figure 5-47). You can choose to have your GitHub repo avatar on your pipeline page.

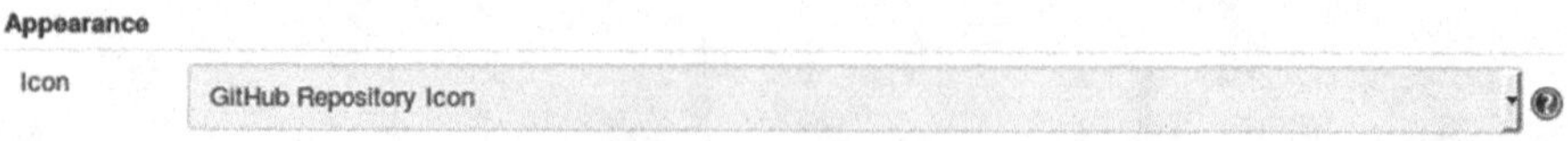

Appearance

Icon   GitHub Repository Icon

Figure 5-47. *Choose the appearance*

5. Click on the **Save** button to save you configuration.

6. The moment you create a multibranch pipeline. Jenkins will immediately fetch the branch details from GitHub and generate a report, as shown in Figure 5-48.

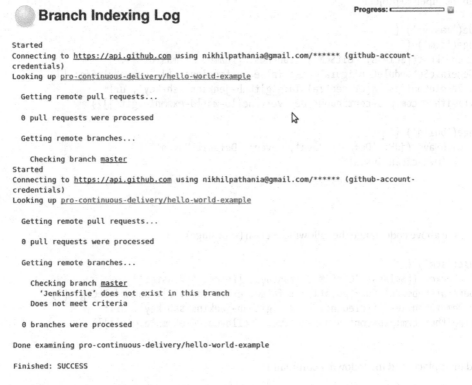

Figure 5-48. *Branch Indexing Log*

7. To access the Branch Indexing Log, click on the **Branch Indexing** link from the Jenkins multibranch pipeline page.

8. From the logs it is clear that the Jenkins multibranch pipeline identified a master branch on the GitHub repo with no Jenkinsfile on it. And hence, it declared the GitHub repository; or to be more specific, the GitHub branch as unsuitable.

9. So let's add a Jenkinsfile to our GitHub repository.

Using a Jenkinsfile

Follow the steps below to use the Jenkinsfile:

1. Take the build script from our previous pipeline project. Shown below is the code from the pipeline project.

    ```
    node('master') {
    stage('scm') {
        checkout([$class: 'GitSCM', branches: [[name: '*/master']],
    doGenerateSubmoduleConfigurations: false, extensions: [], submoduleCfg: [],
    userRemoteConfigs: [[credentialsId: 'github-jenkins-ssh-key', url:
    'git@github.com:pro-continuous-delivery/hello-world-example.git']]])
    }
    stage('build') {
        withMaven(jdk: 'Default Java', maven: 'Default Maven') {
        sh 'mvn clean install'
    }
    }
    }
    ```

2. From the above code delete the following section (scm stage).

    ```
    stage('scm') {
        checkout([$class: 'GitSCM', branches: [[name: '*/master']],
    doGenerateSubmoduleConfigurations: false, extensions: [], submoduleCfg: [],
    userRemoteConfigs: [[credentialsId: 'github-jenkins-ssh-key', url:
    'git@github.com:pro-continuous-delivery/hello-world-example.git']]])
    }
    ```

3. And in its place, add the following command:

    ```
    checkout scm
    ```

4. The resultant code should look as shown below.

    ```
    node('master') {
    checkout scm
    stage('build') {
        withMaven(jdk: 'Default Java', maven: 'Default Maven') {
        sh 'mvn clean install'
    }
    }
    }
    ```

5. Open a text editor and paste the above content in it and save it as **Jenkinsfile**.

6. Add this new **Jenkinsfile** to the cloned repository on your local machine and do a commit + push operation (if you have created a clone of the GitHub repository on your local machine).

7. Or add it directly to your GitHub repo, as shown in Figure 5-49.

Figure 5-49. *Adding Jenkinsfile to GitHub repository*

8. Commit the new **Jenkinsfile** by adding some comments on the master branch, as shown in Figure 5-50.

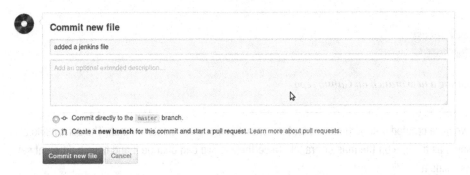

Figure 5-50. *Committing the changes on GitHub*

9. The moment you do so, the multibranch pipeline gets triggered on the Jenkins master. To see this click on our multibranch Jenkins pipeline from the Jenkins Dashboard.

10. As shown in Figure 5-51, you can see a new pipeline, named **master,** gets created inside the multibranch pipeline project.

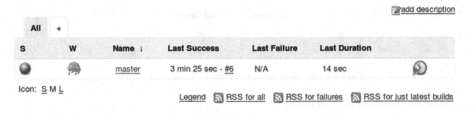

Figure 5-51. *Pipeline for the master branch*

Creating a New Branch on the GitHub Repo

When you create a new branch on the GitHub repo, Jenkins multibranch pipeline will automatically detect it and create a pipeline for it based on the Jenkinsfile. To see this in action, let's create a new branch on Github.

1. As you can see, I am creating a new branch named **feature-branch-1** from the **master** branch (Figure 5-52).

Figure 5-52. *Creating a new branch on Github repo*

■ **Note** Since we have created a branch named feature-branch-1 from the master branch. The Jenkinsfile at this point is the same as the one on the master branch. Nevertheless, we can change it and have a different set of steps and tasks inside it.

---

2. The moment I do so, GitHub notifies Jenkins and the multibranch pipeline project gets triggered. To see this, go to Jenkins Dashboard and click on the multibranch pipeline project. You will see two pipelines inside it. One is for **master** branch and the other one is for **feature-branch-1**, as shown in Figure 5-53.

📖 hello-world-multibranch-pipeline

📝add description

S	W	Name ↓	Last Success	Last Failure	Last Duration	
●	☀	feature-branch-1	5 min 55 sec - #1	N/A	31 sec	🔄
●	☀	master	5 min 54 sec - #1	N/A	30 sec	🔄

Icon: S M L

Legend 📶 RSS for all 📶 RSS for failures 📶 RSS for just latest builds

Figure 5-53. *Pipeline for the feature-branch-1 branch*

3. From the multibranch pipeline project page, click on **Branch Indexing** link. And you will see that Jenkins now has the details about both the branches on the GitHub repo, as shown in Figure 5-54.

 **Branch Indexing Log**

```
Started by timer
Connecting to https://api.github.com using nikhilpathania@gmail.com/****** (github-account-
credentials)
Looking up pro-continuous-delivery/hello-world-example

  Getting remote pull requests...

  0 pull requests were processed

  Getting remote branches...

    Checking branch feature-branch-1
      'Jenkinsfile' exists in this branch
    Met criteria
No changes detected in feature-branch-1 (still at 69f5d39d79494789b261e8b5028c986a62bf86dc)

    Checking branch master
      'Jenkinsfile' exists in this branch
    Met criteria
No changes detected in master (still at 1429f94f16a981c2779692416fa75cef345aaadf)

  2 branches were processed

Done examining pro-continuous-delivery/hello-world-example

Finished: SUCCESS
```

Figure 5-54. *Branch Indexing Log*

A Better Way of Managing GitHub Webhooks

All this time we were using the manual way of creating webhooks on GitHub. However, in the current section, we will discuss some other, better ways to configure webhooks.

1. Using the GitHub services (manual)

2. Using GitHub Plugin in Jenkins (Automatic)

Using the GitHub Services

GitHub has some built-in integration support (services) for popular tools like Jenkins. Using these pre-built services for Jenkins, such as the Jenkins (Git plugin) and the Jenkins (GitHub plugin), you can automatically trigger the Jenkins CI pipeline whenever there is a push on the version control system.

1. Log in to your GitHub account.

2. Open your Repository home page and click on the **Settings** (tab).

3. On the left-hand side menu, click **Webhooks** and delete any existing webhooks that we have configured so far.

4. Next, on the left-hand side menu, click **Integrations & services**.

    a. On the following page, under **Services** section, click on the **Add services** button.

    b. Search for **Jenkins (GitHub plugin)** by typing the same, as shown in Figure 5-55.

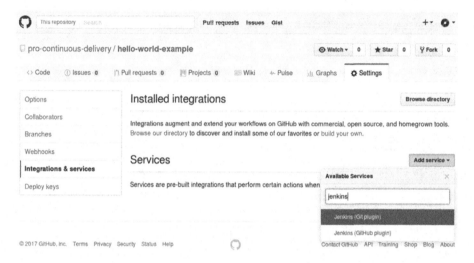

Figure 5-55. *Adding the Jenkins (GitHub plugin) service*

5. On the resultant page (Figure 5-56), do the following,

    a. Add the Jenkins webhook URL under the **Jenkins hook url** field, as shown below.

    b. Click on the **Add Service** button.

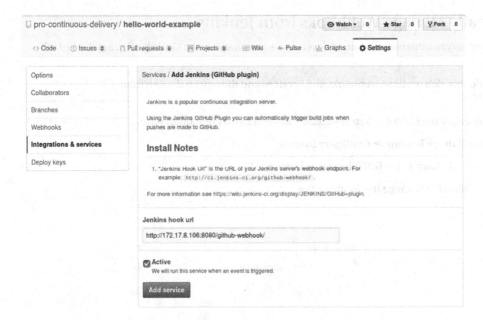

Figure 5-56. Configuring GitHub service

6. The service gets added as shown in Figure 5-57.

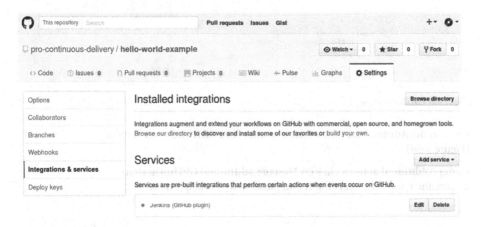

Figure 5-57. New GitHub service

7. Try making some commits on the GitHub repo and see if the new GitHub service works.

Automatically Manage Webhooks from Jenkins

We can make Jenkins create personal token and webhooks automatically on GitHub, all using the GitHub account details:

1. To do this, delete all the webhooks and Services and the personal token from GitHub.

2. Also, delete the GitHub token key created in the Jenkins credentials page.

3. Go to **Manage Jenkins ➤ Configure System**.

   a. Scroll down to the **GitHub** section (Figure 5-58).

   b. Select the **Manage hooks** check box.

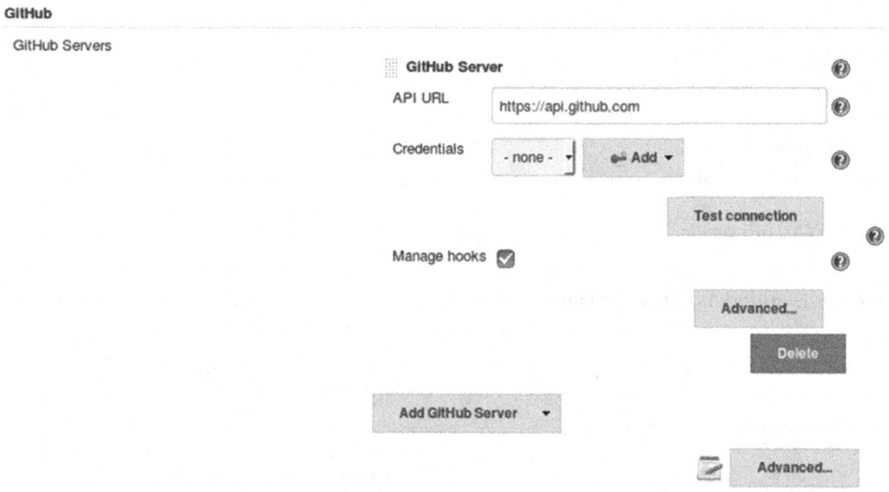

Figure 5-58. *Configuring GitHub plugin 1*

   c. Click on the **Advanced...** button, the one after **Add GitHub Server** button (Figure 5-58).

   d. Under **Additional actions** click on **Manage additional GitHub actions** button and choose **Convert login and password to token** (Figure 5-59).

Re-register hooks for all jobs
Override Hook URL
Specify another hook url for GitHub configuration
Shared secret
- none -
Add
Additional actions
Manage additional GitHub actions
Convert login and password to token
GitHub Enterprise Servers
Add

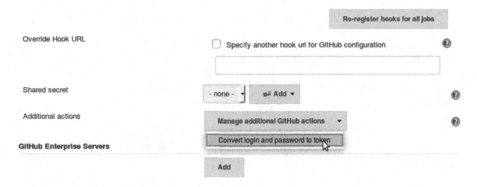

Figure 5-59. *Configuring GitHub plugin 2*

e. You will be presented with some more options (Figure 5-60). Do the following:

f. Under **GitHub API URL** field, add the GitHub URL of your organization, if it's a public repo then leave the field with the default option as shown below.

g. Choose **From credentials** option, and under **Credentials** field, add the GitHub account credentials that we created in the previous sections.

h. Next, press on the **Create token credentials** button. This action will create a personal access token on your GitHub account.

i. Under **Credentials** choose the GitHub account credentials that we created in Jenkins.

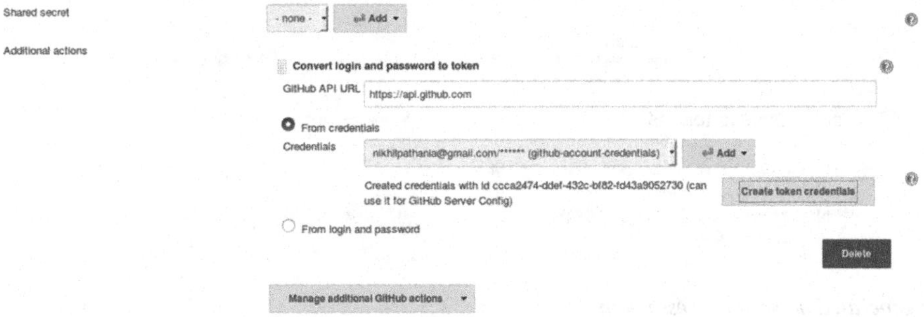

Shared secret
- none -
Add
Additional actions
Convert login and password to token
GitHub API URL
https://api.github.com
From credentials
Credentials
nikhilpathania@gmail.com/****** (github-account-credentials)
Add
Created credentials with id ccca2474-ddef-432c-bf82-fd43a9052730 (can use it for GitHub Server Config)
Create token credentials
From login and password
Delete
Manage additional GitHub actions

Figure 5-60. *Configuring GitHub plugin 3*

j. Click on the **Test connection** button to test the connectivity between Jenkins and GitHub (Figure 5-61).

k. Click on the **Re-register hooks for all jobs** button. This will create all the necessary webhooks on GitHub for both the Jenkins pipelines that we have created so far (Figure 5-61).

GitHub Server

API URL	https://api.github.com
Credentials	GitHub (https://api.github.com) auto generated token credentials for nikhilpathania@gmail.com ▾
	⊶ Add ▾

Credentials verified for user pro-continuous-delivery, rate limit: 4765   [Test connection]

Manage hooks ☑

[Advanced...]

[Delete]

[Add GitHub Server ▾]

Called re-register hooks for 3 items   [Re-register hooks for all jobs]

Override Hook URL   ☐ Specify another hook url for GitHub configuration

Shared secret   GitHub (https://api.github.com) auto generated token credentials for nikhilpathania@gmail.com ▾   ⊶ Add ▾

Additional actions   [Manage additional GitHub actions ▾]

Figure 5-61. *Configuring GitHub plugin 4*

4. Let's log in to GitHub and check the automatically created webhooks and personal access token.

5. Navigate to **Settings (GitHub account)** ➤ **Developer settings** ➤ **Personal access tokens**.

6. You can see a new personal access token, as shown in Figure 5-62.

○ Search GitHub	Pull requests Issues Gist	+▾ ⚙▾

Developer settings	**Personal access tokens**	[Generate new token] [Revoke all]
OAuth applications	Tokens you have generated that can be used to access the GitHub API.	
Integrations		
Personal access tokens	**Jenkins GitHub Plugin token** (http://172.17.8.106:8080/) — Last used within the last day [Edit] [Delete]	
	admin:repo_hook, repo, repo:status	

Figure 5-62. *Auto-generated personal access token*

7. Navigate to **Settings (repository)** ➤ **Developer settings** ➤ **Personal access tokens**.

8. You can see a new webhook, as shown in Figure 5-63.

Figure 5-63. *Auto-generated webhooks*

9. From the Jenkins Dashboard, navigate to **Jenkins ➤ Credentials ➤ System ➤ Global credentials (unrestricted).**

10. You can see the auto-generated personal access token has been added to Jenkins Credentials, as shown in Figure 5-64.

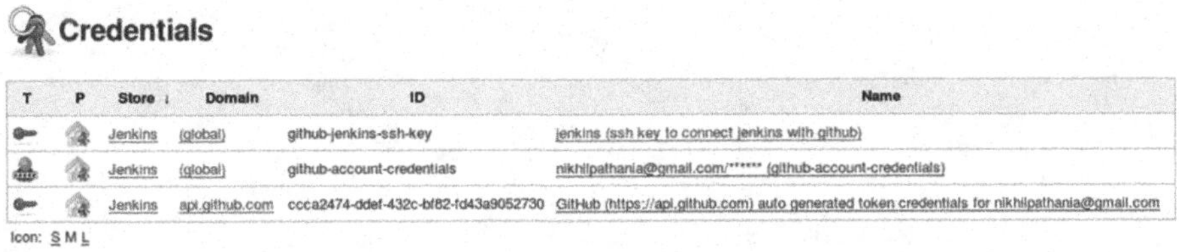

Figure 5-64. *List of credentials*

Summary

In the current chapter we learned to create a simple CI pipeline using the pipeline script (pipeline as a code) with just two stages (scm and build). We also learned to use the Jenkins multibranch pipeline and the Jenkinsfile. Along with these, we also learned to configure webhooks in GitHub and create credentials in Jenkins.

The purpose of this chapter was to introduce its readers to the Jenkins pipeline Job, multibranch pipeline Job, and Jenkinsfile using a simple example. Nevertheless, we will learn more about Jenkins pipeline steps/syntax in the coming chapters.

In the next chapter we will learn to set up a distributed build farm using Docker and Kubernetes. We will also create simple pipelines to test out builds on these build farms. Along with these, pretested commits using Jenkins and GitHub is also a topic of discussion in Chapter 6.

CHAPTER 6

■ ■ ■

Using Containers for Distributed Builds

In the current chapter we will learn to use Docker with Jenkins to provision on-demand Jenkins Slaves. Next, we will learn to use Kubernetes with Jenkins to provision on-demand Jenkins Slaves running across multiple Docker hosts, thus, creating a scalable build farm for running builds.

Distributed Builds Using Docker

In this section we will learn to use Docker containers as Jenkins Slave (build agents), to run our CI pipelines. These Docker containers (build agents) will be created when the CI pipeline runs; the build will be performed inside the container, and once the build is complete the Docker container will be destroyed.

To achieve this we need a Jenkins Master (could be running on any platform: Docker, Windows, Linux, Cloud, etc.). We also need a Docker Server. To set up a Docker server, see the **Installing Docker on Ubuntu** section from **Chapter 4**.

Make sure that your Jenkins Master can talk to GitHub using the **Github Plugin**. See the section **Automatically Manage Webhooks from Jenkins** from **Chapter 5**.

We might also need Java, Git, and Maven configured on your Jenkins Master. See section **Configure Java, Git, and Maven** from **Chapter 5**.

Enabling Docker Remote API

Jenkins (though the Docker Plugin) will use the Docker remote API to communicate with a Docker server. Docker remote API allows external applications to communicate with the Docker server using REST API's. Docker remote API can also be used to get information about all the running containers inside the Docker server.

To enable Docker remote API, we need to modify the Docker's configuration file. Depending on your OS version and the way you have installed Docker on your machine, you might need to choose the right configuration file to modify. Shown below are two methods that work on Ubuntu.

© Nikhil Pathania 2017
N. Pathania, *Pro Continuous Delivery*, DOI 10.1007/978-1-4842-2913-2_6

Modifying the docker.conf file

Follow these steps to modify the docker.conf file. These configurations are important to allow Jenkins to communicate with the Docker Host.

1. Log in to your Docker server, make sure you have sudo privileges.

2. Execute the following command to edit the file **docker.conf**.

   ```
   sudo nano /etc/init/docker.conf
   ```

3. Inside the **docker.conf** file, go to the line containing **DOCKER_OPTS**=.

■ **Note**   You will find **DOCKER_OPTS=** variable at two places inside the **docker.conf** file. First is in the **pre-start script** section and next is in the **post-start script** section. Use the **DOCKER_OPTS=** under the pre-start script section.

---

4. Set the value of **DOCKER_OPTS** to,

   ```
   DOCKER_OPTS='-H tcp://0.0.0.0:4243 -H unix:///var/run/docker.sock'
   ```

5. The above setting will bind the Docker server to the Unix socket as well on TCP port 4243. "0.0.0.0" makes the Docker engine accept connections from anywhere.

■ **Note**   If you want your Docker server to accept connections from only your Jenkins server, then replace "**0.0.0.0**" with your Jenkins Server IP.

---

6. Restart the Docker server using the following command,

   ```
   sudo service docker restart
   ```

7. To check if the configuration has worked, do the following,

   ```
   curl -X GET http://<Docker server IP>:4243/images/json
   ```

■ **Note**   The above command will list all the images present on your Docker server, if any.

Modifying the docker.service File

Follow the steps below to modify the docker.service file.

1. Execute the following command to edit the file **docker.service**.

   ```
   sudo nano /lib/systemd/system/docker.service
   ```

188

2. Inside the **docker.service** file, go to the line containing **ExecStart**=.

3. Set the value of **ExecStart**= as shown below.

```
ExecStart=/usr/bin/docker daemon -H fd:// -H tcp://0.0.0.0:4243
```

4. The above setting will bind the Docker server to the Unix socket as well on TCP port 4243. "0.0.0.0" makes the Docker engine accept connections from anywhere.

■ **Note** If you want your Docker server to accept connections from only your Jenkins server. Then replace **"0.0.0.0"** with your Jenkins Server IP.

---

5. Execute the following command to make the Docker daemon notice the modified configuration.

```
systemctl daemon-reload
```

6. Restart the Docker server using the following command,

```
sudo service docker restart
```

7. To check if the configuration has worked, do the following,

```
curl -X GET http://<Docker server IP>:4243/images/json
```

■ **Note** The above command will list all the images present on your Docker server, if any.

Installing the Docker Plugin

To create Docker containers (build agents) on the fly, we need to install the Docker Plugin for Jenkins. To do this, follow these steps:

1. From the Jenkins Dashboard, click on **Manage Jenkins ➤ Manage Plugins ➤ Available (tab)**. You will be taken to the Jenkins **Manage Plugins** page.

2. Enter "Docker Plugin" in the **Filter** filed, as shown in Figure 6-1.

Figure 6-1. Installing the Docker Plugin

3. Select the **Docker Plugin** from the list and click on the **Install without restart** button.

4. Restart Jenkins if needed.

Configuring the Docker Plugin

Now that we have our Docker Plugin installed, let us configure it.

1. From the Jenkins Dashboard, click **Manage Jenkins ➤ Configure System**.

2. Once on the **Configure System** page, scroll down all the way to the **Cloud** section (Figure 6-2).

   a. Click on the **Add a new cloud** button and choose **Docker** from the available options.

   b. On the resultant page, you will find a good number of settings to configure.

   c. Give your Docker server a name using the **Name** field.

   d. Add your Docker server URL under the **Docker URL** field.

   e. Click on the **Test Connection** button to check if Jenkins can communicate with Docker server.

   f. At the end of the page, click on **Apply** and **Save** button. We will come back here later to make further configurations.

Cloud

Docker	
Name	Default Docker Host
Docker URL	tcp://172.17.8.107:4243/
Docker API Version	
Credentials	- none - Add ▾
Connection Timeout	0
Read Timeout	0
	Version = 1.13.1, API Version = 1.26 Test Connection
Container Cap	100
Images	Add Docker Template ▾
	List of Images to be launched as slaves

Delete cloud

Figure 6-2. *Configuring the Docker Plugin to talk to Docker server*

Creating a Docker Image for Creating Docker Containers (Jenkins Slave)

Enabling the Docker remote API made the communication between Jenkins and the Docker server possible. Now we need a Docker image on the Docker server. This Docker Image will be used by Jenkins to create Docker containers (Jenkins Slaves) on the fly. To do this, follow the steps below:

1. Log in to your Docker server. Give the following command to check the available Docker images.

   ```
   sudo docker images
   ```

2. From the image below you see I have two docker images (ubuntu & hello-world) already on my Docker server.

```
ubuntu@node4:~$ sudo docker images
REPOSITORY          TAG                 IMAGE ID            CREATED             SIZE
ubuntu              latest              f49eec89601e        3 weeks ago         129 MB
hello-world         latest              48b5124b2768        4 weeks ago         1.84 kB
ubuntu@node4:~$ ▮
```

Figure 6-3. *List the Docker Images*

3. If your Docker server is a freshly backed machine, then you will see no images at this point.

4. We will build a Docker Image for our use from the **ubuntu** Docker Image. To do so, download the Docker Image for **ubuntu** using the following command.

   ```
   docker pull ubuntu
   ```

■ **Note**   You can find more Docker Images for various OS on `https://hub.docker.com/`

---

5. One the pull gets completed, give the **sudo docker images** command again. And now you should see a Docker Image for Ubuntu as shown in **Figure** 6-3.

6. We will now upgrade our **ubuntu** Docker Image with all the necessary application that we need to run our build, which are as follows:

   a. Java JDK (Latest)

   b. Git

   c. Maven

   d. A user account to log in into the Docker Container

   e. sshd (to accept ssh connection)

7. Execute the following command to run a Docker container using the Ubuntu Docker Image. This will create a container, and open up its bash shell.

   ```
   sudo docker run -i -t ubuntu /bin/bash
   ```

8. Now, install all the required application as you would do on any normal Ubuntu machine. Let's begin with creating a user **jenkins**.

    a. Execute the following command and follow the user creation steps, as shown in Figure 6-4.

```
adduser jenkins
```

```
ubuntu@node4:~$ sudo docker run -i -t ubuntu /bin/bash
root@81a5d12f6c4a:/# adduser jenkins
Adding user `jenkins' ...
Adding new group `jenkins' (1000) ...
Adding new user `jenkins' (1000) with group `jenkins' ...
Creating home directory `/home/jenkins' ...
Copying files from `/etc/skel' ...
Enter new UNIX password:
Retype new UNIX password:
passwd: password updated successfully
Changing the user information for jenkins
Enter the new value, or press ENTER for the default
        Full Name []: Nikhil Pathania
        Room Number []: 208
        Work Phone []:
        Home Phone []:
        Other []:
Is the information correct? [Y/n] y
root@81a5d12f6c4a:/# ▉
```

Figure 6-4. *Creating a user*

    b. check the new user using the switch user command:

```
su jenkins
```

9. Switch back to the root user by typing **exit**.

10. Next, we will install the SSH server. Execute the following command in sequence.

```
apt-get update
apt-get install openssh-server
mkdir /var/run/sshd
```

11. Next, we will install Git using the following command:

```
apt-get install git
```

12. Install Java JDK using the following command. (You can skip installing Java JDK if you have already configured Java inside Jenkins. See section **Configure Java, Git, and Maven** from **Chapter 5**.)

```
apt-get install openjdk-8-jdk
```

13. Install Maven using the following command. (You can skip installing Maven if you have already configured Maven inside Jenkins. See section **Configure Java, Git, and Maven** from **Chapter 5**.)

```
apt-get install maven
```

14. Next, exit the container by typing **exit**.

15. We need to save (commit) all the changes that we did to our Docker container.

    a. Get the **CONTAINER ID** of the container that we worked on recently by listing all the inactive containers, as shown in Figure 6-5.

```
sudo docker ps -a
```

```
ubuntu@node4:~$ sudo docker ps -a
CONTAINER ID IMAGE    COMMAND      CREATED            STATUS               PORTS  NAMES
81a5d12f6c4a ubuntu   "/bin/bash"  About an hour ago  Exited (0) 2 minutes ago    mystifying_fermat
ubuntu@node4:~$
```

Figure 6-5. *List inactive containers*

    b. Note the **CONTAINER ID**, and execute the following command to commit the changes that we made to our container.

```
sudo docker commit <CONTAINER ID> <new name for the container>
```

    c. I have named my container as **maven-build-slave-0.1** as shown in Figure 6-6:

```
ubuntu@node4:~$ sudo docker commit 81a5d12f6c4a maven-build-slave-0.1
sha256:317fb6ec990f235fc2f2f42beab6f73e44fb4bd2d0bba0479858386c569a7c7d
ubuntu@node4:~$
```

Figure 6-6. *Docker commit command*

    d. Once you have committed the changes, a new Docker Image gets created.

    e. Execute the following Docker command to list images.

```
sudo docker images
```

    f. You can see, our new Docker Image with the name **maven-build-slave-0.1** (Figure 6-7). We will now configure our Jenkins server to use the following Docker image to create Jenkins Slaves (build agents).

```
ubuntu@node4:~$ sudo docker images
REPOSITORY             TAG       IMAGE ID        CREATED            SIZE
maven-build-slave-0.1  latest    317fb6ec990f    About a minute ago 298 MB
ubuntu                 latest    f49eec89601e    3 weeks ago        129 MB
hello-world            latest    48b5124b2768    4 weeks ago        1.84 kB
ubuntu@node4:~$
```

Figure 6-7. *List the Docker Images*

Adding Credentials Inside Jenkins to Access the Docker Container

Follow the below steps to add credentials inside Jenkins to allow it to talk to Docker.

1. From the Jenkins Dashboard, navigate to **Credentials ➤ System ➤ Global credentials (unrestricted)**.

2. Click on the **Add Credentials** link on the left-hand side menu, to create a new credential (Figure 6-8).

   a. Choose **Kind** as **Username and Password**.

   b. Leave the **Scope field** to its default value.

   c. Add a username for your Docker Image (**jenkins** as per our example) under the **Username** field.

   d. Under **the Password** field add the password.

   e. Add an ID under the **ID** field, and some description under the **Description** field.

   f. Once done click on the **OK** button.

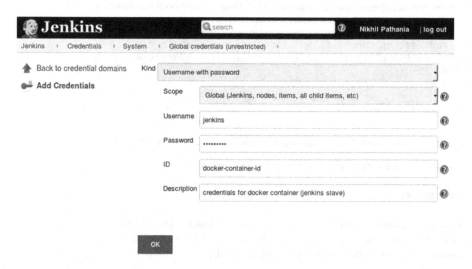

Figure 6-8. *Create credentials inside Jenkins*

Update the Docker Settings Inside Jenkins

Follow the steps below to update the Docker settings.

1. From the Jenkins Dashboard, click on **Manage Jenkins ➤ Configure System**.

2. Scroll all the way down to **Cloud** section (Figure 6-9).

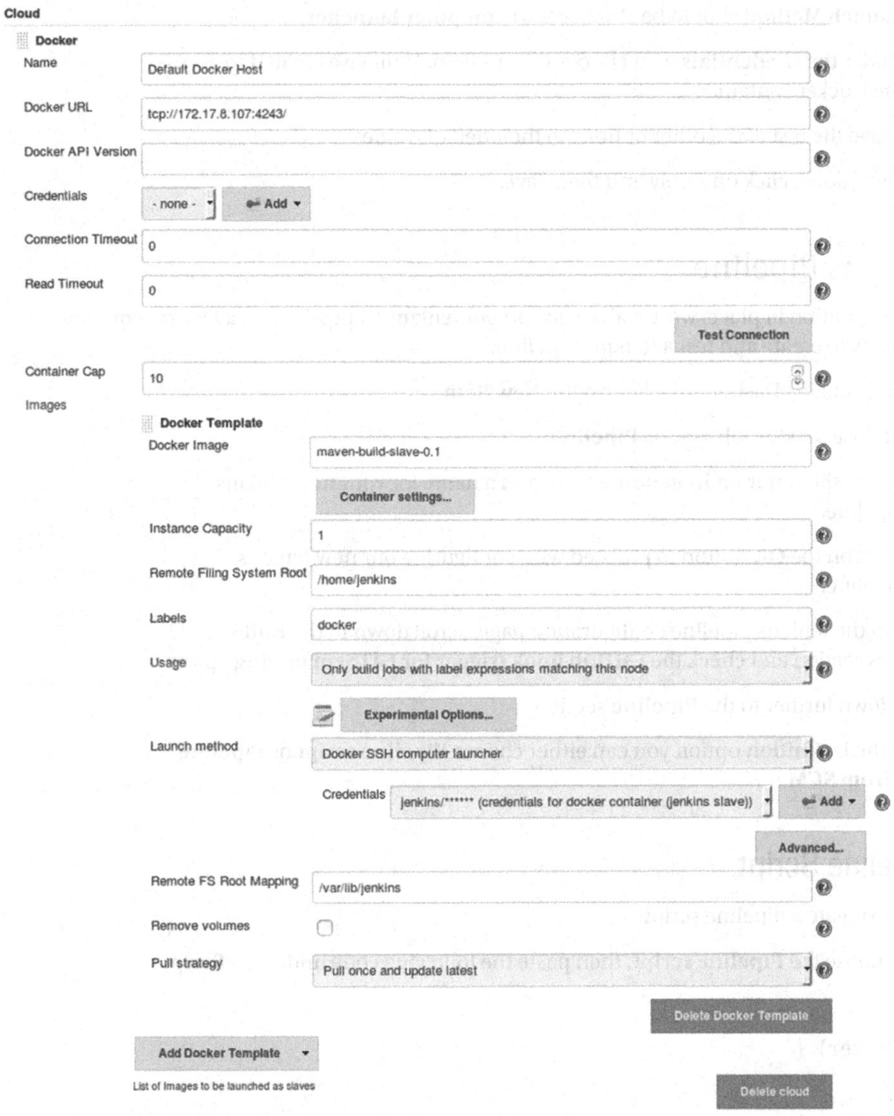

Cloud

Docker

Name	Default Docker Host
Docker URL	tcp://172.17.8.107:4243/
Docker API Version	
Credentials	- none - ▾ ← Add ▾
Connection Timeout	0
Read Timeout	0

Test Connection

Container Cap	10

Images

Docker Template

Docker Image	maven-build-slave-0.1

Container settings...

Instance Capacity	1
Remote Filing System Root	/home/jenkins
Labels	docker
Usage	Only build jobs with label expressions matching this node ▾

Experimental Options...

Launch method	Docker SSH computer launcher ▾
Credentials	jenkins/****** (credentials for docker container (jenkins slave)) ▾ ← Add ▾

Advanced...

Remote FS Root Mapping	/var/lib/jenkins
Remove volumes	☐
Pull strategy	Pull once and update latest ▾

Delete Docker Template

Add Docker Template ▾

List of images to be launched as slaves

Delete cloud

Figure 6-9. *Configuring the Docker Plugin settings*

3. Under the Cloud section, click on the **Add Docker Template** button and choose **Docker Template**.

   a. You will be presented with a lot of settings to configure. However, to keep this demonstration simple, let us stick to the important settings.

   b. Under the **Docker Image** field enter the name of the Docker Image that we created earlier. In my case it is **maven-build-slave-0.1**.

   c. Under the **Labels** field add a label. The Docker container will be recognized using this label by your Jenkins pipeline. I have added a label **docker**.

    d.   **Launch Method** should be **Docker SSH computer launcher**.

    e.   Under the **Credentials** field choose the credentials that we created to access the Docker container.

    f.   Leave the rest of the other options to their default values.

    g.   Once done, click on Apply and then Save.

Create a Jenkins Pipeline

With the entire configuration in place, we are all set to run our Jenkins CI pipeline on a Docker container. Follow the steps below to create and test a Jenkins pipeline:

1.   From the Jenkins Dashboard, click on the **New Item**.

    a.   Choose Jenkins Job type as **Pipeline**.

    b.   Under the **Enter an item name** field, add a name for your new Jenkins pipeline.

    c.   Click on the **OK** button to proceed with configuring our new Jenkins pipeline.

2.   Once on the Jenkins pipeline configuration page, scroll down to the **Build Triggers** section and check the **GitHub hook trigger for GITScm polling** option.

3.   Scroll down further to the **Pipeline** section.

4.   Under the **Definition** option you can either choose **Pipeline script** or **Pipeline script from SCM**.

Using the Pipeline Script

Follow these steps to create a pipeline script.

1.   If you choose the **Pipeline script**, then paste the following code under the **Script** field.

```
node(docker) {

stage('scm') {
    checkout([$class: 'GitSCM', branches: [[name: '*/master']],
doGenerateSubmoduleConfigurations: false, extensions: [], submoduleCfg:
[], userRemoteConfigs: [[credentialsId: 'github-jenkins-ssh-key', url:
'git@github.com:pro-continuous-delivery/hello-world-example.git']]])
}
stage('build') {
    withMaven(jdk: 'Default Java', maven: 'Default Maven') {
    sh 'mvn clean install'
}
}
}
```

■ **Note** The above code is the same that we used in **Chapter 5,** under the section **The Pipeline Syntax Option in Jenkins.** The only difference is in the node name. In the former code it was **master**, and here it's **docker**.

In the above code, change the value of the **credentialsId**: and **url** accordingly.

2. Go straight to **Triggering a Build** section.

Using the Pipeline Script from SCM

If you choose **Pipeline script from SCM** (Figure 6-10), Then do the following,

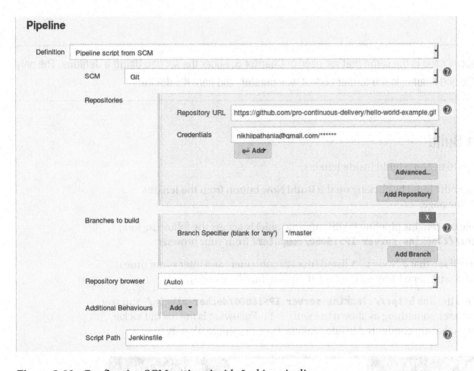

Figure 6-10. Configuring SCM settings inside Jenkins pipeline

1. Choose **Git** as an option for the **SCM** field.

   a. Under the **Repository URL** add your GitHub repo URL.

   b. Under the **Credentials** field choose the credentials for GitHub (it can be the GitHub username and password or SSH key pair to access GitHub account, stored inside Jenkins as credentials).

   c. Click on the **Save** button to save the configuration.

2.   From the Jenkins Dashboard, click on **Manage Jenkins ➤ Configure System**.

3.   Scroll all the way to **GitHub** section and click on the **Re-register hooks for all jobs** button. This will create all the necessary webhooks on GitHub for our new Jenkins pipelines.

4.   Make sure to change the code inside the **Jenkinsfile** present inside the GitHub repository. Replace it with the following:

```
node(docker) {
checkout scm
stage('build') {
    withMaven(jdk: 'Default Java', maven: 'Default Maven') {
    sh 'mvn clean install'
}
}
}
```

■ **Note**   The above code is the same that we used in **Chapter 5,** under the section **Using a Jenkins**. The only difference is in the node name. In the former code it was **master**, and here it's **docker**.

Triggering a Build

Follow these steps to trigger a build inside Jenkins.

1.   Trigger the build by clicking on the **Build Now** button from the Jenkins pipeline page.

2.   While the Jenkins pipeline is still running, quickly access the following link: **http://<Jenkins server IP>:8080/computer/** from your browser.

3.   You will see that a Node gets listed (docker container) and after some time it disappears (depending on the time it takes to build the code).

4.   Access the link **http://<Jenkins server IP>:8080/docker-plugin/**, and you should see something as shown in Figure 6-11. Following is the list of Docker servers that are configured inside Jenkins; in our example it's only one.

Figure 6-11. List of Docker Servers

a.   Click on the available Docker server that we have.

b.   On the resultant page, you will see the details of all the running Docker containers and Docker Images, as shown in Figure 6-12.

Clone the coreos-kubernetes Repository

Follow the below steps to clone the coreos-kubernetes repository.

1. Execute the following command to clone the **coreos-kubernetes** repository from GitHub.

   ```
   git clone https://github.com/coreos/coreos-kubernetes.git
   ```

2. Go to the following directory and list the files inside it, as shown in Figure 6-14.

   ```
   cd coreos-kubernetes/multi-node/vagrant
   ls -lrt
   ```

```
nikhil@dev01:~/coreos-kubernetes/multi-node/vagrant$ ls -lrt
total 49208
-rw-rw-r-- 1 nikhil nikhil      286 Feb 20 20:30 README.md
-rw-rw-r-- 1 nikhil nikhil      404 Feb 20 20:30 etcd-cloud-config.yaml
-rwxrwxr-x 1 nikhil nikhil      297 Feb 20 20:30 conformance-test.sh
-rwxrwxr-x 1 nikhil nikhil 50358448 Feb 20 20:30 kubectl
-rw-rw-r-- 1 nikhil nikhil     6904 Feb 20 23:46 Vagrantfile
-rw-rw-r-- 1 nikhil nikhil      430 Feb 21 00:12 kubeconfig
-rw-rw-r-- 1 nikhil nikhil      147 Feb 21 01:11 config.rb.sample
nikhil@dev01:~/coreos-kubernetes/multi-node/vagrant$ █
```

Figure 6-14. *List of files and utilities*

   a. The Vagrantfile containers instruction for creating a Kubernetes cluster using VirtualBox.

   b. By default the Vagrantfile will create a Kubernetes cluster containing one master node, one worker node, and one etcd node. However, you may choose to create a Kubernetes cluster with your own specifications. To do that we need the config.rb.sample file (rename **config.rb.sample** to **config.rb** before using it).

Starting the Kubernetes Cluster

We will modify the **config.rb.sample** a bit to create 1 master node, 2 worker nodes, and 1 etcd node.

1. Rename the **config.rb.sample** file to **config.rb** file using the mv command:

   ```
   mv config.rb.sample config.rb
   ```

2. Open the file **config.rb** for editing, using either nano or vi editor:

   ```
   nano config.rb
   ```

3. Modify the content of your **config.rb** to look exactly as shown below. As you can see, I have chosen to create two worker nodes.

   ```
   $update_channel="alpha"
   ```

```
$controller_count=1
$controller_vm_memory=1024

$worker_count=2
$worker_vm_memory=2048

$etcd_count=1
$etcd_vm_memory=512
```

4. Run the following vagrant command to start the Kubernetes cluster. It will take a while for Vagrant to provision the machines, depending on your network speed.

    ```
    vagrant up
    ```

5. Once the vagrant has provisioned all the cluster nodes, list the status of the Kubernetes cluster nodes (this is the state of the vagrant nodes, and note the Kubernetes cluster). See Figure 6-15.

    ```
    vagrant status
    ```

```
nikhil@dev01:~/coreos-kubernetes/multi-node/vagrant$ vagrant status
Current machine states:

e1                      running (virtualbox)
c1                      running (virtualbox)
w1                      running (virtualbox)
w2                      running (virtualbox)

This environment represents multiple VMs. The VMs are all listed
above with their current state. For more information about a specific
VM, run `vagrant status NAME`.
nikhil@dev01:~/coreos-kubernetes/multi-node/vagrant$ █
```

Figure 6-15. List of vagrant virtual machines

a. We can see Vagrant has created four virtual machines (e1, c1, w1, and w2).

b. e1 is the etcd node, c1 is the Kubernetes manager node, and w1 and w2 are worker nodes.

6. Open the file **kubeconfig** using your favorite editor. You will find the following three sections, as shown in Figure 6-16.

    clusters
    context
    users

```
apiVersion: v1█
kind: Config
clusters:
- cluster:
    certificate-authority: ssl/ca.pem
    server: https://172.17.4.101:443
  name: vagrant-multi-cluster
contexts:
- context:
    cluster: vagrant-multi-cluster
    namespace: default
    user: vagrant-multi-admin
  name: vagrant-multi
users:
- name: vagrant-multi-admin
  user:
    client-certificate: ssl/admin.pem
    client-key: ssl/admin-key.pem
current-context: vagrant-multi
```

Figure 6-16. *kubeconfig file*

    a.   clusters

```
clusters:
- cluster:
    certificate-authority: ssl/ca.pem
    server: https://172.17.4.101:443
  name: vagrant-multi-cluster
```

The **clusters:** section contains fully qualified URLs (`https://172.17.4.101:443`) of the Kubernetes cluster, as well as the cluster's certificate authority. A cluster has a name (vagrant-multi-cluster), which is used internally within the cluster.

    b.   contexts

```
contexts:
- context:
    cluster: vagrant-multi-cluster
    namespace: default
    user: vagrant-multi-admin
  name: vagrant-multi
```

The **context:** section defines a named cluster, user, and namespace that are used to send requests to the specified cluster using the provided authentication info and namespace. Each of the three is optional; it is valid to specify a context with only one of cluster, user, namespace, or to specify none. Unspecified values, or named values that don't have corresponding entries in the loaded kubeconfig (e.g., if the context specified a pink-user for the above kubeconfig file), will be replaced with the default.

    c.   current-context:

```
current-context: federal-context
```

The **current-context:** section is the nickname or 'key' for the cluster,user,namespace tuple that kubectl will use by default when loading config from this file.

    d.   users:

```
users:
- name: vagrant-multi-admin
  user:
    client-certificate: ssl/admin.pem
    client-key: ssl/admin-key.pem
current-context: vagrant-multi
```

The **users:** section defines client credentials for authenticating to a Kubernetes cluster. A user has a name (nickname) that acts as its key within the list of user entries after kubeconfig is loaded/merged. Available credentials are client-certificate, client-key, token, and username/password.

7.   To load the cluster configuration from the kubeconfig file, execute the following command:

```
export KUBECONFIG="${KUBECONFIG}:$(pwd)/kubeconfig"
kubectl config use-context vagrant-multi
```

8.   You will get a response:

```
Switched to context "vagrant-multi."
```

9.   Give the following command to check the status of the cluster. The Kubernetes application will download all the necessary applications on the cluster nodes; therefore it may take a while for it to get ready. See the response as shown in Figure 6-17.

```
kubectl get nodes
```

```
nikhil@dev01:~/coreos-kubernetes/multi-node/vagrant$ kubectl get nodes
The connection to the server 172.17.4.101:443 was refused - did you specify the
right host or port?
nikhil@dev01:~/coreos-kubernetes/multi-node/vagrant$ ▮
```

Figure 6-17. *Kubernetes cluster coming up*

10.   After a while, you should see the following screen, as shown in Figure 6-18.

```
nikhil@dev01:~/coreos-kubernetes/multi-node/vagrant$ kubectl get nodes
NAME            STATUS                   AGE
172.17.4.101    Ready,SchedulingDisabled 10m
172.17.4.201    Ready                    10m
172.17.4.202    Ready                    10m
nikhil@dev01:~/coreos-kubernetes/multi-node/vagrant$ ▮
```

Figure 6-18. *Kubernetes cluster up and running*

    a.   From the above figure we can see the status of our master as well as two worker nodes.

    b.   **172.17.4.101** is the master node with a **STATUS: Ready, SechedulingDisabled**. This means, the master node is reserved only to provision and manage containers on the worker nodes. There won't be any container running on the master node.

11. To check the configuration that our Kubernetes cluster is running, execute the following command. This will display the current kubeconfig settings, as shown in Figure 6-19.

```
kubectl config view
```

```
nikhil@dev01:~/coreos-kubernetes/multi-node/vagrant$ kubectl config view
apiVersion: v1
clusters:
- cluster:
    certificate-authority: ssl/ca.pem
    server: https://172.17.4.101:443
  name: vagrant-multi-cluster
contexts:
- context:
    cluster: vagrant-multi-cluster
    namespace: default
    user: vagrant-multi-admin
  name: vagrant-multi
current-context: vagrant-multi
kind: Config
preferences: {}
users:
- name: vagrant-multi-admin
  user:
    client-certificate: ssl/admin.pem
    client-key: ssl/admin-key.pem
nikhil@dev01:~/coreos-kubernetes/multi-node/vagrant$ 
```

Figure 6-19. *Configuration in use*

12. We can also fetch the key cluster information using the cluster-info command:

```
kubectl cluster-info
```

13. From the output (Figure 6-20) we can note the Kubernetes dashboard link. However we won't be able to access the link from our client machine.

```
nikhil@dev01:~/coreos-kubernetes/multi-node/vagrant$ kubectl cluster-info
Kubernetes master is running at https://172.17.4.101:443
Heapster is running at https://172.17.4.101:443/api/v1/proxy/namespaces/kube-system/services/heapster
KubeDNS is running at https://172.17.4.101:443/api/v1/proxy/namespaces/kube-system/services/kube-dns
kubernetes-dashboard is running at https://172.17.4.101:443/api/v1/proxy/namespaces/kube-system/services/
kubernetes-dashboard
To further debug and diagnose cluster problems, use 'kubectl cluster-info dump'.
nikhil@dev01:~/coreos-kubernetes/multi-node/vagrant$ 
```

Figure 6-20. *kubectl cluster-info*

The Kubernetes Dashboard

The Kubernetes dashboard is a webpage where we can get information about the whole cluster. For example: Information about the running Pods, Services, Worker nodes, System metrics, etc.

1. To make the dashboard available on the client machine, execute the following command. This will make the Kubernetes dashboard available on localhost port 9090. See Figure 6-21.

```
Kubectl proxy --port=9090
```

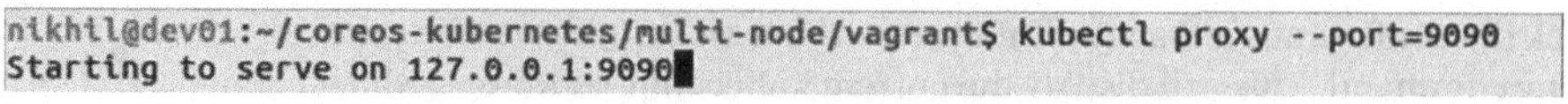

```
nikhil@dev01:~/coreos-kubernetes/multi-node/vagrant$ kubectl proxy --port=9090
Starting to serve on 127.0.0.1:9090█
```

Figure 6-21. *kubectl proxy command*

2. To access the dashboard, enter the following link in your browser.

    **http://localhost:9090/api/v1/proxy/namespaces/kube-system/services/
    kube-dns**

3. The Kubernetes dashboard looks as shown in Figure 6-22.

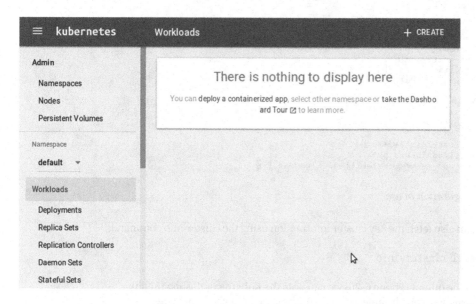

Figure 6-22. *Kubernetes dashboard*

4. From the left-hand side menu, click on the **Namespaces**. You can see the following
    two namespaces: **default** and **kube-system**. As shown in Figure 6-23, all of the
    Kubernetes cluster-related pods run under the **kube-system** namespace. All the
    Jenkins Slave pods that we are going to create will be running under the **default**
    namespaces. You can click on any of the namespaces to see more details about it.

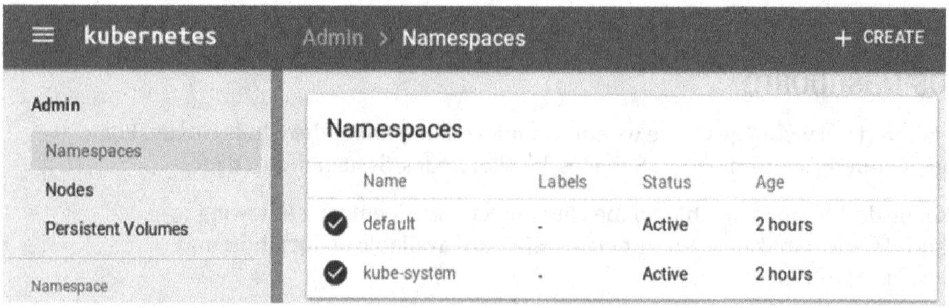

Figure 6-23. *List of namespaces*

5. From the left-hand side menu, click on **Nodes** (Figure 6-24). You can see all the three nodes (1 master and 2 worker nodes). Click on any one of them to see more details about the respective node.

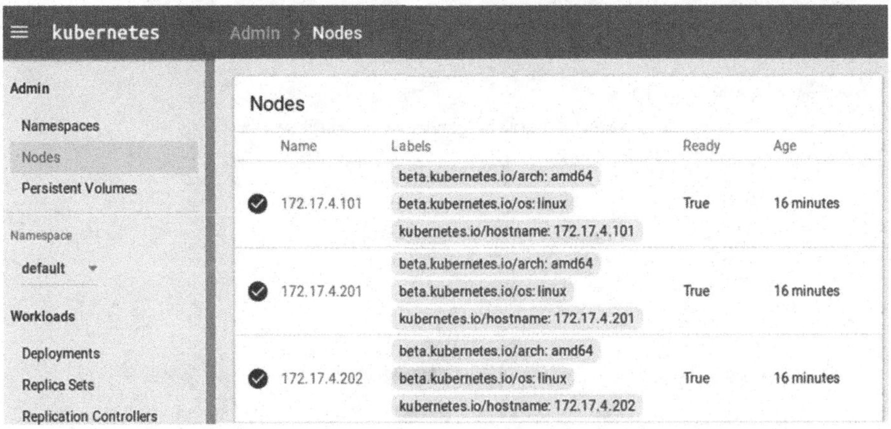

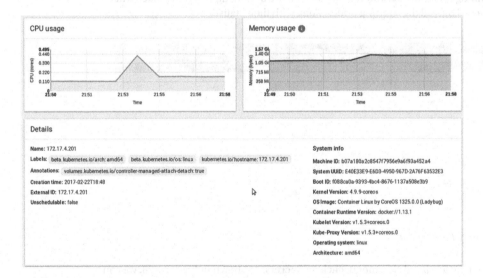

Figure 6-24. *List of nodes*

6. I have clicked on worker node1 (172.17.4.201). As shown in Figure 6-25, we can see the CPU usage and the Memory usage, along with a few details about the respective node.

Figure 6-25. *Node metrics - CPU and Memory usage*

7. Scrolling further down, you can see hardware resource allocated to the node. There is also a section regarding the condition of memory, disk, etc., as shown in Figure 6-26:

Allocated resources							
CPU requests (cores)	%	CPU limits (cores)	%	Memory requests (bytes)	%		Memory limits (bytes)
0.12 / 1	12.00	0.1 / 1	10.00	60 Mi / 1.934 Gi	3.03		50 Mi / 1.934 Gi

Conditions						
Type	Status	Last heartbeat time	Last transition time	Reason	Message	
OutOfDisk	False	-	7 minutes	KubeletHasSufficientDisk	kubelet has sufficient disk space available	
MemoryPressure	False	-	2 hours	KubeletHasSufficientMemory	kubelet has sufficient memory available	
DiskPressure	False	-	2 hours	KubeletHasNoDiskPressure	kubelet has no disk pressure	
Ready	True	-	7 minutes	KubeletReady	kubelet is posting ready status	

Pods								
Name	Status	Restarts	Age	CPU (cores)		Memory (bytes)		
✅ kube-dns-autoscaler-2715466192-vkcnd	Running	1	2 hours		0		21.430 Mi	⦂
✅ kube-proxy-172.17.4.201	Running	1	2 hours		0.114		83.160 Mi	⦂
✅ kubernetes-dashboard-3543765157-2w2wl	Running	2	2 hours		0		17.055 Mi	⦂

Figure 6-26. *Node metrics - Resources, Conditions, and Pods*

8. From the left-hand side menu, click on **Pods**. As you can see we have no nodes running under the **default** namespace (Figure 6-27). But, this is the place where you will find all the running nodes along with their statistics.

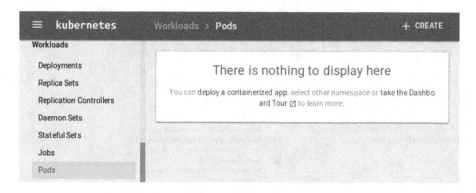

Figure 6-27. *Empty Pods section*

9. From the left-hand side menu, click on **Secrets**. As shown in Figure 6-28, we can see a default secret token. We will need this later to establish communication between Jenkins and the Kubernetes cluster. Click on the token.

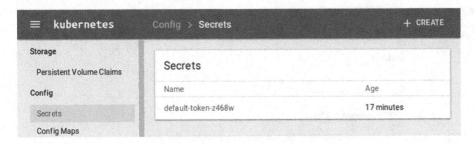

Figure 6-28. *Default Token*

10. On the resultant page you will find some details about the secret token, as shown in Figure 6-29.

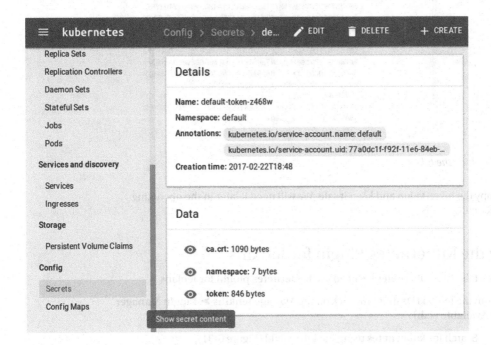

Figure 6-29. *Default Token - details*

11. Under the **Data** section, click on the **token (eye logo)** to un-hide the token value. The token value will be displayed as shown in Figure 6-30.

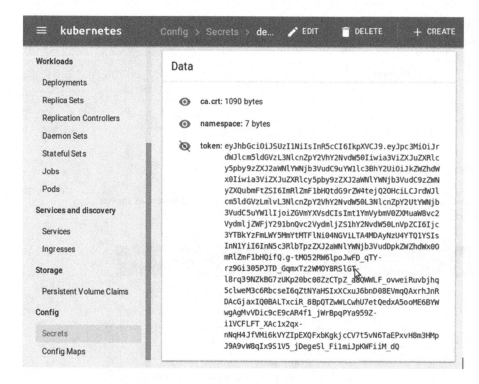

Figure 6-30. *Un-hide the token*

12. Copy the token value and keep it safe. We will need it later in the upcoming section.

Installing the Kubernetes Plugin for Jenkins

To make Jenkins talk with Kubernetes we need the **Kubernetes plugin** for Jenkins.

1. From the Jenkins Dashboard, click on the **Manage Jenkins ➤ Plugin Manager ➤ Available (tab)**.

   a. Search for **kubernetes** using the **Filter** field (Figure 6-31).

   b. Once listed, choose the **kubernetes plugin** and click on **Install without Restart** button.

   c. After the installation, restart Jenkins if needed.

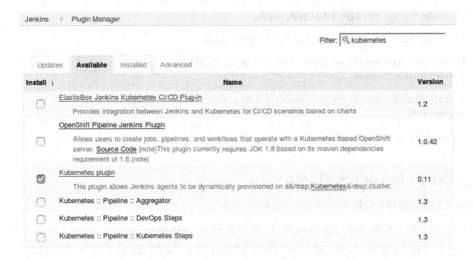

Figure 6-31. *Kubernetes Plugin*

Creating Credentials for Kubernetes Cluster

We need to add credentials for the Kubernetes cluster inside Jenkins to authenticate the connection between Jenkins and Kubernetes.

1. From the Jenkins dashboard, click on **Credentials ➤ System ➤ Global credentials (unrestricted)** (Figure 6-32).

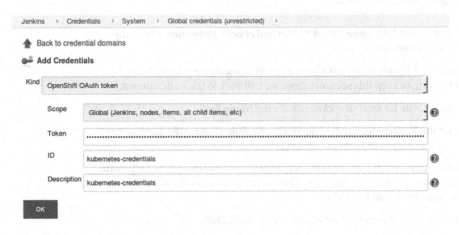

Figure 6-32. *Kubernetes credentials inside Jenkins*

2. On the resultant page, click on **Add Credentials**.

    a. Under the **Kind** field choose **OpenShift OAuth token**.

    b. Under the Token field paste the token key that we copied earlier from the Kubernetes dashboard.

    c. Add an ID and some description under the **ID** and **Description** field respectively.

    d. Click on **OK** Button once done.

Configuring the Kubernetes Plugin

Let us now configure the Kubernetes cluster settings inside Jenkins.

1. From the Jenkins Dashboard, click **Manage Jenkins ➤ Configure System**.

2. Once on the **Configure System** page, scroll down all the way to the **Cloud** section (Figure 6-33).

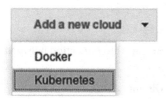

Figure 6-33. *Adding the Kubernetes cloud*

    a. Click on the **Add a new cloud** button and choose **Kubernetes** from the available options.

    b. You will be presented with a lot of options to configure (Figure 6-34). However, to keep this section simple we will stick to the basic options.

    c. Add a name for your new cloud under the **Name** field.

    d. Add the Kubernetes cluster URL under the **Kubernetes URL** field. In our case it's `https://172.17.4.101:443/`.

    e. Make sure to check the **Disable https certificate check** option. Otherwise you need to put the Kubernetes server certificate under the **Kubernetes server certificate key** field.

    f. Under the **Kubernetes Namespace** field add **default**.

    g. Choose the appropriate credentials under the **Credentials** field from the drop-down menu.

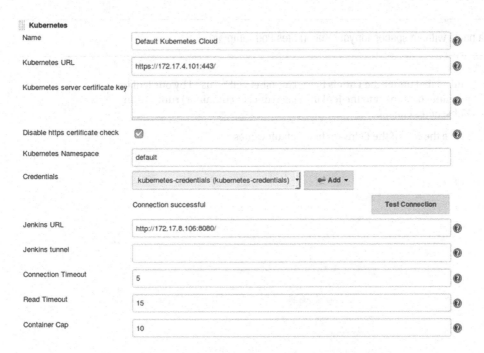

Figure 6-34. *Configuring basic Kubernetes settings*

3. Make sure to add an appropriate value under the **Container Cleanup Timeout** field. I choose to add a value of 30 min (Figure 6-35). The **Container Cleanup Timeout** defines how long to keep a Kubernetes container listed inside Jenkins.

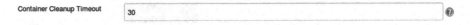

Figure 6-35. *Container Cleanup Timeout*

4. Under the **Images** section, click on the **Add Pod Template** button and choose **Kubernetes** Pod Template, as shown in Figure 6-36.

Figure 6-36. *Adding a Kubernetes Pod Template*

5. You will be presented will a lot more options (Figure 6-37).

   a. Add a name for your Kubernetes Pod Template using the **Name** field.

■ **Note** Add a name without spaces for your Kubernetes Pod Template.

---

b. Add a label under the **Labels** field. This label will be used by our Jenkins pipeline to connect to the Jenkins Slave (docker container) running on Kubernetes cluster.

c. Leave the rest of the fields to their default values.

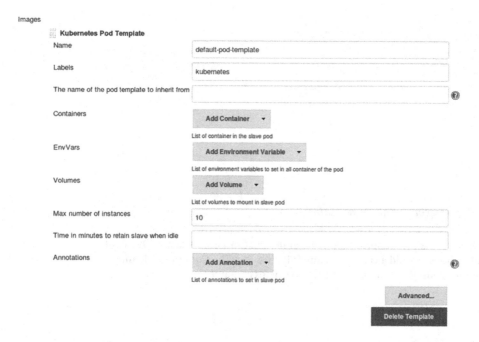

Figure 6-37. *Configuring the Pod Template*

d. Under the **Containers** field click on the **Add Container** button and choose **Container Template** (Figure 6-38).

Figure 6-38. *Adding a Container Template*

e. You will again be presented with a lot more options to configure your Docker image. See Figure 6-39.

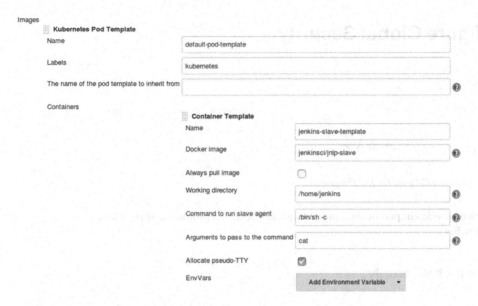

Figure 6-39. *Configuring the Container Template*

    f.   Add a name for your Container Template using the **Name** field.

■ **Note**   Add a name without spaces for your Container Template.

---

    g.   Add **jenkinsci/jnlp-slave** under the **Docker Image** field. This is a Docker Image for Jenkins available on Docker Hub.

    h.   Leave the rest of the fields to their default values.

    6.   Click on the **Apply** and **Save** button at the end of the page.

Configure Global Security

Follow these steps to make modifications to the TCP port settings inside Jenkins. These settings are important to allow Jenkins to spawn containers on the Kubernetes cluster.

    1.   From the Jenkins dashboard, click on **Manage Jenkins ➤ Configure global security**.

    2.   On the Configure Global Security page (Figure 6-40), make sure that the TCP port for JNLP agents is set to **Random**.

Configure Global Security

☑ Enable security ②

TCP port for JNLP agents ○ Fixed : [⌃⌄] ⦿ Random ○ Disable ②

[Agent protocols...]

Figure 6-40. *Configure TCP port for JNLP agents*

3.   Click on the **Agent protocols...** button and choose all the protocols. As shown in Figure 6-41.

Configure Global Security

☑ Enable security ②

TCP port for JNLP agents ○ Fixed : [⌃⌄] ⦿ Random ○ Disable ②

Agent protocols

☑ Jenkins CLI Protocol/1
Accepts connections from CLI clients

☑ Jenkins CLI Protocol/2
Extends the version 1 protocol by adding transport encryption

☑ Java Web Start Agent Protocol/1
Accepts connections from remote clients so that they can be used as additional build agents

☑ Java Web Start Agent Protocol/2
Extends the version 1 protocol by adding a per-client cookie, so that we can detect a reconnection from the agent and take appropriate action

☑ Java Web Start Agent Protocol/3
Extends the version 2 protocol by adding basic encryption but requires a thread per client

☑ Java Web Start Agent Protocol/4
A TLS secured connection between the master and the agent performed by TLS upgrade of the socket.

Figure 6-41. *Configuring Agent protocols*

Creating a Jenkins Pipeline

With the entire configuration in place, we are all set to run our Jenkins CI pipeline on a Kubernetes cluster. Follow the steps below to create and test a Jenkins pipeline:

1.   From the Jenkins Dashboard, click on the **New Item**.

    a.   Choose Jenkins Job type as **Pipeline** (Figure 6-42).

    b.   Under the **Enter an item name** field, add a name for your new Jenkins pipeline.

    c.   Click on the **OK** button to proceed to configure our new Jenkins pipeline.

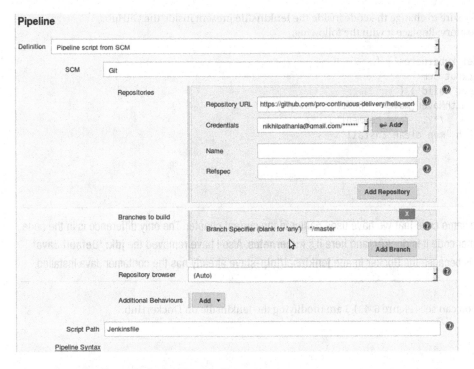

Figure 6-42. *Configuring the Jenkins Pipeline*

2. Once on the Jenkins pipeline configuration page, scroll down to the **Build Triggers** section and check the **GitHub hook trigger for GITScm polling** option.

3. Scroll down further to the **Pipeline** section.

4. Under the **Definition** option you can choose **Pipeline script from SCM**.

   a. Choose **Git** as an option for the **SCM** field.

   b. Under the **Repository URL** add your GitHub repo URL.

   c. Under the **Credentials** field choose the credentials for GitHub (it can be the GitHub username and password or SSH key pair to access GitHub account, stored inside Jenkins as credentials).

   d. Click on the **Save** button to save the configuration.

5. From the Jenkins Dashboard, click on **Manage Jenkins ➤ Configure System**.

6. Scroll all the way to **GitHub** section and click on the **Re-register hooks for all jobs** button. This will create all the necessary webhooks on GitHub for our new Jenkins pipelines.

7. Make sure to change the code inside the **Jenkinsfile** present inside the GitHub repository. Replace it with the following:

```
node('kubernetes') {
checkout scm
stage('build') {
    withMaven(maven: 'Default Maven') {
        /* .. some comment .. */
        sh 'mvn clean install'
    }
  }
}
```

■ **Note**   It's the same code that we have used earlier in the current chapter. The only difference is in the node name. In the former code it is **docker**, and here it's **kubernetes**. Also I have removed the **jdk: 'Default Java'** from line 4. This is because the Docker Image **jenkinsci/jnlp-slave** already has the container Java installed.

---

8. As you can see (Figure 6-43), I am modifying the Jenkinsfile on DockerHub.

Figure 6-43.   *Modifying the Jenkinsfile*

9. And I commit the change by adding a comment. See Figure 6-44.

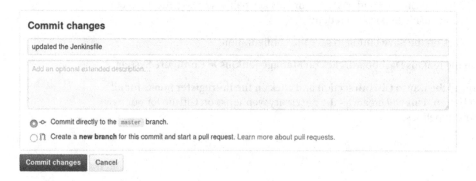

Figure 6-44.   *Commit changes*

Running the Jenkins Pipeline

The moment you commit the changes, Jenkins pipeline gets triggered. As shown in Figure 6-45, it takes a while for Jenkins to create and configure the Jenkins Slave on Kubernetes (using the Docker Image jenkinsci/jnlp-slave).

Figure 6-45. *Jenkins Pipeline in action*

Quickly move to the Kubernetes Dashboard and check the Pods section. In a while you should see a pod getting created, as shown in Figure 6-46.

Figure 6-46. *Pod for Jenkins Slave being created.*

Once the Pod is completely ready the status will change to **Running,** as shown in Figure 6-47.

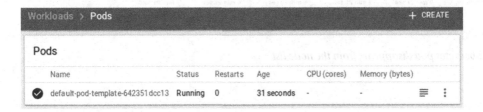

Figure 6-47. *Pod for Jenkins Slave in running state*

Come back to your Jenkins dashboard and go to **Manage Jenkins ➤ Manage Nodes**. You should see the Kubernetes pod listed as a Jenkins Slave (Figure 6-48).

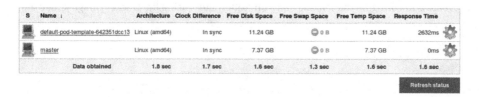

S	Name ↓	Architecture	Clock Difference	Free Disk Space	Free Swap Space	Free Temp Space	Response Time	
🖥	default-pod-template-642351dcc13	Linux (amd64)	In sync	11.24 GB	⊝ 0 B	11.24 GB	2632ms	⚙
🖥	master	Linux (amd64)	In sync	7.37 GB	⊝ 0 B	7.37 GB	0ms	⚙
	Data obtained		1.8 sec	1.7 sec	1.6 sec	1.3 sec	1.6 sec	1.6 sec

Refresh status

Figure 6-48. *Kubernetes pod listed inside Jenkins*

Check your Jenkins pipeline. It should have been completed successfully by now. In the Console Output of your Jenkins pipeline you should see the Kubernetes pod name on which the build ran, as shown in Figure 6-49.

⬤ Console Output

```
Started by user Nikhil Pathania
 > git rev-parse --is-inside-work-tree # timeout=10
Fetching changes from the remote Git repository
 > git config remote.origin.url https://github.com/pro-continuous-delivery/hello-world-example.git # timeout=10
Fetching upstream changes from https://github.com/pro-continuous-delivery/hello-world-example.git
 > git --version # timeout=10
using GIT_ASKPASS to set credentials
 > git fetch --tags --progress https://github.com/pro-continuous-delivery/hello-world-example.git +refs/heads/*
   :refs/remotes/origin/*
 > git rev-parse refs/remotes/origin/master^{commit} # timeout=10
 > git rev-parse refs/remotes/origin/origin/master^{commit} # timeout=10
Checking out Revision 177c71c873cc72e243936b773ff834718b862bcb (refs/remotes/origin/master)
 > git config core.sparsecheckout # timeout=10
 > git checkout -f 177c71c873cc72e243936b773ff834718b862bcb
First time build. Skipping changelog.
[Pipeline] node
Still waiting to schedule task
Waiting for next available executor
Running on default-pod-template-642351dcc13 in /home/jenkins/workspace/pipeline to build inside kubernetes
[Pipeline] {
[Pipeline] checkout
```

Figure 6-49. *Jenkins Logs stating Kubernetes pod*

Soon after the Jenkins pipeline gets completed, the Kubernetes Jenkins Slave disappears from the list of available nodes (Figure 6-50).

S	Name ↓	Architecture	Clock Difference	Free Disk Space	Free Swap Space	Free Temp Space	Response Time	
🖥	master	Linux (amd64)	In sync	7.37 GB	⊝ 0 B	7.37 GB	0ms	⚙
	Data obtained	6 min 21 sec	6 min 21 sec	6 min 21 sec	6 min 20 sec	6 min 21 sec	6 min 21 sec	

Refresh status

Figure 6-50. *Kubernetes pod disappears from the node list*

Summary

In the current chapter we learned to use Docker as well as Kubernetes along with Jenkins to run builds on dynamically provisioned build agents (Docker container).

In the next chapter we will learn about Pre-tested commits using Jenkins and GitHub.

CHAPTER 7

■ ■ ■

Pre-tested Commits Using Jenkins

In the current chapter we will learn about pre-tested commits and the means to achieve them using Jenkins. We will do this by leveraging the **Distributed nature** of Git and **Merge before build** feature of Jenkins.

Pre-tested Commits

Continuous Integration requires developers to publish each and every change (commit) to the Integration/Master branch. All these changes (on the Integration/Master branch) are built, tested, and analyzed for quality, and only after this we know if a change is good or bad. Pre-tested commits (Gated Check-in), on the other hand, ensures that not all, but only those changes that are good, should be allowed on the Integration/Master branch. Pre-tested commits (Gated check-in) ensure that only good changes are published to the Integration/Master branch by performing a check (build, test, analyze) on them.

Both Continuous Integration (CI) and Pre-tested commits (Gated Check-in) have their own advantages. Pre-tested commits are good if you have a large number of developers with average development skills, as it prevents bad code getting into the Integration/Master branch. But, at the same time it also increases the time it takes for a change to be made available to everyone.

CI makes sure that each and every change is made available to everyone as soon as possible. It is also suitable in cases where the build time is less (less than an hour). If a build, test, and analyze cycle takes more than an hour, Gated Check-in is more suitable.

Tools such as Microsoft TFS have a feature to perform Gated Check-in. However, in the current chapter we will learn to leverage the **Distributed nature** of Git and **Merge before build** feature of Jenkins to achieve Pre-tested commits (Gated Check-in).

Pre-tested Commits Using Jenkins and Git

Let us understand how Gated Check-in works. We will start by making the following assumptions:

- We will assume a role of a developer.

- The version control system in use is Git or GitHub.

- On the version control system we have Integration/Master branch and a Feature-1 branch.

- We are using Jenkins as our CI server, which will also perform pre-tested commits.

- Only Jenkins is allowed to push changes on the Integration/Master branch (remote repository).

© Nikhil Pathania 2017
N. Pathania, *Pro Continuous Delivery*, DOI 10.1007/978-1-4842-2913-2_7

Stage 1: Developer Clones the Remote Repository

In stage 1, the developer clones the GitHub repository on his local machine, as shown in Figure 7-1.

Figure 7-1. Stage 1

Stage 2: Developer Works on His Local Copy of the Code

In stage 2 the developer does the following steps (Figure 7-2).

- a. Developer makes some changes on the Feature-1 (local repository) branch and commits the change.

- b. Developer then performs a build and unit test on his local machine.

- c. If the build passes, developer pushes his changes to the Feature-1 branch on the remote repository.

- d. Meanwhile, the master branch (remote repository) has also changed.

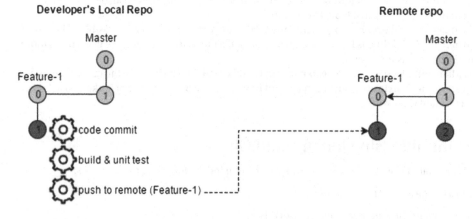

Figure 7-2. Stage 2

Stage 3: Jenkins Performs a Pre-test on the Code

The following steps take place in stage 3 (Figure 7-3).

- a. As soon as Jenkins identifies a change on Feature-1 branch (remote repository), the pipeline to pre-test commit is initiated.

b. First, Jenkins clones the remote repository.

c. Next, Jenkins performs a merge from Feature-1 branch (local repository) to the Master branch (local repository).

d. If the merge is successful, Jenkins performs a build on the Master branch (local repository).

e. If the build and unit test are successful, Jenkins pushes the code to the Master branch on the remote repository.

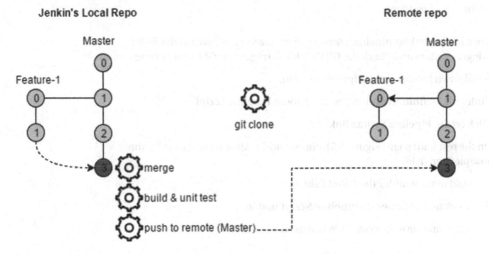

Figure 7-3. *Stage 3*

Creating a Jenkins Pipeline to Perform Pre-tested Commits

Now let us create a Jenkins pipeline to achieve the scenario discussed in the previous section.

1. From the Jenkins Dashboard, click on the **New Item.**

    a. Choose Jenkins Job type as **Pipeline** (Figure 7-4).

    b. Under the **Enter an item name** field, add a name for your new Jenkins pipeline.

    c. Click on the **OK** button to proceed with configuring our new Jenkins pipeline.

Figure 7-4. Jenkins pipeline script

2. Once on the Jenkins pipeline configuration page, scroll down to the Build Triggers section and check the **GitHub hook trigger for GITScm polling** option.

3. Scroll down further to the **Pipeline** section.

4. Under the **Definition** option you can choose **Pipeline script**.

5. Click on the **Pipeline Syntax** link.

6. On the resultant page (Figure 7-5), choose **node: Allocate node** under the **Sample Step** field.

   a. Add **master** under the **Label** field.

   b. Click on the **Generate Pipeline Script** button.

   c. Copy and save the code. (We will need it later.)

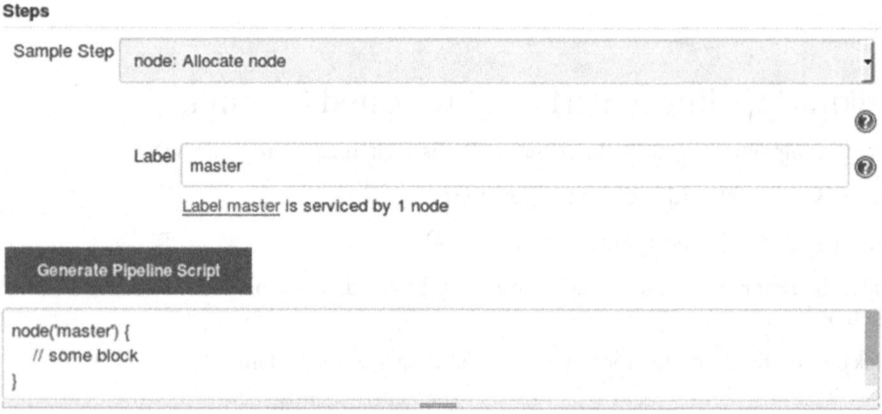

Figure 7-5. Pipeline code for allocating node

7. Next, choose **stage: Stage** option from the **Sample Step** field (Figure 7-6).

   a. Under the **Stage Name** field add **scm**.

   b. Click on the **Generate Pipeline Script** button.

   c. Copy and save the code. (We will need it later.)

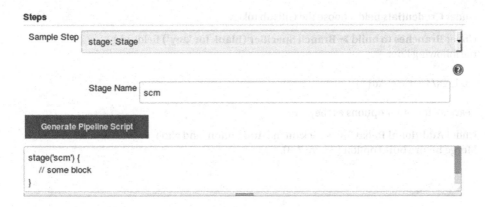

Figure 7-6. *Pipeline code for creating stage*

8. Create code for another stage named **build** and **push**. Copy the generated code. (We will need it later.)

9. Next, choose **checkout: General SCM** option from the **Sample Step** field (Figure 7-7). When you do so, the page refreshes with a new set of configurable items.

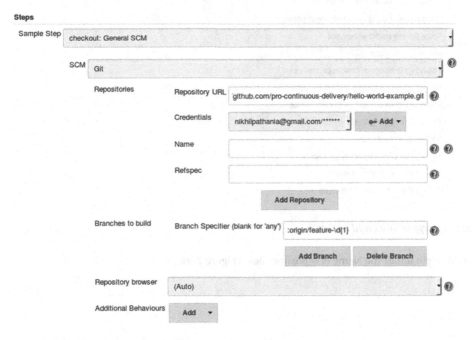

Figure 7-7. *Generating code for SCM*

a. Choose **Git** for the **SCM** field.

b. Under **Repositories ➤ Repository URL**, add the GitHub repository's (http link).

    c.   Under **Credentials** field, choose the GitHub token.

    d.   Under **Branches to build ➤ Branch Specifier (blank for 'any')** field, add
        the following line:

```
:origin/feature-\d{1}
```

    e.   Leave all the other options as they are.

    f.   Under **Additional Behaviours** click on the **Add** button, and choose
        Merge before build option (Figure 7-8).

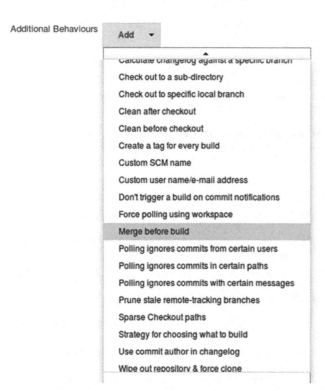

Figure 7-8. *Using the Merge before build option*

    g.   Add origin under the Name of repository field (Figure 7-9).

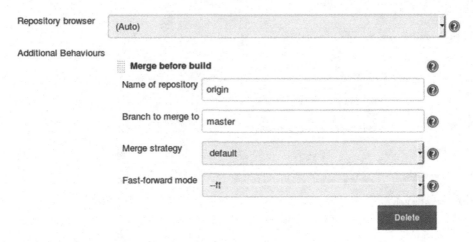

Figure 7-9. *Configuring the Merge before build settings*

    h.   Add master under the Branch to merge to field.

    i.   Leave the rest of the options to their default values.

    j.   Click on the **Generate Pipeline Script** button (Figure 7-10).

Figure 7-10. *Generated code for SCM*

    k.   Copy and save the code. (We will need it later.)

■ **Note** Remove the following line of code from the generated pipeline code: **mergeStrategy: <object of type org.jenkinsci.plugins.gitclient.MergeCommand.Strategy>**

---

10.   Next, choose **withMaven: Provide Maven environment** option from the **Sample Step** field. When you do so, the page refreshes with a new set of configurable items (Figure 7-11).

    a.   choose **Default Maven** under the **Maven** field.

    b.   Choose **Default JDK** under the **JDK** field.

    c.   Click on the **Generate Pipeline Script** button.

    d.   Copy and save the code. (We will need it later.)

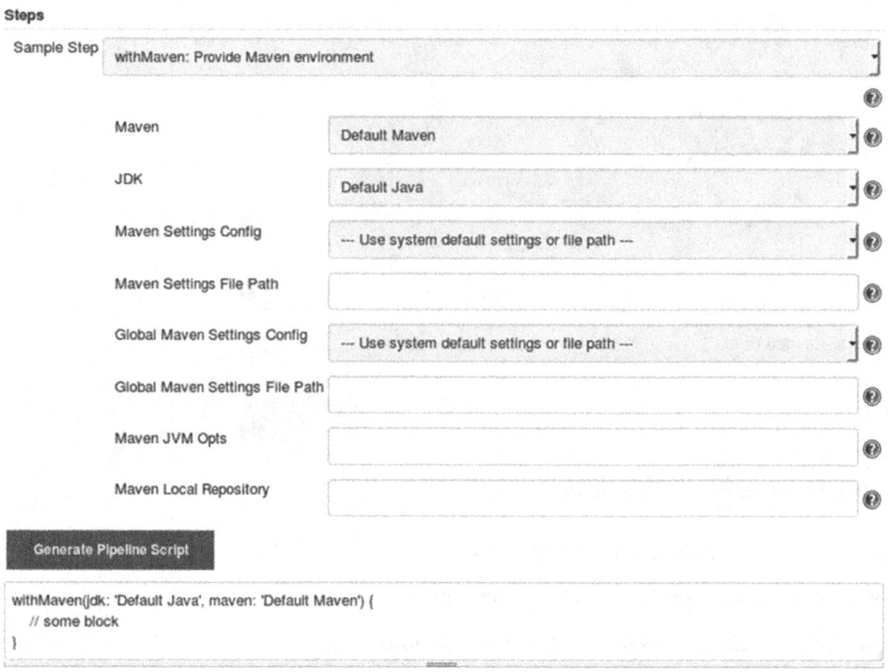

Steps

| Sample Step | withMaven: Provide Maven environment |

Maven	Default Maven
JDK	Default Java
Maven Settings Config	--- Use system default settings or file path ---
Maven Settings File Path	
Global Maven Settings Config	--- Use system default settings or file path ---
Global Maven Settings File Path	
Maven JVM Opts	
Maven Local Repository	

Generate Pipeline Script

```
withMaven(jdk: 'Default Java', maven: 'Default Maven') {
    // some block
}
```

Figure 7-11. *Generated code for Maven*

11.   Add the following line of code under the withMaven code block:

```
add sh ('mvn clean install')
```

12.   Next, choose **withCredentials: Bind credentials to variables** option from the **Sample Step** field. When you do so, the page refreshes with a new set of configurable items (Figure 7-12).

a.   Click on the add button and choose **Binfings Secret text** from the options.

b.   add github-token under the Variable field.

c.   choose the GitHub token under the Credentials field.

d.   Click on the **Generate Pipeline Script** button.

e.   Copy and save the code. (We will need it later.)

Steps

Sample Step   withCredentials: Bind credentials to variables

Bindings

Secret text

Variable   github-token

Credentials   GitHub (https://api.github.com) auto generated token credentials for nikhilpathania@gmail.com

➡ Add ▾

Delete

Add ▾

Generate Pipeline Script

```
withCredentials([string(credentialsId: '9d4d09c5-3fc8-46ec-97ff-84d3974f3504', variable: 'github-token')]) {
    // some block
}
```

Figure 7-12. *Generated code for withCredentials*

13. Add the following line of code under the push stage code block:

```
sh("git tag -a ${BUILD_NUMBER} -m 'Jenkins'")
sh("git push https://${credentials}@github.com/pro-continuous-delivery/
hello-world-example.git HEAD:master --tags")
```

14. Finally the complete combined code should look as shown below:

```
node('master'){

stage('scm'){
checkout changelog: true, poll: true, scm: [$class: 'GitSCM', branches:
[[name: ':origin/feature-\\d{1}']], doGenerateSubmoduleConfigurations:
false, extensions: [[$class: 'PreBuildMerge', options:
[fastForwardMode: 'FF', mergeRemote: 'origin', mergeTarget:
'master']]], submoduleCfg: [], userRemoteConfigs: [[credentialsId:
'github-account', url: 'https://github.com/pro-continuous-delivery/
hello-world-example.git']]]
}

stage('build'){
    withMaven(jdk: 'Default Java', maven: 'Default Maven') {
    sh ('mvn clean install')
}
}
```

```
stage('push'){
    withCredentials([string(credentialsId: '9d4d09c5-3fc8-46ec-97ff-
    84d3974f3504', variable: 'credentials')]) {
    sh("git tag -a ${BUILD_NUMBER} -m 'Jenkins'")
    sh("git push https://${credentials}@github.com/pro-continuous-
delivery/hello-world-example.git HEAD:master --tags")
    }
    }


}
```

15. On the pipeline configuration page, add the above code inside the **Script** field (Figure 7-13).

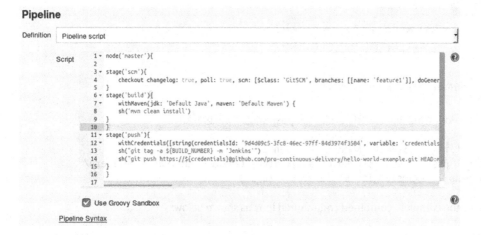

Figure 7-13. Adding the code to the script field

16. Save the configuration by clicking on the **Save** button at the end of the page.

Creating Feature Branch on Github

We will create a feature branch to make some changes on our code. The changes made on the feature branch will be tested by Jenkins. If the tests are successful, then Jenkins will merge the changes made on feature branch to the master branch.

1. Log in to your GitHub account, and under your repository create a new branch named **feature-1** as shown in Figure 7-14:

Figure 7-14. *Creating a feature branch*

2. Switch to the feature-1 branch and modify your Message.java file. I have modified the return message from Hello World! To Hi, How are you? (line number 5), as shown in Figure 7-15.

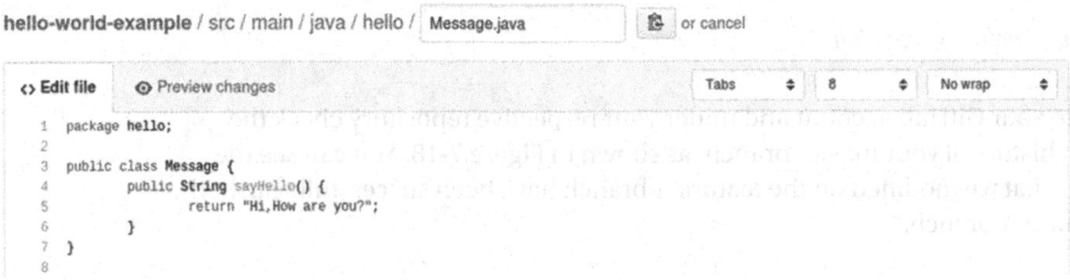

Figure 7-15. *Modifying the Message.java file*

3. Modify the MessageTest.java file to make sure our test passes. I have modified the containersString from **Hello** to **Hi,** (line number 14), as shown in Figure 7-16.

hello-world-example / src / test / java / hello / MessageTest.java   or cancel

```
1   package hello;
2
3   import static org.hamcrest.CoreMatchers.containsString;
4   import static org.junit.Assert.*;
5
6   import org.junit.Test;
7
8   public class MessageTest {
9
10      private Message message = new Message();
11
12      @Test
13      public void messageSaysHello() {
14          assertThat(message.ssyHello(), containsString("Hi,"));
15      }
16
17  }
```

Figure 7-16. *Modifying the MessageTest.java file*

4. Commit both the files to trigger a build in Jenkins.

5. Move to the Jenkins dashboard and click on the Jenkins pipeline, In our case its **pre_test_commits_using_Jenkins.** As shown in Figure 7-17, you can see the pipeline is a success, and the code has been pushed successfully to the remote master branch after a successful build.

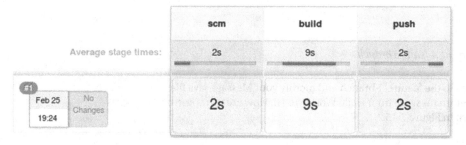

Figure 7-17. Jenkins pipeline stage view

6. Log in to your GitHub account and under your respective repository check the commit history of your master branch, as shown in Figure 7-18. You can see the two files that we modified on the feature-1 branch have been successfully pushed to the master branch.

Figure 7-18. Commit history on the master branch

Simulating a Failure

We will deliberately fail the build by modifying our unit test code in order to check if Jenkins pushes the code change to the Master branch on the remote repository.

1. Modify the MessageTest.java file so that our unit test fails. I am modifying the code, as shown in Figure 7-19.

hello-world-example / src / test / java / hello / [MessageTest.java]   🖺 or cancel

```
<> Edit file      ⊙ Preview changes                                    Tabs  ♦  8  ♦    No wrap  ♦
 1  package hello;
 2
 3  import static org.hamcrest.CoreMatchers.containsString;
 4  import static org.junit.Assert.*;
 5
 6  import org.junit.Test;
 7
 8  public class MessageTest {
 9
10      private Message message = new Message();
11
12      @Test
13      public void messageSaysHello() {
14          assertThat(message.sayHello(), containsString("Hello,"));
15      }
16
17  }
```

Figure 7-19. *Modifying the MessageTest.java file*

2. The moment you commit the file on GitHub, a build is triggered in Jenkins.

3. Move to the Jenkins dashboard to check the pipeline status. You should see something as shown in Figure 7-20.

pre_test_commits_using_Jenkins - Stage View

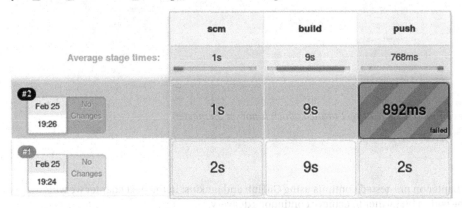

Figure 7-20. *Jenkins pipeline stage view*

4. Also check the Console Output for the Jenkins pipeline. And you will see that the build failed due to a failed unit test, as shown in Figure 7-21.

```
--------------------------------------------------------
 T E S T S
--------------------------------------------------------
Running hello.MessageTest
Tests run: 1, Failures: 1, Errors: 0, Skipped: 0, Time elapsed: 0.212 sec <<< FAILURE!
messageSaysHello(hello.MessageTest)  Time elapsed: 0.049 sec  <<< FAILURE!
java.lang.AssertionError:
Expected: a string containing "Hello,"
     but: was "Hi,How are you?"
```

Figure 7-21. *Jenkins pipeline Console Output logs*

5. Move to the GitHub. Under your repository page (while you are on the master branch), you will see that there is a new change on the Feature-1 branch that is not yet merged to the master (Figure 7-22).

Figure 7-22. *New commit on the feature-1 branch which is not yet on master*

Summary

This was a small chapter on pre-tested commits using GitHub and Jenkins. In the next chapter we will extend our pipeline code a bit further to achieve continuous delivery.

■ ■ ■

## CHAPTER 8

Continuous Delivery Using Jenkins Pipeline

In the current chapter we will learn to implement continuous delivery using Jenkins along with the relevant DevOps tool chain needed for it. We will begin the chapter by installing and configuring Artifactory and SonarQube. Next, we will create Docker images for our Integration and Performance test environments. To keep things short, we will see only two types of testing in the current chapter; however, in the real world, you can have multiple Docker images to describe all the testing environments that you would use. The current chapter will demonstrate continuous delivery using the tools described in Table 8-1. Nevertheless, you may have an alternative choice of tools.

Table 8-1. *Continuous Delivery tool chain*

Tools Used	Purpose	Alternative Tools
Jenkins	Main orchestrator for the Continuous Delivery	Teamcity, Atlassian Bamboo, ThoughtWorks Go…(may or may not have the option of pipeline as a code)
Artifactory	The binary repository to store build artifacts	Sonatype Nexus…
SonarQube	To perform Static Code Analysis	Squale, Kalistick, MetrixWare, Cast…
Apache Jmeter	To perform performance testing	LoadRunner, Testing Anywhere…
Junit	To perform unit testing and Integration testing	The list is huge depending on the project code…
Maven	To build Java project	Ant, MSBuild (.net, c#, c++)…
GitHub	Version Control repository	Git, Bitbucket, SVN, Mercurial…
Docker	To provision on-demand Jenkins Slaves	Kubernetes, Amazon EC2…

Setting Up the Artifactory Server

In the following section we will learn the following:

- Installing an Artifactory Server on Ubuntu

- Creating a generic repository inside Artifactory

- Creating user credentials inside Jenkins to access Artifactory

- Installing and configuring the Artifactory plugin for Jenkins

© Nikhil Pathania 2017
N. Pathania, *Pro Continuous Delivery*, DOI 10.1007/978-1-4842-2913-2_8

Installing and Configuring Artifactory

In the following section we will set up Artifactory on Ubuntu 16.04.

Install Java and Set the JAVA_HOME Path

Follow the steps below to install Java.

1. Update the package index:

```
sudo apt-get update
```

2. Next, install Java. The following command will install the Java Runtime Environment (JRE).

```
sudo apt-get install default-jre
```

3. To set the **JAVA_HOME** environment variable, first get the Java installation location. Do this by executing the following command. You should see a response as shown in Figure 8-1.

```
update-java-alternatives -l
```

```
root@07c8b33b80d9:/tmp# update-java-alternatives -l
java-1.8.0-openjdk-amd64        1081        /usr/lib/jvm/java-1.8.0-openjdk-amd64
root@07c8b33b80d9:/tmp# ▮
```

Figure 8-1. *List of available Java installations*

4. Copy the resultant path and update the **JAVA_HOME** variable inside the file **/etc/ environment** file, as shown below:

```
JAVA_HOME="/usr/lib/jvm/java-1.8.0-openjdk-amd64"
```

Downloading the Artifactory Package

Follow the steps below to download the Artifactory package.

1. Download the latest version of Artifactory installation package from the link: `https://www.jfrog.com/open-source/`

2. Unzip the archive package into your home directory ($HOME).

```
unzip Jfrog-artifactory-oss-5.1.0.zip -d $HOME/
```

3. Move to the extracted folder and list its content.

```
cd $HOME/artifactory-oss-5.1.0
```

```
ls -lrt
```

■ **Note** **bin/** folder contains all the scripts to install and start Artifactory. **logs/** folder contains the Artifactory logs.

Starting the Artifactory Server

Follow the steps below to start the Artifactory server.

1. Move to the **$HOME/artifactory-oss-5.1.0/bin/** folder and run the **installService.sh** script.

   ```
   sudo ./installService.sh
   ```

2. Executing the above command will give the following output.

   ```
   Installing artifactory as a Unix service that will run as user artifactory
   Installing artifactory with home /home/ubuntu/artifactory-oss-5.1.0
   Creating user artifactory...creating... DONE

   Checking configuration link and files in /etc/opt/jfrog/artifactory...
   Moving configuration dir /home/ubuntu/artifactory-oss-5.1.0/etc /home/ubuntu/
   artifactory-oss-5.1.0/etc.original...creating the link and updating dir... DONE
   Creating environment file /etc/opt/jfrog/artifactory/default...creating... DONE
   ** INFO: Please edit the files in /etc/opt/jfrog/artifactory to set the correct
   environment
   Especially /etc/opt/jfrog/artifactory/default that defines ARTIFACTORY_HOME,
   JAVA_HOME and JAVA_OPTIONS

   Initializing artifactory service with update-rc.d... DONE

   Setting file permissions... DONE

   *********** SUCCESS ***************
   Installation of Artifactory completed

   Please check /etc/opt/jfrog/artifactory, /home/ubuntu/artifactory-oss-5.1.0/
   tomcat and /home/ubuntu/artifactory-oss-5.1.0 folders
   Please check /etc/init.d/artifactory startup script
   ```

3. Start the Artifactory service using any of the following commands (Figure 8-2):

   ```
   sudo service artifactory start
   ```

   (or)

   ```
   sudo /etc/init.d/artifactory start
   ```

   (or)

   ```
   sudo systemctl start artifactory
   ```

4. You can check Artifactory installation by executing any of the following command:

```
service artifactory check
```

(or)

```
/etc/init.d/artifactory check
```

(or)

```
sudo ./artifactoryctl check
```

```
ubuntu@node5:~/artifactory-oss-5.1.0/bin$ sudo ./artifactoryctl check
Artifactory is running, on pid=17436

ubuntu@node5:~/artifactory-oss-5.1.0/bin$
```

Figure 8-2. *Artifactory running status*

5. Access the Artifactory dashboard using the following link:

```
http://<Server IP Address>:8081/artifactory
```

6. The default login credentials to the Artifactory server are:

```
username: admin
password: password
```

Reset the Default Credentials

Follow the steps below to reset Artifactory credentials.

1. From the Artifactory dashboard, click on **Welcome, admin ➤ Edit Profile**.

2. Enter your current password in the **Current Password** field and press the **Unlock button**.

3. On the resultant page, under **Personal Settings** add your e-mail ID and new credentials.

4. Once done, click on the **Save** button.

Creating a Repository in Artifactory

In the following section we will create a genetic repository inside Artifactory. The repository will be used to store the build artifacts.

1. From the Artifactory dashboard, on the left-hand side menu, click on **Admin ➤ Repositories ➤ Local**, as shown in Figure 8-3.

Figure 8-3. *Creating a Local repository in Artifactory*

2. The resultant page will show you all the available local repositories currently available, as shown in Figure 8-4.

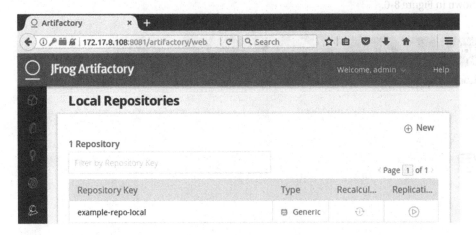

Figure 8-4. *List of all the Local Repositories*

3. Click on the **New** button at the top-right corner to create a new local repository (Figure 8-4).

4. You will be presented with a pop-up window with a list of various types of repositories to choose from. As shown below, choose the **Generic** type (Figure 8-5).

Figure 8-5. Option to choose various types of repositories.

5. Give your repository a name by adding a value under the **Repository Key*** field, as shown in Figure 8-6.

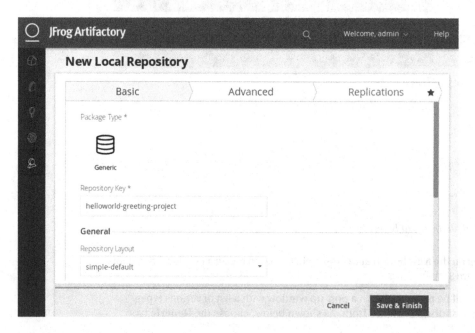

Figure 8-6. Naming our new local repository

6. Once done, click on the **Save & Finish** button.

7. Now we have our new local repository, as shown in Figure 8-7.

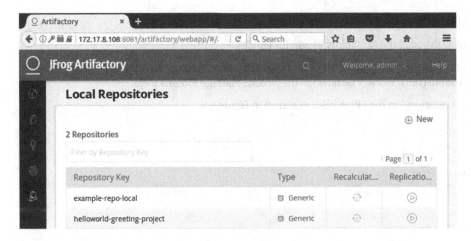

Figure 8-7. Our newly created local repository

Adding Artifactory Credentials Inside Jenkins

Follow the steps below to create credentials inside Jenkins to talk to Artifactory.

1. From the the Jenkins dashboard click on **Credentials ➤ System ➤ Global credentials (unrestricted)**.

2. Click on the **Add Credentials** link on the left-hand side menu, to create a new credential (Figure 8-8).

   a. Choose **Kind** as **Username and Password.**

   b. Leave the **Scope field** to its default value.

   c. Add the Artifactory username under the **Username** field.

   d. Under **the Password** field add the password.

   e. Add an ID under the **ID** field, and some description under the **Description** field.

   f. Once done click on the **OK** button.

Figure 8-8. Adding artifactory credentials inside Jenkins

Installing Artifactory Plugin

Follow the step below to install the Artifactory Plugin for Jenkins.

1. From the Jenkins Dashboard, click on **Manage Jenkins ➤ Manage Plugins ➤ Available (tab)**. You will be taken to the Jenkins **Manage Plugins** page.

2. Enter "Artifactory" in the **Filter** field, as shown in Figure 8-9.

Figure 8-9. Installing the Artifactory plugin

3. Select the **Artifactory Plugin** from the list and click on **Install without restart** button.

4. Restart Jenkins if needed.

Configuring Artifactory Plugin

Now that we have our Artifactory Plugin installed, let us configure it.

1. From the Jenkins Dashboard, click **Manage Jenkins ➤ Configure System.**

2. Once on the **Configure System** page, scroll down all the way to the **Artifactory** section.

3. Under the **Artifactory** section, click on the **Add** button.

   a. You will be presented with the following settings to configure, as shown below.

   b. Name your Artifactory server a name using the **Server ID** field.

   c. Enter the Artifactory server URL under the **URL** field.

   d. Add Artifactory credentials under the **Default Deployer Credentials**, as shown in Figure 8-10.

   e. Click on the **Test Connection** button to test the Jenkins connection with Artifactory.

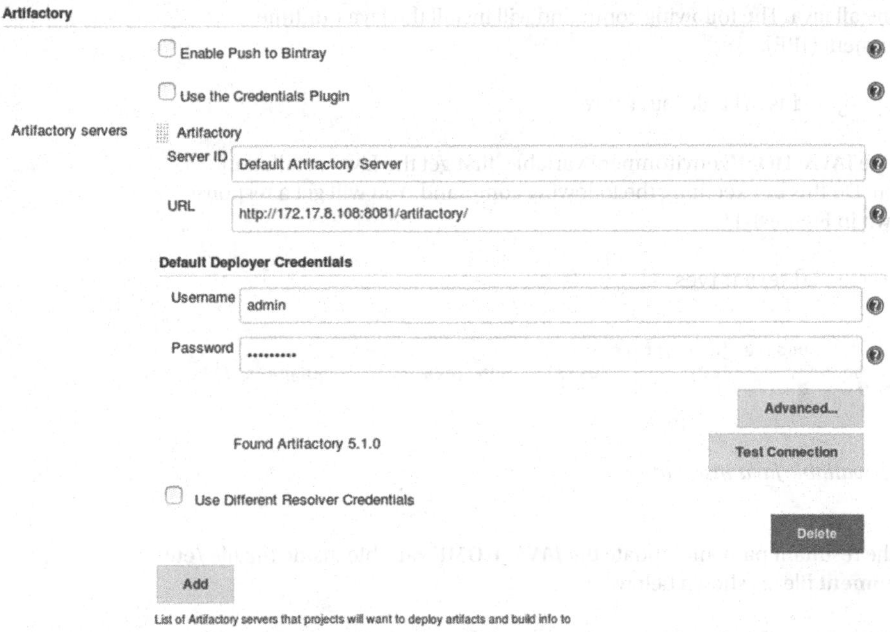

Artifactory

    ☐ Enable Push to Bintray   ❓

    ☐ Use the Credentials Plugin   ❓

Artifactory servers   ⠿ Artifactory

    Server ID   Default Artifactory Server   ❓

    URL   http://172.17.8.108:8081/artifactory/   ❓

Default Deployer Credentials

    Username   admin   ❓

    Password   •••••••••   ❓

                       Advanced...

    Found Artifactory 5.1.0   Test Connection

    ☐ Use Different Resolver Credentials

                               Delete

    Add

    List of Artifactory servers that projects will want to deploy artifacts and build info to

Figure 8-10.   *Configuring the Artifactory plugin*

    4.   Once done, click on the **Save** button at the end of the page to save the settings.

Setting Up the SonarQube Server

In the following section we will learn the following:

    a.   Installing a SonarQube Server on Ubuntu

    b.   Creating a project inside SonarQube

    c.   Installing and configuring the SonarQube Plugin for Jenkins

Installing and Configuring SonarQube

In the following section we will set up SonarQube on Ubuntu 16.04. Make sure you have latest version of Java installed with JAVA_HOME path set.

Install Java and Set the JAVA_HOME Path

Follow the steps below to install Java.

    1.   Update the package index:

```
sudo apt-get update
```

2. Next, install Java. The following command will install the Java Runtime Environment (JRE).

```
sudo apt-get install default-jre
```

3. To set the **JAVA_HOME** environment variable, first get the Java installation location. Do this by executing the following command. You will get a response as shown in Figure 8-11.

```
update-java-alternatives -l
```

```
root@07c8b33b80d9:/tmp# update-java-alternatives -l
java-1.8.0-openjdk-amd64        1081        /usr/lib/jvm/java-1.8.0-openjdk-amd64
root@07c8b33b80d9:/tmp# █
```

Figure 8-11. *List of available Java installations*

4. Copy the resultant path and update the **JAVA_HOME** variable inside the file **/etc/environment** file, as shown below:

```
JAVA_HOME="/usr/lib/jvm/java-1.8.0-openjdk-amd64"
```

Downloading the SonarQube Package

Follow the steps below to download the SonarQube package.

1. Download the latest version of SonarQube installation package using the link: https://www.sonarqube.org/downloads/

2. Unzip the archive package into you home directory ($HOME).

```
unzip sonarqube-5.6.6.zip -d $HOME/
```

3. cd to the extracted folder and list its content.

```
cd $HOME/sonarqube-5.6.6
```

■ **Note**   **bin/** folder contains all the scripts to install and start SonarQube. **logs/** folder contains the SonarQube logs.

Starting the SonarQube Server

Follow the steps below to start the SonarQube Server.

1. Move to the **$HOME/sonarqube-5.6.6/bin/linux-x86-64/**. (In our current example we are starting SonarQube on a 64-bit Linux OS.)

```
cd $HOME/sonarqube-5.6.6//bin/linux-x86-64/
```

2. Run the **sonar.sh** script to start SonarQube, as shown below.

```
./sonar.sh start
```

3. Access the SonarQube dashboard using the following link:

```
http://<Server IP Address>:9000
```

4. The default login credentials to the SonarQube server are:

```
username: admin
password: admin
```

Reset the Default Credentials and Generate a Token

Follow the steps below to reset the credentials and generate a token.

1. From the dashboard, click on **Administrator ➤ My Account ➤ Security (tab)**.

2. On the resultant page, under the **Change password** section, do the following:

   a. Add your old password (admin) under the field **Old Password**.

   b. Add a new password under the **New Password** field.

   c. Reconfirm your new password by adding it again in the field **Confirm Password**.

   d. Once done, click on the **Change Password** button.

3. On the same page there is an option to generate token. Jenkins can use this token to access SonarQube. Do the following steps to generate a new token.

   a. Look for the **Tokens** section on the **Security** Page (Figure 8-12).

   b. Under the **Tokens** section, add a name for your new token using the **Generate Tokens** field and click on the **Generate** Button.

   c. A new token will get generated as shown below.

   d. Save this token as we will need it later.

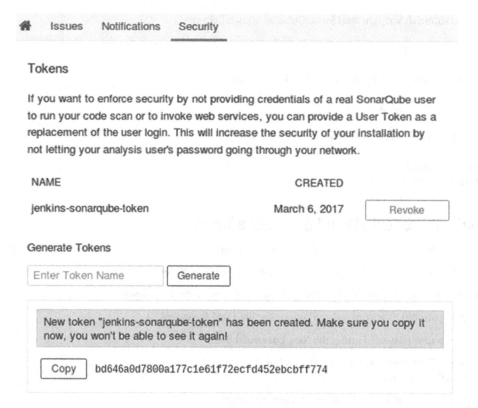

Figure 8-12. *Creating a token inside SonarQube*

Creating a Project in SonarQube

In the following section we will create a project inside SonarQube. The project will be used to display the static code analysis for our example project.

1. From the SonarQube dashboard click on **Administration ➤ Projects ➤ Management**.

2. On the resultant page click on **Create Project** button.

3. On the resultant pop-up window, do the following (Figure 8-13):

   a. Add a name under the **Name** field.

   b. Add a key under the **Key** field.

   c. Click on the **Create** button.

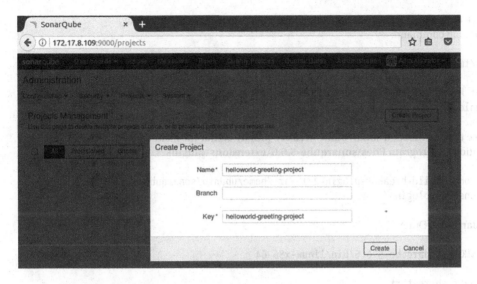

Figure 8-13. *Creating a project inside SonarQube*

    4. You can see your newly created project on the Project Management page, as shown in Figure 8-14.

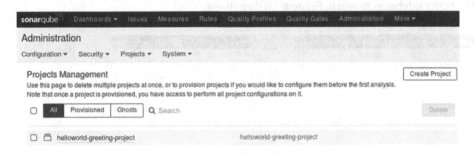

Figure 8-14. *Newly created project inside SonarQube*

Installing the Build Breaker Plugin for Sonar

The build breaker plugin is a SonarQube Plugin. This plugin allows the Continuous Integration system (Jenkins) to forcefully fail a Jenkins Build if a "Quality Gate" condition is not satisfied.

To install the build breaker plugin, login to the SonarQube server and follow the steps as mentioned below:

    1. Before downloading the plugin, first refer the compatibility table. This will help us in downloading the right plugin version. The compatability table is available on the following link: `https://github.com/SonarQubeCommunity/sonar-build-breaker`

    2. Download the build breaker plugin from the following link: `https://github.com/SonarQubeCommunity/sonar-build-breaker/releases`

3. Move to the **tmp** location and download the build breaker plugin using the following command:

    ```
    cd /tmp
    ```

    ```
    wget https://github.com/SonarQubeCommunity/sonar-build-breaker/releases/
    download/2.1/sonar-build-breaker-plugin-2.1.jar
    ```

4. Place the downloaded **sonar-build-breaker-plugin-2.1.jar** file inside the location **C:\Program Files\sonarqube-5.6.6\extensions\plugins**.

    ```
    cp sonar-build-breaker-plugin-2.1.jar /home/ubuntu/sonarqube-5.6.6/
    extensions/plugins/
    ```

5. Restart SonarQube.

    ```
    cd $HOME/sonarqube-5.6.6/bin/linux-x86-64
    ```

    ```
    ./sonar.sh restart
    ```

6. After a successful restart, go to the SonarQube dashboard and log in as admin.

7. Click on the **Administration** link from the menu options.

8. On the **Administration** page you will find the **Build Breaker** option under the **CATEGEORY** sidebar as shown in Figure 8-15, do nothing.

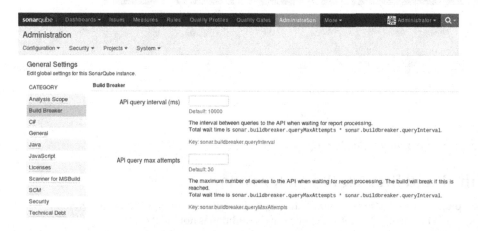

Figure 8-15. *Build Breaker plugin settings inside SonarQube*

Creating a Quality Gate in SonarQube

In the following section we will create a Quality Gate inside SonarQube. If any build crosses the threshold set by the Quality Gate, in that case the build breaker plugin will fail the build.

1. From the SonarQube Dasboard, click on **Quality Gates** link from the top menu bar.

2. On the resultant page, click on the **Create** button.

3. You will get a pop-up window as shown in Figure 8-16. Add a name for your Quality Gate under the **Name** field, and click on the **Create** Button.

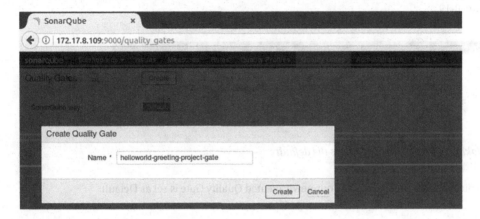

Figure 8-16. *Creating a new Quality Gate*

4. You will see your new Quality Gate listed under the Quality Gates, as shown in Figure 8-17.

Figure 8-17. *Our new Quality Gate*

5. Let us now add a condition to our Quality Gate by choosing one from the **Add Condition** menu.

6. Shown below is a condition named **Major Issues**. If it's greater than 1 but less than 3, it's a warning. And if it's greater than 3, it's an error. This is just an example. You can configure any number of conditions you like, as shown in Figure 8-18.

Figure 8-18. *Configuring the Quality Gate*

7. Now let's make our newly created Quality Gate as the default Quality Gate. We do so by clicking on the **Set as Default** option at the top-right corner, as shown in Figure 8-19.

Figure 8-19. *Making our new Quality Gate as the default*

8. As you can see from Figure 8-20, our newly created Quality Gate is set as Default.

Figure 8-20. *Our new Quality Gate is now set to default*

Installing the SonarQube Plugin

Follow the steps below to install the SonarQube plugin for Jenkins.

1. From the Jenkins Dashboard, click on **Manage Jenkins** ➤ **Manage Plugins** ➤ **Available (tab)**. You will be taken to the Jenkins **Manage Plugins** page.

2. Enter "SonarQube Plugin" in the **Filter** field, as shown in Figure 8-21.

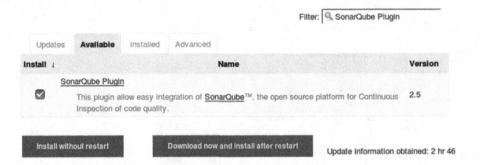

Figure 8-21. Installing the SonarQube Plugin

3. Select the **Artifactory Plugin** from the list and click on **Install without restart** button.

4. Restart Jenkins if needed.

Configuring SonarQube Plugin

Now that we have our SonarQube Plugin installed, let us configure it.

1. From the Jenkins Dashboard, click **Manage Jenkins ➤ Configure System**.

2. Once on the **Configure System** page, scroll down all the way to the **SonarQube servers** section.

3. Under the **SonarQube servers** section, click on the **Add SonarQube** button.

    a. You will be presented with the following settings to configure, as shown in Figure 8-22.

    b. Name your SonarQube server a name using the **Name** field.

    c. Enter the SonarQube server URL under the **Server URL** field.

    d. Add Artifactory credentials under the **Default Deployer Credentials**, as shown below.

    e. Add the token that we created inside SonarQube under the **Server authentication token** field.

    f. Click on the **Test Connection** button to test the Jenkins connection with Artifactory.

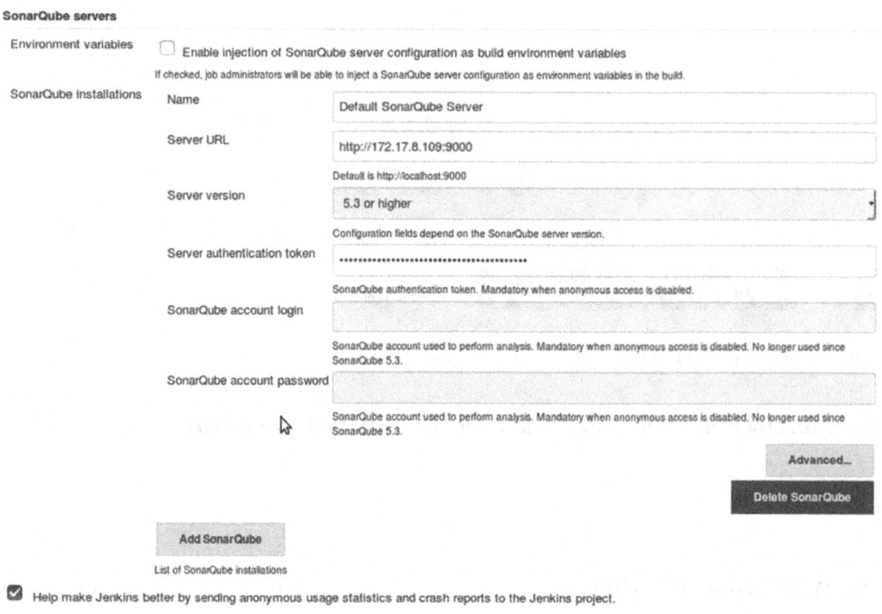

Figure 8-22. Configuring the SonarQube Plugin

4. Once done, click on the **Save** button at the end of the page to save the settings.

Analyzing with SonarQube Scanner for Maven

Ideally we need SonarQube Scanner to perform static code analysis on a project. However, we will use the SonarQube Scanner utility for Maven instead, as the example source code that we are using in the current chapter is a Maven project.

To do so, add the following code to your pom file:

```
<properties>
    <project.build.sourceEncoding>UTF-8</project.build.sourceEncoding>
    <sonar.language>java</sonar.language>
</properties>
```

Creating a Docker Image for Integration Testing

In the following section we will create a Docker image that will serve as our Integration Testing Environment. This Docker Image will be used by Jenkins to create Docker containers (Jenkins Slaves) on the fly. To do this follow the steps below:

1. Log in to your Docker server. Give the following command to check the available Docker images.

   ```
   sudo docker images
   ```

2. If you are following the example discussed in the previous chapter, then you will see the following Docker images, as shown in Figure 8-23.

```
ubuntu@node4:~$ sudo docker images
REPOSITORY                TAG        IMAGE ID         CREATED        SIZE
maven-build-slave-0.1     latest     317fb6ec990f     2 weeks ago    298 MB
ubuntu                    latest     f49eec89601e     6 weeks ago    129 MB
hello-world               latest     48b5124b2768     7 weeks ago    1.84 kB
ubuntu@node4:~$ █
```

Figure 8-23. *List the Docker Images.*

3. If your Docker server is a freshly backed machine, then you will see no images at this point.

4. We will build a Docker Image for our use from the **ubuntu** Docker Image. To do so, download the Docker Image for **ubuntu** using the following command. But if you already have it, then skip this step.

    ```
    docker pull ubuntu
    ```

■ **Note**   You can find more Docker Images for various OS on `https://hub.docker.com/`

---

5. One the pull gets completed, give the **sudo docker images** command again. And now you should see a Docker Image for Ubuntu as shown in **Figure** 8-23.

6. We will now upgrade our **ubuntu** Docker Image with all the necessary applications that we need to run our build, Static Code Analysis, and Integration Testing. The applications are mentioned as follows:

    a. Java JDK (Latest)

    b. Git

    c. Maven

    d. A user account to log into the Docker Container

    e. sshd (to accept ssh connection)

7. Execute the following command to run a docker container using the **ubuntu** Docker Image. This will create a container, and will open up a bash shell.

    ```
    sudo docker run -i -t ubuntu /bin/bash
    ```

8. Now, install all the required applications as you would on any normal Ubuntu machine.

Create a User Jenkins

Let's begin with creating a user **jenkins**.

1. Execute the following command and follow the user creation steps, as shown in Figure 8-24.

    ```
    adduser jenkins
    ```

```
root@07c8b33b80d9:/# adduser jenkins
Adding user `jenkins' ...
Adding new group `jenkins' (1000) ...
Adding new user `jenkins' (1000) with group `jenkins' ...
Creating home directory `/home/jenkins' ...
Copying files from `/etc/skel' ...
Enter new UNIX password:
Retype new UNIX password:
passwd: password updated successfully
Changing the user information for jenkins
Enter the new value, or press ENTER for the default
        Full Name []: Nikhil Pathania
        Room Number []: 208
        Work Phone []:
        Home Phone []:
        Other []:
Is the information correct? [Y/n] y
root@07c8b33b80d9:/# ▮
```

Figure 8-24. *Creating a user*

2. Check the new user using the switch user command:

    ```
    su jenkins
    ```

3. Switch back to the root user by typing **exit**.

Install SSH Server

To install the SSH server, execute the following command in sequence:

```
apt-get update
```

```
apt-get install openssh-server
```

```
mkdir /var/run/sshd
```

Install Java and Set the JAVA_HOME Path

Follow the below steps to install Java.

1. Update the package index:

    ```
    sudo apt-get update
    ```

2. Next, install Java. The following command will install the Java Runtime
    Environment (JRE).

    ```
    sudo apt-get install default-jre
    ```

Install Git, Maven, and Nano Text Editor

Follow the step below to install Git, Maven, and a text editor.

1. Install Git using the following command:

    ```
    apt-get install git
    ```

2. Install Maven using the following command:

    ```
    apt-get install maven
    ```

3. Install the nano package if required using the following apt-get command:

    ```
    apt-get install nano
    ```

Configure the Maven Installation to Work with SonarQube

In the following section we will configure the Maven installation to allow it to work with SonarQube.

1. Edit the **settings.xml** file, located in **$MAVEN_HOME/conf** or ~/**.m2**, to set the plugin prefix and optionally the SonarQube server URL.

    ```
    cd ~/.m2
    ```

    (or)

    ```
    cd /usr/share/maven/
    ```

2. Open the **settings.xml** file using the nano editor.

    ```
    nano settings.xml
    ```

3. Inside the **settings.xml** file, navigate to the <PluginGroup></PluginGroup> section and add the following lines.

    ```
    <pluginGroups>
            <pluginGroup>org.sonarsource.scanner.maven</pluginGroup>
    </pluginGroups>
    ```

4. Next, inside the same **settings.xml** file, navigate to the <profiles></profiles> section and add the following lines.

    ```
    <profiles>
            <profile>
                <id>sonar</id>
                <activation>
                    <activeByDefault>true</activeByDefault>
                </activation>
                <properties>
                    <!-- Optional URL to server. Default value is http://localhost:9000 -->
    ```

```
            <sonar.host.url>
               http://<sonarqube server ip>:9000
            </sonar.host.url>
         </properties>
      </profile>
   </profiles>
```

Save the Changes Made to the Docker Image

Follow the steps below to save all the changes that we made to the Cocker image.

1. Exit the container by typing **exit**.

2. We need to save (commit) all the changes that we made inside the Docker container.

    a. Get the **CONTAINER ID** of the container that we worked on recently by listing all the inactive containers, as shown in Figure 8-25.

        ```
        sudo docker ps -a
        ```

```
ubuntu@node4:~$ sudo docker ps -a
CONTAINER ID   IMAGE    COMMAND       CREATED         STATUS                    PORTS   NAMES
9e96f9b335bb   ubuntu   "/bin/bash"   17 minutes ago  Exited (1) 7 seconds ago          amazing_shaw
f8b14a252e77   ubuntu   "/bin/bash"   23 hours ago    Exited (0) 23 hours ago           wonderful_allen
81a5d12f6c4a   ubuntu   "/bin/bash"   2 weeks ago     Exited (0) 2 weeks ago            mystifying_fermat
ubuntu@node4:~$
```

Figure 8-25. *List inactive containers*

    b. Note the **CONTAINER ID**. And execute the following command to commit the changes that we made to our container.

        ```
        sudo docker commit <CONTAINER ID> <new name for the container>
        ```

    c. I have named my container as **integration-test-agent-0.1** as shown in Figure 8-26:

```
ubuntu@node4:~$ sudo docker commit 9e96f9b335bb integration-test-agent-0.1
sha256:465ed4ab3eff915dba4bdd3685752391e056280aff83105365d42c10adaa553e
ubuntu@node4:~$
```

Figure 8-26. *Docker commit command*

    d. Once you have commited the changes, a new Docker Image gets created.

    e. Execute the following Docker command to list images, as shown in Figure 8-27.

        ```
        sudo docker images
        ```

```
ubuntu@node4:~$ sudo docker images
REPOSITORY                     TAG        IMAGE ID        CREATED         SIZE
integration-test-agent-0.1     latest     465ed4ab3eff    57 seconds ago  652 MB
maven-build-slave-0.1          latest     317fb6ec990f    2 weeks ago     298 MB
ubuntu                         latest     f49eec89601e    6 weeks ago     129 MB
hello-world                    latest     48b5124b2768    7 weeks ago     1.84 kB
ubuntu@node4:~$ █
```

Figure 8-27. *List the Docker Images*

    f.   You can see our new Docker Image with the name **integration-test-agent-0.1**. We will now configure our Jenkins server to use the following Docker image to create Jenkins Slaves (build agents).

Adding Docker Image Credentials Inside Jenkins

Follow the below steps to create credentials inside Jenkins to allow it to talk to Docker.

    1.   From the Jenkins Dashboard, navigate to **Credentials ➤ System ➤ Global credentials (unrestricted).**

    2.   Click on the **Add Credentials** link on the left-hand side menu to create a new credential (Figure 8-28).

        a.   Choose **Kind** as **Username and Password.**

        b.   Leave the **Scope field** to its default value.

        c.   Add a username for your Docker Image (**jenkins** as per our example) under the **Username** field.

        d.   Under **the Password** field add the password.

        e.   Add an ID under the **ID** field, and some description under the **Description** field.

        f.   Once done click on the **OK** button.

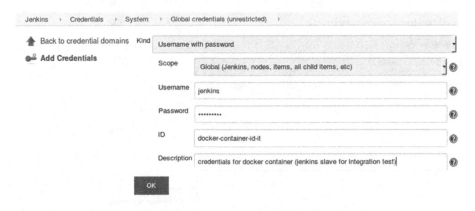

Figure 8-28. *Add credentials for the Docker Image*

Update the Docker Settings Inside Jenkins

Follow the steps below to update the Docker settings inside Jenkins.

1. From the Jenkins Dashboard, click on **Manage Jenkins ➤ Configure System**.

2. Scroll all the way down to **Cloud** section.

3. Under the Cloud section, click on the **Add Docker Template** button and choose **Docker Template**.

   a. You will be presented with a lot of settings to configure. However, to keep this demonstration simple, let us stick to the important settings (Figure 8-29).

   b. Under the **Docker Image** field enter the name of the Docker Image that we created earlier. In my case it is **integration-test-agent-0.1**.

   c. Under the **Labels** field add a label. The Docker container will be recognized using this label by your Jenkins pipeline. I have added a label **docker_it**.

   d. **Launch Method** should be **Docker SSH computer launcher**.

   e. Under the **Credentials** field choose the credentials that we created to access the Docker container.

   f. Leave the rest of the other options to their default values.

   g. Once done, click on Apply and then Save.

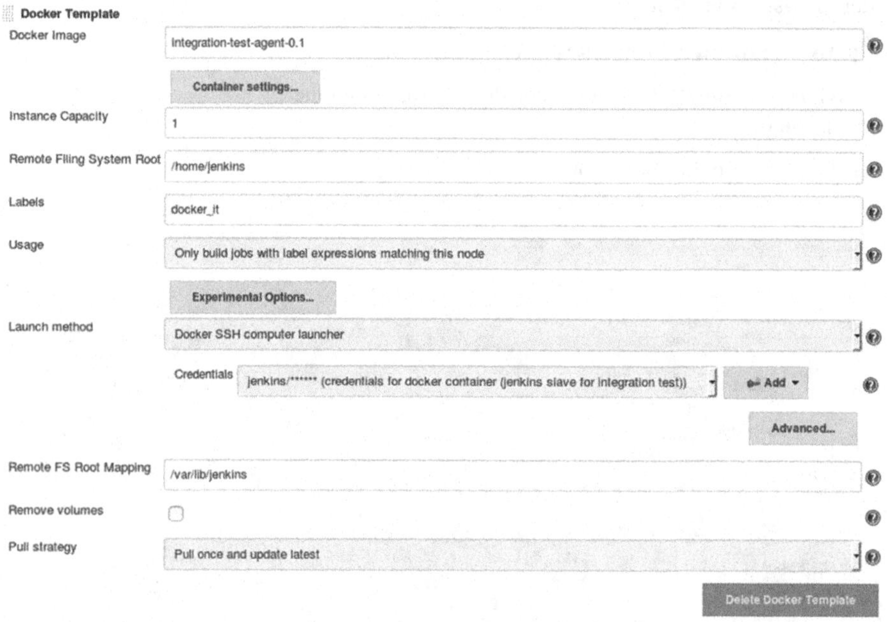

Figure 8-29. *Creating a Docker Template for Integration testing*

Creating Docker Image for Performance Testing

1. Log in to your Docker server. Give the following command to check the available Docker images.

   ```
   sudo docker images
   ```

2. You should see something as shown in Figure 8-30.

```
ubuntu@node4:~$ sudo docker images
REPOSITORY                  TAG       IMAGE ID        CREATED           SIZE
integration-test-agent-0.1  latest    465ed4ab3eff    57 seconds ago    652 MB
maven-build-slave-0.1       latest    317fb6ec990f    2 weeks ago       298 MB
ubuntu                      latest    f49eec89601e    6 weeks ago       129 MB
hello-world                 latest    48b5124b2768    7 weeks ago       1.84 kB
ubuntu@node4:~$ 
```

Figure 8-30. *List the Docker Images.*

3. We will build a new Docker image for running our PT using the **ubuntu** Docker Image.

4. We will now upgrade our **ubuntu** Docker Image with all the necessary applications that we need to run our build, which are as follows:

   a. Java JDK (Latest)

   b. Apache Tomcat (8.5)

   c. Apache Jmeter

   d. A user account to log into the Docker Container

   e. sshd (to accept ssh connection)

   f. curl

5. Execute the following command to run a docker container using the ubuntu Docker Image. This will create a container, and open up its bash shell.

   ```
   sudo docker run -i -t ubuntu /bin/bash
   ```

6. Now, install all the required application as you would do on any normal Ubuntu machine. Let's begin with creating a user **jenkins**.

Creating a User Jenkins

Follow the steps below to create a user inside named Jenkins.

1. Execute the following command and follow the user creation steps, as shown in Figure 8-31.

   ```
   adduser jenkins
   ```

```
root@9e96f9b335bb:/# adduser jenkins
Adding user `jenkins' ...
Adding new group `jenkins' (1000) ...
Adding new user `jenkins' (1000) with group `jenkins' ...
Creating home directory `/home/jenkins' ...
Copying files from `/etc/skel' ...
Enter new UNIX password:
Retype new UNIX password:
passwd: password updated successfully
Changing the user information for jenkins
Enter the new value, or press ENTER for the default
        Full Name []: Nikhil Pathania
        Room Number []: 208
        Work Phone []:
        Home Phone []:
        Other []:
Is the information correct? [Y/n] y
root@9e96f9b335bb:/# █
```

Figure 8-31. *Creating a user*

2. Check the new user using the switch user command:

   su jenkins

3. Switch back to the root user by typing **exit**.

Install SSH Server

Next, we will install the SSH server. Execute the following command in sequence.

apt-get update

apt-get install openssh-server

mkdir /var/run/sshd

Install Java and Set the JAVA_HOME path

Follow the steps below to install Java.

1. Update the package index:

   sudo apt-get update

2. Next, install Java. The following command will install the Java Runtime Environment (JRE).

   sudo apt-get install default-jre

Install Apache Tomcat

Follow the steps below to install Apache Tomcat.

1. The best way to install Tomcat 8.5 is to download the latest binary release, then configure it manually.

2. Move to the **tmp/** directory and download the Apache Tomcat 8.5 using the following commands:

```
cd /tmp
```

```
wget http://mirrors.dotsrc.org/apache/tomcat/tomcat-8/v8.5.11/bin/apache-tomcat-8.5.11.tar.gz
```

3. We will install Tomcat inside the **$HOME** directory. To do so, create a directory **tomcat** inside **$HOME.**

```
mkdir $HOME/tomcat
```

4. Then extract the archive to it:

```
tar xzvf apache-tomcat-8*tar.gz -C $HOME/tomcat --strip-components=1
```

Install Apache JMeter

Apache JMeter is a good tool to perform Performance Testing. It's free and open source. It can run in both GUI and command-line mode, which makes it a suitable candidate for automating Performance Testing.

1. Move to the tmp/ directory.

```
cd /tmp
```

2. Download the apache-jmeter-3.1.tgz or whichever is the latest stable version from http://jmeter.apache.org/download_jmeter.cgi

```
wget http://ftp.download-by.net/apache//jmeter/binaries/apache-jmeter-3.1.tgz
```

3. We will install Jmeter inside the **opt/jmeter/** directory. To do so create a **jmeter** directory inside **opt/**.

```
mkdir /opt/jmeter
```

4. Then extract the archive to it:

```
tar xzvf apache-jmeter-3*.tgz -C /opt/jmeter --strip-components=1
```

Saving the Changes Made to the Docker Image

Follow the steps below to save all the changes that we made to the Docker image.

1. Exit the container by typing **exit**.

2. We need to save (commit) all the changes that we made to our Docker container.

   a. Get the **CONTAINER ID** of the container that we worked on recently by listing all the inactive containers, as shown in Figure 8-32.

   ```
   sudo docker ps -a
   ```

```
ubuntu@node4:~$ sudo docker ps -a
CONTAINER ID   IMAGE    COMMAND       CREATED        STATUS                      PORTS   NAMES
f8b14a252e77   ubuntu   "/bin/bash"   30 minutes ago Exited (0) About a minute ago        wonderful_allen
81a5d12f6c4a   ubuntu   "/bin/bash"   2 weeks ago    Exited (0) 2 weeks ago               mystifying_fermat
ubuntu@node4:~$
```

Figure 8-32. *List inactive containers.*

b.   Note the **CONTAINER ID**. And execute the following command to commit the changes that we made to our container.

   ```
   sudo docker commit <CONTAINER ID> <new name for the container>
   ```

c.   I have named my container as **performance-test-agent-0.1** as shown in Figure 8-33:

```
ubuntu@node4:~$ sudo docker commit f8b14a252e77 performance-test-agent-0.1
sha256:5218edfb90a9d3391393e5b11a2188f6fe8e1f85fd7e92a12d9bac558cc33e41
ubuntu@node4:~$
```

Figure 8-33. *Docker commit command*

d.   Once you have commited the changes, a new Docker Image gets created.

e.   Execute the following Docker command to list images, as shown in Figure 8-34.

   ```
   sudo docker images
   ```

```
ubuntu@node4:~$ sudo docker images
REPOSITORY                    TAG      IMAGE ID       CREATED         SIZE
integration-test-agent-0.1    latest   465ed4ab3eff   57 seconds ago  652 MB
performance-test-agent-0.1    latest   5218edfb90a9   23 hours ago    720 MB
maven-build-slave-0.1         latest   317fb6ec990f   2 weeks ago     298 MB
ubuntu                        latest   f49eec89601e   6 weeks ago     129 MB
hello-world                   latest   48b5124b2768   7 weeks ago     1.84 kB
ubuntu@node4:~$
```

Figure 8-34. *List the Docker Images.*

f.   You can see our new Docker Image with the name **performance-test-agent-0.1**. We will now configure our Jenkins server to use the following Docker image to create Jenkins Slaves (build agents).

Adding Docker Image Credentials Inside Jenkins

Follow the steps below to create credentials inside Jenkins to allow it to talk to Docker.

1.   From the Jenkins Dashboard, navigate to **Credentials ➤ System ➤ Global credentials (unrestricted)**.

2.   Click on the **Add Credentials** link on the left-hand side menu to create a new credential (Figure 8-35).

a.   Choose **Kind** as **Username and Password**.

b.   Leave the **Scope field** to its default value.

    c.   Add a username for your Docker Image (**jenkins** as per our example) under the **Username** field.

    d.   Under **the Password** field add the password.

    e.   Add an ID under the **ID** field, and some description under the **Description** field.

    f.   Once done, click on the **OK** button.

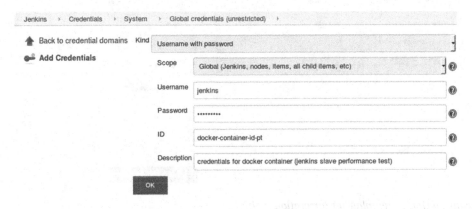

Figure 8-35. *Create credentials inside Jenkins*

Update the Docker Settings Inside Jenkins

Follow the steps below to update the Docker settings inside Jenkins.

1.   From the Jenkins Dashboard, click on **Manage Jenkins ➤ Configure System**.

2.   Scroll all the way down to **Cloud** section.

3.   Under the Cloud section, click on the **Add Docker Template** button and choose **Docker Template**.

    a.   You will be presented with a lot of settings to configure (Figure 8-36). However, to keep this demonstration simple, let us stick to the important settings.

    b.   Under the **Docker Image** field, enter the name of the Docker Image that we created earlier. In my case it is **performance-test-agent-0.1**.

    c.   Under the **Labels** field add a label. The Docker container will be recognized using this label by your Jenkins pipeline. I have added a label **docker_pt**.

    d.   **Launch Method** should be **Docker SSH computer launcher**.

    e.   Under the **Credentials** field choose the credentials that we created to access the Docker container.

    f.   Leave the rest of the other options to their default values.

    g.   Once done, click on Apply and then Save.

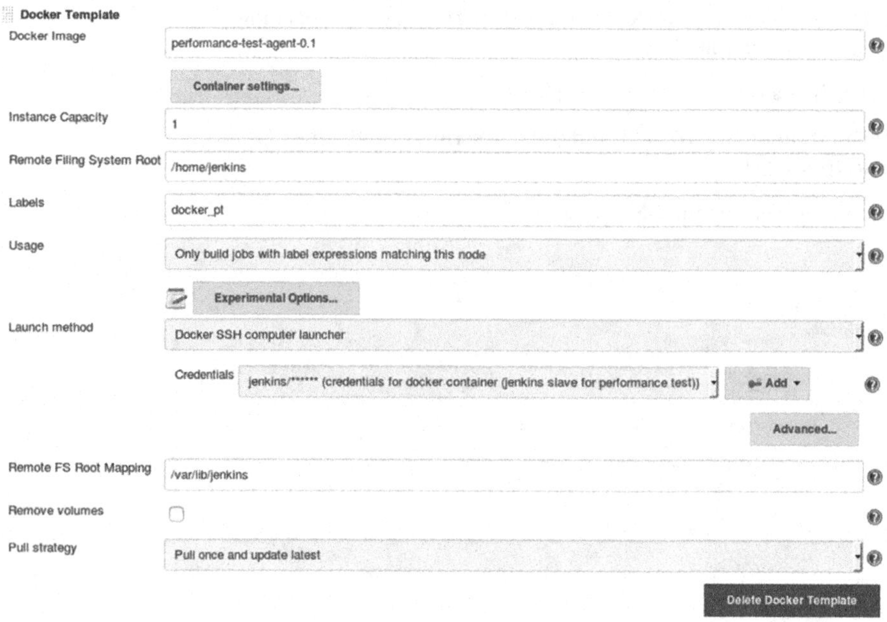

Figure 8-36. *Creating a Docker Template for Integration testing*

Creating a Performance Test Using Jmeter

In the following section we will learn to create a simple performance test using the tool Jmeter.

Install Java and Set the JAVA_HOME Path

Follow the steps below to install Java.

1. Update the package index:

   ```
   sudo apt-get update
   ```

2. Next, install Java. The following command will install the Java Runtime Environment (JRE).

   ```
   sudo apt-get install default-jre
   ```

3. To set the **JAVA_HOME** environment variable, first get the Java installation location. Do this by executing the following command.

   ```
   sudo update-alternatives --config java

   <image showing the output of the above command>
   ```

4. Copy the resultant path and update the **JAVA_HOME** variable inside the file /etc/environment.

   ```
   <image showing the /etc/environment file>
   ```

Install Apache JMeter

Follow the steps below to install apache JMeter.

1. Move to the **tmp/** directory.

    ```
    cd /tmp
    ```

2. Download the apache-jmeter-3.1.tgz or whichever is the latest stable version from http://jmeter.apache.org/download_jmeter.cgi

    ```
    wget http://ftp.download-by.net/apache//jmeter/binaries/apache-jmeter-3.1.tgz
    ```

3. We will install Jmeter inside the **opt/jmeter/** directory. To do so, create a **jmeter** directory inside **opt/**.

    ```
    mkdir /opt/jmeter
    ```

4. Then extract the archive to it:

    ```
    tar xzvf apache-jmeter-3*.tgz -C /opt/jmeter --strip-components=1
    ```

Starting Jmeter

Follow the steps below to start Jmeter.

1. To start Jmeter, move to the Jmeter installation directory and run the **jmeter.sh** script using the following command:

    ```
    cd /opt/jmeter/bin
    ```

    ```
    ./jmeter.sh
    ```

2. You will see the Jmeter GUI utility open up in a new Window.

Creating a Performance Test Case

By default you will see an example test plan. We will create a new test plan by modifying the existing template.

1. Rename the test plan to **Hello World Test Plan** as shown in Figure 8-37.

Figure 8-37. *Creating a test plan*

2. Save it inside the **examples** folder by clicking on the save button from the menu items or by clicking Ctrl+S, as shown in Figure 8-38.

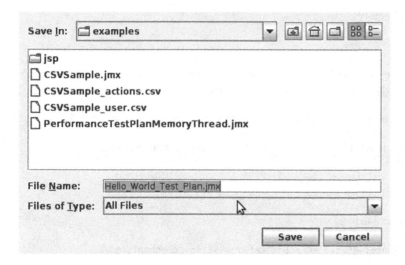

Figure 8-38. *Saving the test plan*

Creating a Thread Group

Follow the steps below to create a thread group.

1. Add a thread group. To do so, right-click on the **Hello World Test Plan** and select **Add ➤ Threads (Users) ➤ Thread Group** (Figure 8-39).

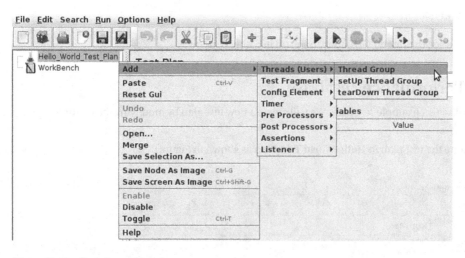

Figure 8-39. *Creating a thread group*

2. In the resultant page. Give your thread group a name. And fill in the option as follows (Figure 8-40).

    a. Select **Continue** for the option **Action to be taken after a Sampler error**.

    b. Add **Number of Threads (users) = 1**

    c. Add **Ramp-Up Period (in seconds) = 1**

    d. Add **Loop Count =1**

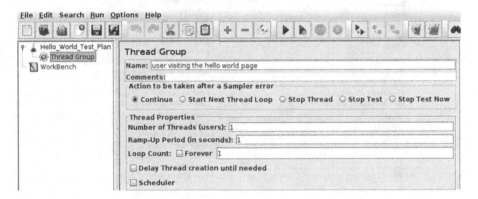

Figure 8-40. *Configuring a thread group*

Creating a Sampler

Follow the steps below to create a Sampler.

1. To do so, right-click on the **Hello_World_Test_Plan** and select **Add ➤ Sampler ➤ Http Request** (Figure 8-41).

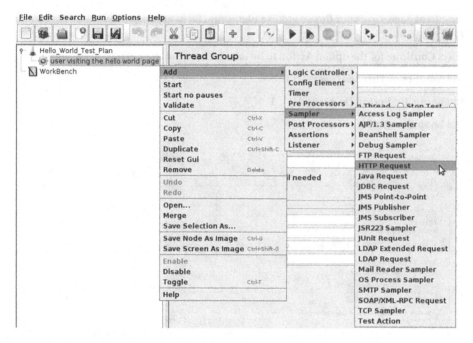

Figure 8-41. *Adding a Sampler*

2. Name the HTTP Request appropriately. And fill in the options as follows (Figure 8-42).

   a. Add **Server Name or IP = <ip address of your Testing Server machine ➤**

   b. Add **Port Number = 8080**

   c. Add **Path = /payslip-0.0.1/**

Figure 8-42. *Configuring a sampler*

Adding a Listener

Follow the steps below to add a listener.

1. To do so, right-click on the **Hello_World_Test_Plan** and select **Add ➤ Listener ➤ View Results Tree** (Figure 8-43).

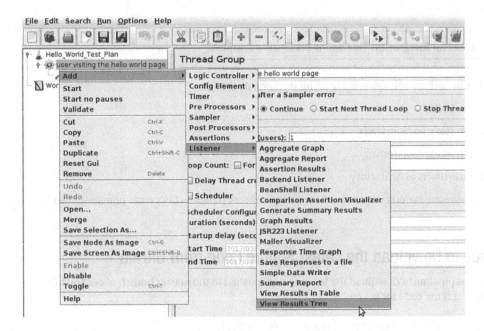

Figure 8-43. Adding a Listener

2. Do nothing. Leave all fields as they are.

3. Save the whole configuration by clicking on the save button in the menu items or by clicking Ctrl+S.

4. Copy the **.jmx** file from **/opt/jmeter/bin/examples**.

5. Under your Maven project create a folder named **pt** inside the **src** directory. And add the .jmx file inside it.

6. Upload the code to github.

Creating Jenkins CD Pipeline

We have all the required tools and the Docker images ready. In the following section we will create a pipeline in Jenkins that will describe our continuous delivery process.

Creating Pipeline Script

Lets us build our pipeline code for Continuous Delivery step-by-step:

Pipeline Code for Spawning a Docker Container for the Integration Testing

First, let us create a pipeline code that will create a Cocker container (Jenkins Slave) using the Docker image for Integration testing **integration-test-agent-0.1**.

```
node('docker_it') {
}
```

docker_it	Label for **integration-test-agent-0.1** Docker Template.

We would like to perform the following tasks on the node **docker_it**.

- a. perform build
- b. perform static code analysis
- c. perform Integration testing
- d. publish artifacts to Artifactory

All the tasks above are various stages of our continous delivery pipeline. Let's write pipeline code for each one of them.

Pipeline Code to Download the Latest Source Code from GitHub

We want our Jenkins pipeline to download the latest change pushed to the master branch of our GitHub repository. Following is the code for it:

```
checkout([$class: 'GitSCM', branches: [[name: '*/master']],
doGenerateSubmoduleConfigurations: false, extensions: [], submoduleCfg: [],
userRemoteConfigs: [[credentialsId: 'github-account',
url: 'https://github.com/pro-continuous-delivery/hello-world-greeting.git']]])
```

credentialsId:	The credentials saved inside Jenkins to access GitHub.
url:	https or ssh link of your GitHub repository.
name:	GitHub repository branch to build.

Wrap the step above inside a stage called **Poll**.

```
stage('Poll') {
    checkout([$class: 'GitSCM', branches: [[name: '*/master']],
doGenerateSubmoduleConfigurations: false, extensions: [], submoduleCfg: [],
userRemoteConfigs: [[credentialsId: 'github-account', url: 'https://github.com/pro-
continuous-delivery/hello-world-greeting.git']]])
}
```

Pipeline Code to Perform a Build

The example project that we are using in the current chapter is a Maven project. Therefore the pipeline code for the build is a simple shell script that runs the **mvn clean** command:

```
sh 'mvn clean verify -DskipITs=true';
```

-DskipITs=true	Option to skip Integration test and perform only the build.

Wrap the step above inside a stage called **Build**.

```
stage('Build'){
        sh 'mvn clean verify -DskipITs=true';
}
```

Pipeline Code to Perform Static Code Analysis

The pipeline code to perform static code analysis is a simple shell script that will run the Maven command, as shown below. This is made possible using the SonarQube Scanner utility for Maven. Remember the configuration that we did in the sections **Analyzing with SonarQube Scanner for Maven** and **Configure the Maven Installation to Work with SonarQube.**

```
sh 'mvn clean verify sonar:sonar';
```

Wrap the step above inside a stage called **Static Code Analysis**.

```
stage('Static Code Analysis'){
    sh 'mvn clean verify sonar:sonar';
}
```

Pipeline Code to Perform Integration Testing

The pipeline code to perform Integration testing is a shell script that will run the Maven command, as shown below:

```
sh 'mvn clean verify -Dsurefire.skip=true';
```

-Dsurefire.skip=true	Option to skip Unit testing and perform only the Integration testing.

Wrap the step above inside a stage called **Integration Test**.

```
stage ('Integration Test'){
    sh 'mvn clean verify -Dsurefire.skip=true';
}
```

Pipeline Code to Publish Build Artifacts to Artifactory

To upload the build artifacts to Artifactory we will use the **File Specs**. The **File Specs** code looks as shown below:

```
"files": [
    {
        "pattern": "[Mandatory]",
        "target": "[Mandatory]",
        "props": "[Optional]",
        "recursive": "[Optional, Default: 'true']",
        "flat" : "[Optional, Default: 'true']",
        "regexp": "[Optional, Default: 'false']"
    }
  ]
```

pattern	[Mandatory]
	Specifies the local file system path to artifacts that should be uploaded to Artifactory. You can specify multiple artifacts by using wildcards or a regular expression as designated by the regexp property.
	If you use a regexp, you need to escape any reserved characters (such as " . ", "?", etc.) used in the expression using a backslash "\".
	Version 2.9.0 of the Jenkins Artifactory plugin and version 2.3.1 of the TeamCity Artifactory plugin the pattern format has been simplified and uses the same file separator "/" for all operating systems, including Windows.
target	[Mandatory]
	Specifies the target path in Artifactory in the following format: [repository_name]/[repository_path]
	If the pattern ends with a slash, for example, "repo-name/a/b/", then "b" is assumed to be a folder in Artifactory and the files are uploaded into it. In the case of "repo-name/a/b", the uploaded file is renamed to "b" in Artifactory.
	For flexibility in specifying the upload path, you can include placeholders in the form of {1}, {2}, {3}…that are replaced by corresponding tokens in the source path that are enclosed in parentheses. For more details, please refer to Using Placeholders.
props	[Optional]
	List of "key=value" pairs separated by a semi-colon (;) to be attached as properties to the uploaded properties. If any key can take several values, then each value is separated by a comma (,). For example, "key1=value1;key2=value21,value22;key3=value3".
flat	[Default: true]
	If true, artifacts are uploaded to the exact target path specified and their hierarchy in the source file system is ignored. If false, artifacts are uploaded to the target path while maintaining their file system hierarchy.
recursive	[Default: true]
	If true, artifacts are also collected from sub-directories of the source directory for upload. If false, only artifacts specifically in the source directory are uploaded.
regexp	[Default: false]
	If true, the command will interpret the pattern property, which describes the local file-system path of artifacts to upload, as a regular expression. If false, the command will interpret the pattern property as a wild-card expression.

Following is the **File Specs** code that we will use in our pipeline:

```
def server = Artifactory.server 'Default Artifactory Server'
def uploadSpec = """{
    "files": [
    {
      "pattern": "target/hello-0.0.1.war",
      "target": "helloworld-greeting-project/${BUILD_NUMBER}/",
      "props": "Integration-Tested=Yes;Performance-Tested=No"
    }
        ]
}"""
server.upload(uploadSpec)
```

def server = Artifactory.server'Default Artifactory Server'	The following line tells Jenkins to use the existing Artifactory Server configured in Jenkins. In our example its Default Artifactory Server.
Default Artifactory Server	This is the name of the Artifactory Server configured inside Jenkins.
"pattern": "target/hello-0.0.1.war",	The following line of code will look like a file named hello-0.0.1.war inside the directory target, which is again inside the Jenkins workspace directory.
"target": "helloworld-greeting-project/${BUILD_NUMBER}/",	The following line of code will try to upload the build artifacts to the Artifactory repository named helloworld-greeting-project. **It will place the artifact inside a folder named after the build number inside the Artifactory repository**.
${BUILD_NUMBER}	The Jenkins environment variable for the build number.
"props": "Integration-Tested=Yes;Performance-Tested=No"	The following code creates two key/value pairs and assigns them to the uploaded code. These key/value pairs can be used as labels for code promotion in Artifactory. Integration-Tested=Yes Performance-Tested=No

Wrap the step above inside a stage called **Publish to Artifactory**.

```
stage ('Publish to Artifactory'){
    def server = Artifactory.server 'Default Artifactory Server'
    def uploadSpec = """{
    "files": [
    {
      "pattern": "target/hello-0.0.1.war",
      "target": "helloworld-greeting-project/${BUILD_NUMBER}/",
      "props": "Integration-Tested=Yes;Performance-Tested=No"
    }
        ]
}"""
    server.upload(uploadSpec)
}
```

Pipeline Code to Stash the Build Artifacts

Jenkins pipeline has a feature to pass build artifacts across nodes using a feature called **stash**. In the following step we will stash a few build artifacts that we wish to pass to the node **docker_pt** wherein we will perform our performance test.

```
stash includes: 'target/hello-0.0.1.war,src/pt/Hello_World_Test_Plan.jmx', name: 'binary'
```

name:	Name for the stash
includes:	Comma separated files to include

Combined Code for Node docker_it

Following is the complete combined code that will run inside the node **docker_it**.

```
node('docker_it') {
stage('Poll') {
    checkout([$class: 'GitSCM', branches: [[name: '*/master']],
doGenerateSubmoduleConfigurations: false, extensions: [], submoduleCfg: [],
userRemoteConfigs: [[credentialsId: 'github-account', url: 'https://github.com/
pro-continuous-delivery/hello-world-greeting.git']]])
}
stage('Build'){
        sh 'mvn clean verify -DskipITs=true';
}
stage('Static Code Analysis'){
    sh 'mvn clean verify sonar:sonar';
}
stage ('Integration test'){
    sh 'mvn clean verify -Dsurefire.skip=true';
}
stage ('Publish to Artifactory'){
    def server = Artifactory.server 'Default Artifactory Server'
    def uploadSpec = """{
    "files": [
    {
     "pattern": "target/hello-0.0.1.war",
     "target": "helloworld-greeting-project/${BUILD_NUMBER}/",
         "props": "Integration-Tested=Yes;Performance-Tested=No"
  }
        ]
}"""
server.upload(uploadSpec)
}
    stash includes: 'target/hello-0.0.1.war,src/pt/Hello_World_Test_Plan.jmx', name: 'binary'
}
```

Pipeline Code for Spawning a Docker Container for the Performance Testing

First, let us create a pipeline code that will create a docker container (Jenkins Slave) using the Docker image for performance testing **performance-test-agent-0.1**.

```
node('docker_pt') {
}
```

docker_pt	Label for **performance-test-agent-0.1** Docker Template.

We would like to perform the following tasks on the node **docker_pt**.

a. Start tomcat.

b. Deploy the build artifacts to tomcat.

c. Perform performance testing.

d. Promote the build artifacts inside Artifactory.

All the tasks above are various stages of our continous delivery pipeline. Let write pipeline code for each one of them.

Pipeline Code to Start Apache Tomcat

The pipeline code to start Apache Tomcat on the performance testing agent is a simple shell script that will run the **./startup.sh** script present inside the Tomcat installation directory.

```
sh '''cd /home/jenkins/tomcat/bin
./startup.sh''';
```

Wrap the above step inside a stage called **Start Tomcat**.

```
stage ('Start Tomcat'){
    sh '''cd /home/jenkins/tomcat/bin
    ./startup.sh''';
}
```

Pipeline Code to Deploy Build Artifacts to the Tomcat's Webapps Directory

The pipeline code to deploy build artifacts happens in two steps. First, we will unstash the binary package that we stashed from the previous node **docker_it**. Then we deploy the unstashed files into the **webapps** folder inside the Tomcat installation directory. Following is the code:

```
unstash 'binary'

sh 'cp target/hello-0.0.1.war /home/jenkins/tomcat/webapps/';
```

Wrap the step above inside a stage called **Deploy to Testing Env.**

```
stage ('Deploy to Testing Env'){
    unstash 'binary'
    sh 'cp target/hello-0.0.1.war /home/jenkins/tomcat/webapps/';
}
```

Pipeline Code to Execute Performance Testing

The pipeline code to execute the performance testing is a simple shell script that invokes the jmeter.sh script and passes the .jmx file to it. The test result is stored inside a .jtl file that is then archived. Following is the code:

```
sh '''cd /opt/jmeter/bin/
./jmeter.sh -n -t /home/jenkins/workspace/helloworld-greeting-cd/src/pt/Hello_World_Test_
Plan.jmx -l /home/jenkins/workspace/helloworld-greeting-cd/test_report.jtl''';

step([$class: 'ArtifactArchiver', artifacts: '**/*.jtl'])
```

./jmeter.sh -n -t <path to the .jmx file> -l <path to save the .jtl file>	Following is the jmeter command to execute the performance test plan (.jmx files) amd generate a test result (.jtl files).
step([$class: 'ArtifactArchiver', artifacts: '**/*.jtl'])	The following line of code will archive all files with the .jtl extention.

Wrap the step above inside a stage called **Performance Testing.**

```
stage ('Performance Testing'){
    sh '''cd /opt/jmeter/bin/
    ./jmeter.sh -n -t /home/jenkins/workspace/helloworld-greeting-cd/src/pt/Hello_World_
    Test_Plan.jmx -l /home/jenkins/workspace/helloworld-greeting-cd/test_report.jtl''';
    step([$class: 'ArtifactArchiver', artifacts: '**/*.jtl'])

}
```

Pipeline Code to Promote Build Artifacts in Artifactory

The way we are going to promote build artifacts in Artifactory is using the properties (key/value pair) feature. All builds that have passed Performance testing will be applied a tag **Performance-Tested=Yes**. Following is the code:

```
withCredentials([usernameColonPassword(credentialsId: 'artifactory-account', variable:
'credentials')]) {
sh 'curl -u${credentials} -X PUT "http://172.17.8.108:8081/artifactory/api/storage/
helloworld-greeting-project/${BUILD_NUMBER}/hello-0.0.1.war?properties=Performance-
Tested=Yes"';
}
```

withCredentials([usernameColonPassword(credentialsId: 'artifactory-account', variable:'credentials')]) {
 	
}
	We are using the withCredentials Plugin inside Jenkins to pass Artifactory credentials to the curl command.

curl -u<username>:password -X PUT "<artifactory server URL>/api/storage/<artifactory repository name>?properties=key-value"	Following is the curl command to update the property (key/value pair) on the build artifact present inside Artifactory. The curl command makes use of the REST API features of Artifactory.

Wrap the step above inside a stage called **Promote build in Artifactory**.

```
stage ('Promote build in Artifactory'){
    withCredentials([usernameColonPassword(credentialsId: 'artifactory-account', variable:
    'credentials')]) {
        sh 'curl -u${credentials} -X PUT "http://172.17.8.108:8081/artifactory/api/storage/
        helloworld-greeting-project/${BUILD_NUMBER}/hello-0.0.1.war?properties=Performance-
        Tested=Yes"';
    }
}
}
```

Combined Code for Node docker_pt

Following is the complete combined code that will run inside the node **docker_pt**.

```
node('docker_pt') {
stage ('Start Tomcat'){
    sh '''cd /home/jenkins/tomcat/bin
    ./startup.sh''';
}
stage ('Deploy to Testing Env'){
    unstash 'binary'
    sh 'cp target/hello-0.0.1.war /home/jenkins/tomcat/webapps/';
}
stage ('Performance Testing'){
    sh '''cd /opt/jmeter/bin/
    ./jmeter.sh -n -t /home/jenkins/workspace/helloworld-greeting-cd/src/pt/Hello_World_
    Test_Plan.jmx -l /home/jenkins/workspace/helloworld-greeting-cd/test_report.jtl''';
    step([$class: 'ArtifactArchiver', artifacts: '**/*.jtl'])
}
  stage ('Promote build in Artifactory'){
    withCredentials([usernameColonPassword(credentialsId: 'artifactory-account', variable:
    'credentials')]) {
        sh 'curl -u${credentials} -X PUT "http://172.17.8.108:8081/artifactory/api/storage/
        helloworld-greeting-project/${BUILD_NUMBER}/hello-0.0.1.war?properties=Performance-
        Tested=Yes"';
    }
}
}
}
```

Complete Pipeline Script

Combining the pipeline code that runs inside **docker_it** and **docker_pt,** we get the following code:

```
node('docker_it') {
stage('Poll') {
    checkout([$class: 'GitSCM', branches: [[name: '*/master']], doGenerateSubmoduleConfigurations:
    false, extensions: [], submoduleCfg: [], userRemoteConfigs: [[credentialsId: 'github-account',
    url: 'https://github.com/pro-continuous-delivery/hello-world-greeting.git']]])
}
stage('Build'){
        sh 'mvn clean verify -DskipITs=true';
}
stage('Static Code Analysis'){
    sh 'mvn clean verify sonar:sonar';
}
stage ('Integration Test'){
    sh 'mvn clean verify -Dsurefire.skip=true';
}
stage ('Publish to Artifactory'){
    def server = Artifactory.server 'Default Artifactory Server'
    def uploadSpec = """{
    "files": [
    {
      "pattern": "target/hello-0.0.1.war",
      "target": "helloworld-greeting-project/${BUILD_NUMBER}/",
          "props": "Integration-Tested=Yes;Performance-Tested=No"
    }
          ]
}"""
server.upload(uploadSpec)
}
    stash includes: 'target/hello-0.0.1.war,src/pt/Hello_World_Test_Plan.jmx', name: 'binary'
}
node('docker_pt') {
stage ('Start Tomcat'){
    sh '''cd /home/jenkins/tomcat/bin
    ./startup.sh''';
}
stage ('Deploy to Testing Env'){
    unstash 'binary'
    sh 'cp target/hello-0.0.1.war /home/jenkins/tomcat/webapps/';
}
stage ('Performance Testing'){
    sh '''cd /opt/jmeter/bin/
    ./jmeter.sh -n -t /home/jenkins/workspace/helloworld-greeting-cd/src/pt/Hello_World_
    Test_Plan.jmx -l /home/jenkins/workspace/helloworld-greeting-cd/test_report.jtl''';
    step([$class: 'ArtifactArchiver', artifacts: '**/*.jtl'])
}
```

```
stage ('Promote build in Artifactory'){
    withCredentials([usernameColonPassword(credentialsId: 'artifactory-account', variable:
    'credentials')]) {
        sh 'curl -u${credentials} -X PUT "http://172.17.8.108:8081/artifactory/api/storage/
        helloworld-greeting-project/${BUILD_NUMBER}/hello-0.0.1.war?properties=Performance-
        Tested=Yes"';
}
}
}
```

Creating Pipeline in Jenkins

Follow the steps below to create a new pipeline in Jenkins.

1. From the Jenkins Dashboard, click on the **New Item**.

    a. Choose Jenkins Job type as **Pipeline**.

    b. Under the **Enter an item name** field, add a name for your new Jenkins pipeline.

    c. Click on the **OK** button to proceed with configuring our new Jenkins pipeline.

2. Once on the Jenkins pipeline configuration page, scroll down to the **Build Triggers** section and check the **GitHub hook trigger for GITScm polling** option.

3. Scroll down further to the **Pipeline** section.

4. Under the **Definition** option, choose **Pipeline script** (Figure 8-44).

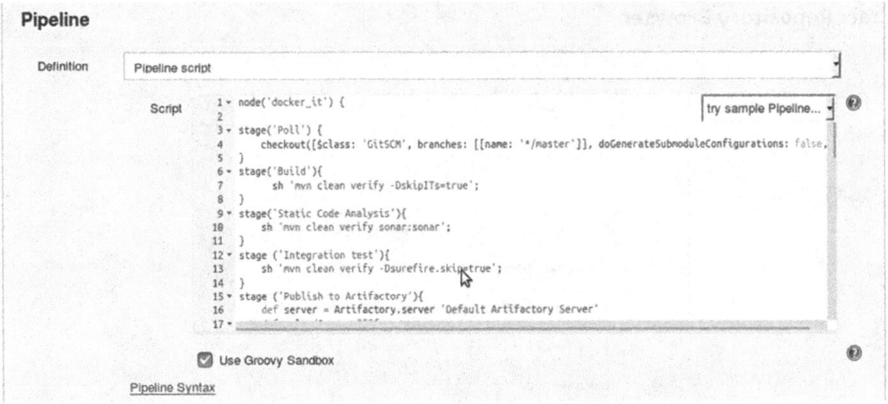

Figure 8-44. Jenkins pipeline script

5. Paste the pipeline code created in the previous section under the **Script** field.

6. Click on the save button at the end of the page.

Jenkins Continuous Delivery Pipeline in Action

Make some changes on your GitHub code or just trigger the Jenkins pipeline from the Jenkins dashboard.

To see the pipeline in action, from the Jenkins dashboard click on the **Jenkins pipeline Job ➤ Full Stage View**. You should see something similar, as shown in Figure 8-45.

helloworld-greeting-cd - Stage View

	Poll	Build	Static Code Analysis	Integration test	Publish to Artifactory	Start Tomcat	Deploy to Testing Env	Performance Testing	Promote build in Artifactory
Average stage times:	5s	37s	43s	11s	4s	3s	914ms	8s	400ms
#28 Mar 11 20:44 No Changes	5s	37s	43s	11s	4s	3s	914ms	8s	400ms

Figure 8-45. Jenkins cd pipeline in action

Log in to the Artifactory server to see if the code has been uploaded and promoted using the properties (Figure 8-46).

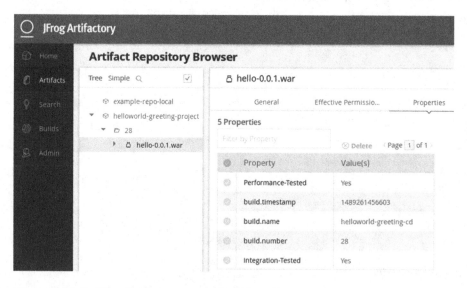

Figure 8-46. Build artifact being promoted inside artifactory

Log in to the SonarQube server to see if there is any Static Code Analysis that happened on the code (Figure 8-47).

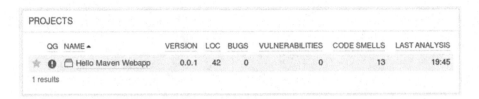

Figure 8-47. *Static Code analysis on the Maven project*

From Figure 8-48, you can see that the total number of Major issues is 13, which is greater than 1 but less than 20. Hence, its considered as a warning.

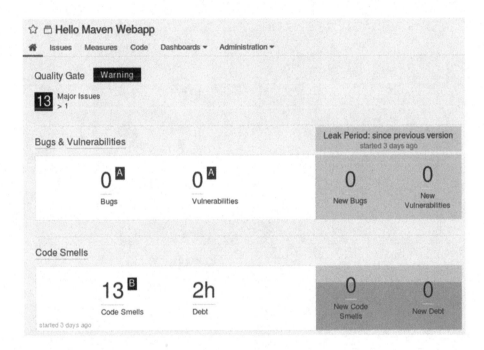

Figure 8-48. *Static Code analysis report on the project*

Summary

In the current chapter we learned to set up the DevOps tool chain required for continuous delivery. We also created a few more Docker images for our testing enviroments. And finally, we created and tested out Jenkins continuous delivery pipeline.

Index

Get the eBook for only $5!

Why limit yourself?

With most of our titles available in both PDF and ePUB format, you can access your content wherever and however you wish—on your PC, phone, tablet, or reader.

Since you've purchased this print book, we are happy to offer you the eBook for just $5.

To learn more, go to http://www.apress.com/companion or contact support@apress.com.

Apress®